TRAINING THE TIMI
HYPNOTIC AND CONDITIONING APPROACHES

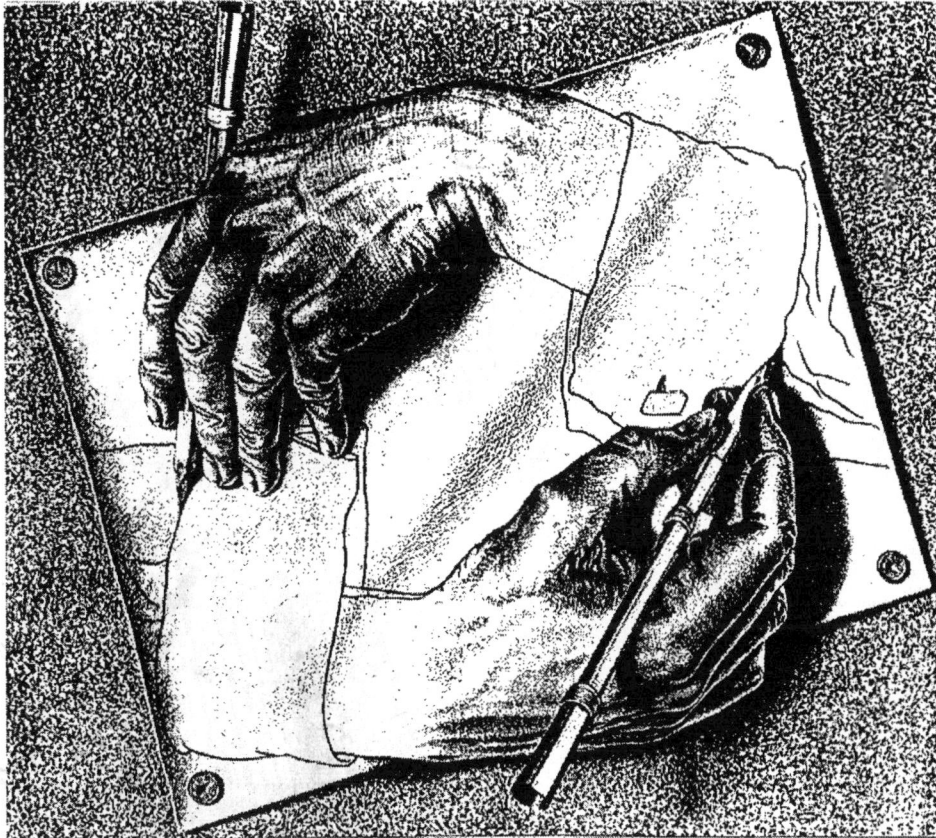

Dr. Robert F. Morgan

Including material by Linn Cooper, Elizabeth Erickson, Milton Erickson, Gary Marshall, Christina Maslach, Robert Morgan, Paul Sacerdote, and Philip Zimbardo.

Morgan Foundation Publishers
305 Mission Serra Terrace
Chico, CA 95926

TRAINING THE TIME SENSE: HYPNOSIS & CONDITIONING

ISBN 1-885679-10-6

Printed in the United States of America by:
Amazing Experiences Press
1908 Keswick Lane
Concord, CA 94518
925-691-5204
http://www.booksprinted.com

10   9   8   7   6   5   4   3   2   1

For Becky

This book is dedicated to the memory of contributor Milton Erickson and his genius. It is also dedicated to memories past and memories to come from my wife, Becky Owl Morgan, my parents, my brother, Nelson Morgan, my sister, Patricia Norman, my daughters, Cinnamon Camo, Angel Kwan-Yin Morgan, and their families.

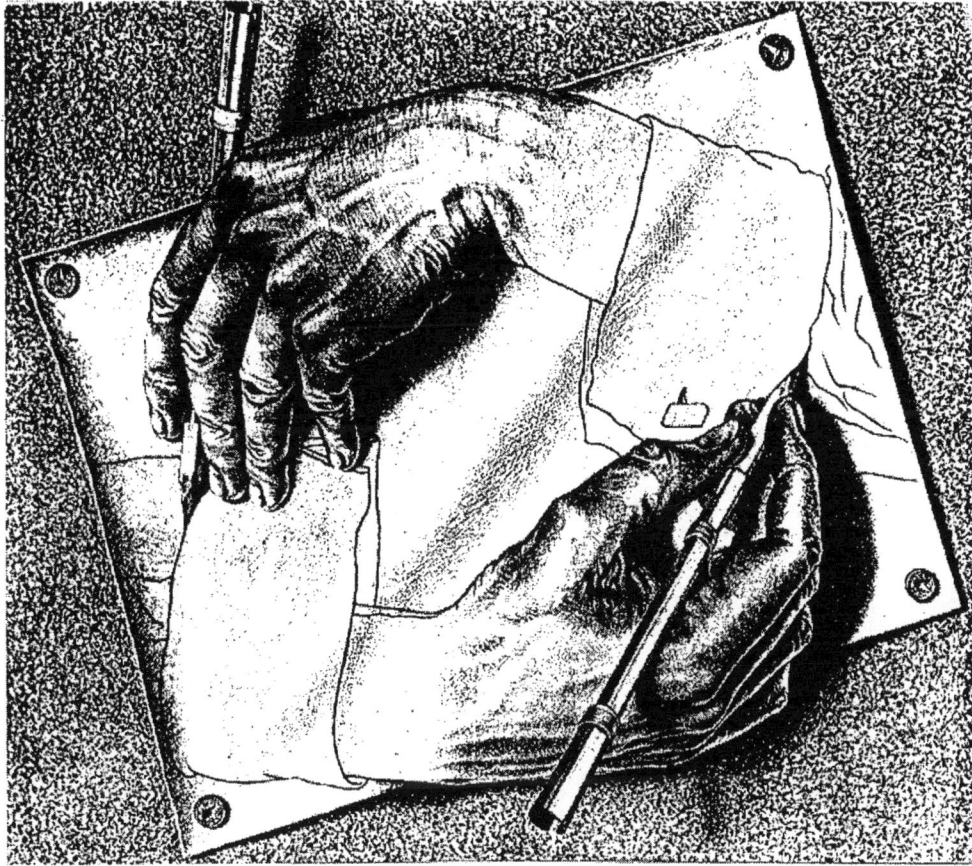

Drawing Hands – M. C. Escher 1948

ACKNOWLEDGEMENTS

First and foremost, the years of encouragement and collaboration from the late Stanley C. Ratner must be acknowledged. Also of extreme help in the temporal conditioning portion of the research in this manuscript were Michigan State University psychologists Abram Barch and M. Ray Denny, Michigan State University zoologist John A. King, and Simon Fraser University psychologist Paul Bakan.

The temporal conditioning research done by the author was supported in part by a grant from the Public Health Service's National Institute of Mental Health.

I am particularly grateful for the pioneering and imaginative contributions of the many innovators in temporal psychology over the last several decades, particularly those whose work is quoted or reprinted here: (in order of appearance) Jacob von Uexkull, Philip Zimbardo, Gary Marshall, Christina Maslach, Linn Cooper, Milton Erickson, Elizabeth Erickson, and Paul Sacerdote.

And, just as Stanley Ratner was the leading force for me in the temporal conditioning area, so must I credit the impressive and distinguished. leadership of David Cheek for opening the modern frontiers of hypnosis these many decades.

In California, I have had helpful exchanges with faculty, staff, and students during the final drafting of this work. Don Hudson was particularly helpful in developing the indexes, and Wendy Speciale in printing format. I also appreciate the journalistic exposure of this work by Gurney Williams, Liz Lufkin and others (excerpts follow beginning with the next page). Jon Herron's editing and printing also deserve recognition. My wife, Rebecca Owl Morgan, deserves applause for her patience, support, ideas and time.

Finally, I dedicate this work to my late grandparents, both sides of the family, whose cumulative total of 23 children underlines the great importance of temporal methods.

INTRODUCTION

One day my two daughters came home from their Reno grade school with bumper stickers reading "I LIKE IT AT NIGHT" and another "I LIKE IT IN THE MORNING". Their school was running a contest between the morning and afternoon newspapers. Each parent was expected to subscribe to one paper or the other, with the appropriate bumper sticker returning to school on the child's shirt. Whichever paper won the contest would donate substantially to the school. I thought it a strangely adult double entendre for a grade school, but probably appropriate to Nevada. In any case, as a bachelor parent, I preferred to save money and buy papers from the stands as needed. So I handcrafted a return sticker for each, sans subscription, which read "I LIKE IT WHEN I CAN AFFORD IT."

Time, whether diurnal facets (such as morning vs evening) or more long-term aspects, is a central portion of human existence. As we get older. we take a longer view. Time seems to accelerate and the light of increasingly extensive past experience begins to illuminate future choices.

At the close of the millennium, this was particularly true. With individual clients in therapy, whatever other issues arise, the approach of a decade birthday is a particular stressor. Moving into ones 30s, 40s, 50s, 60s, etc triggers a reasonably predictable set of events. Particularly in the year before, one can anticipate a review of personal expectations what was supposed to have been completed prior to entry into that new decade. There is a flurry of activity to get there before the crucial (arbitrary) deadline. Relationships end, others begin. Jobs end, new careers begin. It is a time for introspection and reminiscence. We look backward though our decade and our life. We become nostalgic. It is a backward-looking time with many changes under pressure. Once we have passed through the dreaded temporal gateway, we become more relaxed and more forward-looking, identifying more with our future and less with past (even repudiating the past). This process is a specific application of the well known anniversary neurosis; only it is normative and, more often than not, we survive it. Once into a new decade we have time. After crossing, there are ten years to the next decade transition. As with individuals, so also with the culture. As the year 2000 approached (Y2K), we collectively faced a new decade and a new century and a new millennium. All were arbitrary points and yet the full range of global apocalyptic thinking occurred. Movies, books, television: all were retrospective, remakes generated sequels and other remakes. Nations divided and reunited. It was, as the Chinese curse goes, "interesting times". The worst of the century made "curtain calls," only to be dismissed, once the transition was over, as "20th century thinking." Everything now must be new. As a society we now have time.

In San Francisco, Mayor Willie Brown, arguably one of the best the city ever had, was under ongoing pressure to get the Muni buses more punctual. Complying with temporal demand is a central issue in contemporary life and yet not easy in a democratic society. I'll be retrospective for a minute:

IT WAS MORE THAN THREE DECADES INTO THE 20TH CENTURY AND ITALY'S RAILROADS WERE A MESS. MUSSOLINI RODE INTO POWER WITH THE PLEDGE TO MAKE THE TRAINS RUN ON TIME. WITH THE FORCE OF A FASCIST STATE HE KEPT HIS WORD AND ALONG WITH THAT TERRORIZED THE POPULACE FOR YEARS. ONE DAY MUSSOLINI WAS OVERTHROWN, HUNG FROM THE PUBLIC SQUARE, AND FASCISM LEFT ITALY. THE NEXT MORNING ITALIANS ALL OVER THE COUNTRY WERE ABLE TO ANNOUNCE WITH PRIDE: "MY TRAIN WAS LATE" AND EVERYONE CHEERED.

(Note: In November of 1998, the nearly elected Speaker of the House, Robert Livingston, who would have replaced Newt Gingrich, was reported to promise he would "make the trains run on time." The reporter, possibly unaware of the history of this expression found the promise "prosaic" — NEWS-WEEK 11/23/98.)

Is there a humane way to synchronize with time, to meet our practical responsibilities and personal explorations without hurting anyone? This book offers a few possibilities.

Keep the ideas and techniques discussed here in context. They have power but there is an ethical ecology to everything.

One last example of this: Roger Ullrich, a behavior modification expert, gave this case history. A young couple, newlyweds, were attending college together. They had just moved into a small 1-room married housing studio apartment. They came into counseling for a variety of problems: insomnia, arguments, difficulty concentrating on their studies, and reduced sexual satisfaction. The psychologist learned that, due to the lack of space in their apartment, they used their bed for sleep, sex, fighting, and studying. He told them they had stimulus competition going on and needed to separate time if not space. To do this, he prescribed a light with red and green bulbs as well as standard white. The sleep activity was with no light, study with only white light, fighting only in green light, and sex only in red light. In this manner they differentiated their limited space by altered states in time, color coded. According to the case history, it worked perfectly. Sex became fun again, study concentration improved, sleep was full, and arguments decreased. The colors kept the bed from eliciting sleep or wakefulness at the wrong time, or fighting from interfering with sex. A success without a long analysis.

And yet, I wondered what happened when they drove in traffic?

Use these hypnotic and learning approaches well: we have time.

—Robert Morgan, Editor

Additional Reading

In psychology, and related fields, we have leaned to short term "cross-sectional" research. This is rooted in the present with matched groups and short term outcomes. Such work fits a fast tempo society with deadlines for dissertations and research grants, promotions and competitions. The alternative is "longitudinal" research which tracks people through their future. Often taking decades or lifetimes, but more typically requiring at least 5 years for remission/cure outcomes, these projects are being reconsidered. As we live longer we are beginning to take a look at the tong term consequences of our actions. I find myself, for example, now I am entering my 4th decade as a psychologist, publishing followup studies over decades on clinical cases (Morgan, 1996, 1999) or tests with long histories (Morgan, 1994) or Cultural PTSD (Duran & Duran 1995). Longitudinal research, or at least, 5 year+ followups, are another future direction based on a longer view of time.

I would particularly recommend reading James Birren's books in this regard (see below). For contemporary hypnosis applications beyond those in this present book, I would recommend David Cheek's work (also below).

Birren, J.E., Kenyon, G.M., Ruth, J., Schroots, J.J.F, Svenson, T. AGING & BIOGRAPHY: EXPLORATIONS IN ADULT DEVELOPMENT. New York: Springer, 1996.

Cheek, D,B, HYPNOSIS: THE APPLICATION OF IDEOMOTOR TECHNIQUES. Needham Heights, Mass: Allyn & Bacon, 1994.

Duran, E. & Duran, B. NATIVE AMERICAN POSTCOLONIAL PSYCHOLOGY. Albany: State University of New York Press, 1995.

Morgan, R.F. ELECTROSHOCK: THE CASE AGAINST OVER FOUR DECADES. Fair Oaks, CA: Morgan Foundation Publishers, 1999.

Morgan, R.F. NO PLACE LIKE HOME in P. Breggin's PSYCHOSOCIAL APPROACHES TO DEEPLY DISTURBED PERSONS. Hazelton, PA: Haworth Press, 141—183, 1996.

Morgan, R.F. DECADES OF RESEARCH AND PRACTICE WITH THE ADULT GROWTH EXAMINATION, A BRIEF STANARDIZED TEST OF ADULT AGING in A. Balin, HUMAN BIOLOGICAL AGE DETERMINATION. Boca Raton: FL: CRC Press, Ch. 12, 181—211, 1994.

Two magazine reports on our work, reprinted with permission, follow with the main articles of this book presented thereafter.

A PRACTICAL GUIDE TO THE ART AND SCIENCE OF STAYING YOUNG

LONGEVITY

VOL.1, NO.10   JULY 1989

SLOWING HOW FAST TIME RUNS OUT The idea of tinkering with time in order to live "longer" and lower body age may sound off-the-wall. It's not. A small, persistent band of researchers are working to reset the clock of life. . . And not a minute too soon.

By Gurney Williams III.

PHOTOGRAPH BY WALTER WICK

SLOWING
HOW FAST TIME
RUNS OUT
BY GURNEY WILLIAMS III

Time flew, and it wasn't any fun. Charlie, 18, would stand in a long line at the bank and, it seemed, barely have a moment to pull out his checkbook before the teller yelled "Next!' at him. He would sit down for a chat with his wife and no sooner start talking before she would tell him an hour had passed. It seemed as though his life was skittering by in fast motion, like a Keystone Kops comedy. If Charlie lived to be 150, he would have felt shortchanged on time. Robert F. Morgan, Ph.D., then a graduate student at Michigan State University, tool the blame. He knew immediately when Charlie— not his real name—came back to see him a week later that his experiment with time had gone too far. By manipulating a simple laboratory situation, Morgan had created a man who was living at fast-forward speed. Charlie was a student volunteer in a time-conditioning experiment Morgan was running at Michigan State. When he began, Morgan had no idea that it would so radically reset anyone's body clock. His goal had been simply to see whether people could improve. their ability to guess how much time had passed between two events.

The experiment wasn't complicated. Charlie sat in a room bathed in dim red light. There were few comforts: chicken, lemonade, a glass urinal. The focus of the room was a 100-watt frosted light bulb a foot and a half in front of Charlie. It blinked on briefly, once an hour, for 16 hours. Charlie's only task was to guess when the light would go on and to say "Now!" just before the expected flash. No one told him how much time would pass between blinks. He had no idea how long the experiment would last.

In a separate room, Morgan monitored the experiment. Subjects wore two small electrically sensitive rings on their fingers to register the production of sweat, a sign of arousal or excitement. It was clear to Morgan as he watched the continuous readouts that his subjects felt a physiological twinge of anticipation just before they said "Now!" The signal that turned on the sweat, he concluded, came from some kind of mental clock.

In the course of 16 hours, the "clock" became more and more accurate in anticipating the next flash. After the first few hours, guesses frequently came within seconds of the light. But paradoxically, at the end of the 16-hour experiment Charlie and other subjects emerged bleary-eyed from the red room without any idea of what time it was.

Charlie told Morgan that he thought the whole session had taken just an hour, with the light blinking every four minutes. That's why he never ate any chicken or used the urinal, he explained: There just hadn't been time. He returned to daily life as a man running at 33 revolutions per minute (rpm) in a 78-rpm world. Acutely uncomfortable, he soon returned to Morgan for help.

To 'reset" Charlie, Morgan put him back into the red-glowing room, told him again to try to anticipate when the light would go on and gradually shortened the period between flashes until the frosted bulb was blinking once every 60 seconds. It worked. Charlie's perception of time returned to normal. There was even a small payoff for his pain: Like most of the other subjects in Morgan's research, he stopped needing an alarm clock. His sense of time became acute enough to bounce him out of bed when he had to wake up.

Now a psychologist at the Pacific Graduate School of Psychology in San Francisco, Morgan is one of a mere handful of researchers exploring the passage of time. Their work helps explain why some car-accident victims review their whole lives in the split second before a crash. It's part of a primitive survival mechanism, according to David Cheek, M.D., a California obstetrician and a widely recognized expert on hypnotic states. "It's very important for animals to have instant replay of what permitted them to get out of trouble before, Cheek says. In humans the sudden deceleration of time as they hurtle toward collision allows for evasion or escape.

Perhaps most important, researchers have learned that no one needs to be a prisoner of time. Using autohypnotic techniques, there are ways to change our perceptions of how we're aging. Some therapists today are helping people travel in time—not only backward to retrieve the memories of youth but also forward to tap the wisdom of old age. Morgan's basic message: Time is largely subjective, every person's province to be conquered and controlled.

HOW LONG IS A MOMENT?

All of us experience time distortion, Morgan says. Classic childhood summers can seem to last forever, while the great getaway vacation often seems gone in an instant. 'The older we get," says Morgan, "the more time seems to speed' by." By contrast, some researchers speculate, everything seems sluggish to a newborn. The late anthropologist Margaret Mead once pointed out that the one-day-old child who has been

TIME-ZONE DEFENSE

Sometimes navigating between past, present and future takes the skills of a detective, psychologist Robert Morgan says. In one of his most memorable cases, a woman in her late 30s went to him for therapy because she suffered continual stomachaches. A series of gastrointestinal tests had turned up no obvious medical problems.

Her life story wasn't remarkable. She had moved from London to California 17 years before Morgan saw her, and she returned to London for occasional visits. She was married.

"How do you spend your day?" Morgan asked her. She said she drank a six-pack of Pepsi in the morning and smoked two packs of cigarettes by 2 p.m. Many therapists and physicians might have stopped there, having pinpointed a potential danger to her health. Sensitive to time, Morgan pressed on. "When do you eat?" he asked her. She said that at 2 p.m. she ate the first meal of the day. She felt hungry again at about 10 p.m. but fasted until well after midnight, when she ate a snack.

Morgan scribbled some time-zone calculations that led him to the root of her problems.

"You're living on London time," he told her, "and it isn't jet lag." Pepsi in the morning, California time, took the place of the tea Londoners were sipping at the same time. Her 2 p.m. meal coincided with a late dinner in London. The hunger pangs at 10 p.m. marked the time for breakfast in Hyde Park. But, like many Londoners, she skipped breakfast and ate only a light lunch—at three in the morning on the West Coast of the United States.

She had chosen to "live" in a comforting time zone, Morgan reports, far from the husband, whom—she soon acknowledged—she disliked and subsequently divorced. Then she automatically switched her body clock to local time.

wearing a wet diaper for half a day has been wet half his life. At any age, pain or frustration decelerates time an takes us back to that infantile sense that life is a river of molasses. Heavy traffic slows clocks. Bank lines seem to wind forever.

Animal studies reveal that at least some of our time perception is hardwired at birth. Different animals have divergent perceptions of how fast or slowly the world turns. The studies show that each species has a moment, the smallest

Perceivable time fragment. For humans the moment is one eighteenth of a second. If a reed vibrates more rapidly than that, you hear the vibration as a single tone. Eighteen taps applied to human skin in one second feel like a continuous touch. And 18 pictures projected per second on a screen look like one picture; our moment makes movies possible.

For the fighting fish, a freshwater animal that survives by catching fast-moving prey, research shows that the moment is one fiftieth of a second. To such a fish our movies would look choppy, and human swimmers would seem to move in slow motion. A snail moment, though, is only a third to a quarter of a second. Meandering brooks probably seem like white-water rapids to snails.

Although humans share a single moment, we differ in our personal time perspectives, according to Philip G. Zimbardo, a psychology professor at Stanford University. The perspective or "time zone," you're in, Zimbardo speculates, may reveal something about your health and potential longevity.

HAZARDOUS TIME ZONES

Zimbardo and Alexander Gonzalez, chairman of the psychology department at California State University, Fresno, discovered seven such zones while studying over 12,000 responses to a national magazine reader survey. One zone, for example, is occupied by "Present, Fatalistic" people likely to say: "If things don't get done on time, I don't worry about it." Denizens of the "Present, Hedonis-

REWINDING THE BRAIN STEM
Recently I asked Sidney Rosen, M.D., a New York City Psychiatrist, to teach me how to distort my sense of the passage of time while under hypnosis. Here are portions of a transcript from a recent session. Rosen is speaking. I am awake at the start.

"What we're going to do is get you to focus your attention on one thing. . . .It could be a thought you focus on, or it could be a word or a sound, a sensation. . . .

"You can go into as deep a trance as you want, simply by focusing attention on whatever phenomenon interests you. . . .Your curiosity will guide you and lead you more and more into your trance.

"Your breathing has become slower, your muscle tone has become more relaxed. . . .You can have a dream or see a movie right now. Your dream is just about ready to start, isn't it? Now. . . .[Twenty seconds pass.] is the dream all finished?

"I'm going to count backward slowly from 20 to 1. I'd like you to come out of your trance one twentieth with every number that I count toward one, so by the count of one your eyes are open. You feel relaxed, rested, refreshed, wider and wider awake. . . ."

He counted me out of the trance. When he told me to dream, I had climbed a tree self-consciously. It was a birch with scratchy white bark. I thought of Robert Frost's poem "Birches." At the top I looked around and saw dark skies and sensed the penetrating eyes of Sidney Rosen. The events in the dream seemed to take about a minute to unfold—but Rosen assured me that practice would help me "stretch" my experience of elapsed time in a hypnotic state. A *paradox*, I thought: *It takes time to get more time.*

tic" time zone believe that "getting together with friends to party is one of life's important pleasures" and say, 1 do things impulsively, making decisions on the spur of the moment." By contrast, future-oriented people—who occupy any of four distinct "Future" zones—are likely to map out their day every morning, take responsibility for deadlines and buy life insurance. The last of the time zones, the "Time Press" zone, is the realm of people inordinately preoccupied with punctuality and maintaining a tight schedule.

Zimbardo is currently mapping out the health-maintenance habits of people with different time perspectives. His suspicion: Life in some of the time zones may be hazardous to your health.

"Present, Hedonistic people are most prone to addictions," Zimbardo says, "things that feel good regardless of their long-term consequences. So I expect you get a high percentage of mortality among them because they get addicted to drugs, food, cigarettes." They are also less likely to carry out simple health-maintenance duties, such as setting up routine medical checkups. Beyond disco dancing, they tend to sit out strenuous exercise. Zimbardo lacks sufficient data to make similar predictions about Present, Fatalistic people, but chances are that their tendency to see life as something beyond their control puts them in at least as much jeopardy as their hedonistic counterparts.

People of the various Future zones are more likely to watch Their diets; exercise wisely and get the medical support they need.

Zimbardo doesn't see much hope of transporting Present zone people into a healthier time zone. But Zimbardo and other researchers say that people in all chronological zones can change their *perceptions* of the passage of time. They point to the classic work done some 40 years ago by Milton H. Erickson, M.D., and Linn F. Cooper MID., who used hypnosis to create the human equivalent of the fighting fish—people who can, in effect, live "longer" by experiencing the passage of time more slowly.

PUTTING THE CLOCK ON HOLD

Erickson and Cooper called one of' their prize subjects 'E." Under hypnosis E. was 'told to imagine herself doing a repetitive task.' She used to have a job packing cookies, she said. Erickson told her to picture herself counting the cookies as she packaged them. After a set time, he told her to stop and describe everything that she had imagined herself doing.

She had been in a basement, she said, putting cookies into sacks. She counted out loud for Erickson to show how fast she had been working: one cookie per second. She had done it for 23 minutes, she said, time enough to pack about 1,400 cookies.
But there had been distractions. She had had a sneezing fit. The phone had rung for almost half the time she had been working. She let it ring and kept her count. By the end of the work session, she had packed 1,003 cookies.

"Was it real?" Erickson asked E. of her hypnotic dream.

"Yes," she said. Erickson had kept careful track of how much clock time had elapsed. E.'s 23 minutes had actually taken ten seconds.

Starting at the fifth second, Erickson had sounded a single note on a pitch pipe. E. said the phone had begun to ring as she was packing the four-hundred-ninety-eighth cookie, almost exactly halfway through her work.

Psychologists today who know Erickson's work are using trances as a means of "stretching" time. Jeffrey Zeig, Ph.D., director of the Milton H. Erickson Foundation in Phoenix, follows Erickson's lead by punctuating his work as a therapist with personal mental forays into altered states where time seems to slow down.

I set my mind on an idea, like *creativity* or *comfort,*" he says. Then he opens himself up to spontaneous images from his unconscious mind. His noonday trances last no more than 10 or 15 minutes each.

Zeig says each of his trance states "seems pretty long," although he has never measured the dream events in his trances the way Erickson did to record the time expansion. "It's not a panacea," he cautions. "I'm still tired at the end of work." But the time distortion does help him attain a simple goal shared by most people: "I want to make five minutes of rest seem as long, as possible," he says.

SLOWING TIME TO LIVE LONGER MAY SEEM NUTS. IT'S NOT.

A BRAKE ON AGING

Hypnotic time manipulation may offer more than relaxation. Although the evidence is sketchy, some therapists say hypnotic suggestion can directly slow the aging process or at least help in the treatment of physical and mental disorders. When Leonard Elkind, Ph.D., a clinical psychologist in private practice in North San Diego, was a doctoral candidate in the early Seventies, he tested the anti-aging potential of hypnotic suggestion. Nineteen women took part in his experiment. Some were told: "Your body can become younger." All were given an examination called the AGE test, designed to assess how their bodies were aging. The 15-minute test, developed by Robert Morgan, measures hearing level at high frequency, the ability to read print close to the eyes and systolic, blood pressure, then generates a numerical "age" score that often differs from a subjects chronological age. Elkind's subjects, ages 39 to 56, had "body age" scores that ranged from 23 to 66.

Nine of the women were then hypnotized. "The body is a self-repairing organism," they were told while in their trance states. "Through hypnosis your body can become younger; not like a child but like a healthy, vigorous adult. . . .Let yourself feel younger. Feel the vigor and health that is yours. . . ." The remaining ten women served as controls.

Three weeks after the hypnotic session the whole group retook the AGE test. The , members of the control group showed modest changes in body age. No subject's score differed more than four points from her first score, and some of them tested "older." But every member of the hypnotized group enjoyed a *drop* in body age, from three to 18 years. The median drop was 11 years.

In a related experiment cited by Morgan, a 59-year-old Canadian woman named Marg [sic] Meston, who had volunteered for a television demonstration, registered a body age score of 61 when first tested. Two months later, after posthypnotic suggestion, her body age had dropped to 40.

Elkind has not performed follow-up studies on his 19 subjects, nor have many investigators pursued this avenue of longevity research. The prospect of embarking on a longitudinal study in which the most salient data—dates of death—are, many decades away may be inherently daunting. Nonetheless, time distortion has become a mainstay of Elkind's work as a therapist. For many patients he prescribes what he calls a "time wedge." He tells patients to envision a place that's special to them. It may be a vacation retreat or a mountaintop with unlimited vistas. "Then at some point I'll remind them that in hypnosis, all time is *now* and that they have all the time they need for productive dreams." Patients wake up from these . five-minute trances feeling as though they've been "gone" for an hour—almost doubling their therapy time. Most important, says Elkind, patients in a time wedge may gain more freedom of choice.

"I call it a time Wedge because people sometimes find themselves in points in their lives when they see everything as black or white, either-or. The time wedge disrupts this either-or proposition." In a time-wedge trance, Elkind says, his patients have the extra time they need to consider new options for their lives.

He cites the case of a woman once tortured by a phobia about leaving her house and driving a long way to work on a California freeway. In hypnosis she has since learned to see the trip differently, helped by Elkind's suggestions that the frightening quantum leap from home to office is really just a connected series of short trips between freeway exits. The trance state gave her time to rehearse the journey in her mind until it wasn't alarming anymore. As a result, she has virtually stopped taking tranquilizers.

Using similar time wedges, therapists such as Jeffrey Zeig have helped women in childbirth stretch out periods of comfort between contractions. And by making the contractions themselves seem shorter, time-distortion techniques have reduced the demand for palliative drugs, making the birth process safer for mother and child.

FUTURE TENSE

Techniques that alter time perception offer fundamental gifts of longevity, Morgan says: a bonus of good time in your life. But you can also learn to live better in the present by mentally traveling to other times—most intriguingly, the future.

A 37-year-old Colorado woman was ambivalent about a divorce. Morgan hypnotized her, then told her to visualize her own face at age 57—two decades later—and listen to advice from herself. "She made contact," Morgan says, "and saw herself very dearly, but it was a tense encounter. It wasn't that she disliked her future face. The problem was like a broken TV: She saw a picture with no sound."

Explaining the uneasy silence, Morgan told her, "You don't want to hear what you're going to say." In several subsequent sessions he taught the woman that she was just as free to ignore advice from her future self as from anyone else. With that reassurance, she began to hear her own voice, warning her against staying with her husband. She later acknowledged that she had been afraid that the figure in her future would tell her to avoid divorce at all costs—counseling that her mother might have given her.

"The permission to get the divorce wasn't just advice from a mother or wise person," Morgan says. It came from someone in her future who could reassure her—better than anyone else—that things were going to work out.

Whether the goal is resetting one's biological time clock, lowering body age, gaining an hour's worth of rest in a five-minute trance, using a time wedge to sort out tough choices—or even asking advice from an older and wiser version of oneself—the common message of time-oriented therapists and physicians is that you can use your mind to put time to work for you. The payoff may even be a longer life span, and if not that, then at least the *experience* of a longer life, with greater well-being. That, in the end, is arguably what longevity is all about.

Gurney Williams III is a writer and a lecturer on science, health and the future. He is also the **former editor of Omni.**

In this era of faxing and Fed-Ex-ing you may feel the need to stay in fifth gear. But going too fast can be hazardous to your health

SLOW DOWN, YOU MOVE TOO FAST: THE TIME-SICKNESS CURE

BY LIZ LUFKIN

THEY ANXIOUSLY GLANCE AT their watches in elevators. They pace before meetings; they fidget in the car. And they're likely to fly off the handle when something—anything—gets in the way of their frantic race to get things done. They are suffering from time sickness, a syndrome that's on the upswing in today's sped-up world of Filofaxes, fax machines and Federal Express.

People who are time-sick feel harassed by the clock and oppressed by a sense of urgency. For them life is like peddling up a never-ending hill. Everything seems to take an incredibly long time, and there are never enough hours in a day to accomplish what they want to do.

"Lots of people believe the whole universe will grind to a halt unless they're doing something every second," explains Joan Borysenko, Ph.D., the president of Mind/Body Health Sciences Inc. and a stress expert who used to suffer from the disorder herself. "It's almost a badge of honor to run yourself into the ground."

THE HURRY-UP EPIDEMIC

In the past 50 years our culture has sped up at an accelerating rate, says Robert R Morgan, Ph.D., vice president of the Pacific Graduate School of Psychology in Palo Alto, California, and author of *Training the Time Sense*. "If someone were transplanted from the '40s to the '90s, they'd be amazed at how fast things go, from the speed of our cars to the pace of our movies."

Humans used to operate on the yearly, monthly and daily cycles of the sun and moon, tides and seasons; but increasingly we are living in a new, artificial kind of time that clicks by at the lightning-fast pace of computers. While the most fundamental human time reference is 60 seconds, a computer operates in nanoseconds—and one-billionth of a second is a unit of time beyond our ability to experience. Snapping your fingers—once the symbol of instant response—takes 500 *million* nanoseconds.

"All the high-tech devices that are supposed to give us more free time have had the opposite effect," observes stress expert Larry Dossey, MD, author of *Recovering the Soul*. One need never be further out of touch than the nearest car phone or fax machine-and many people find it impossible to escape. In the past decade the average American workweek has skyrocketed from 41 hours to 47 hours.

"We're reaching the point of diminishing returns," says Jeremy Rifkin, president of the Foundation of Economic Trends in Washington, DC, and author of *Time Wars: the Primary Conflict in Human History*. "We're actually getting back very little [from our high-speed gadgets]—and we're losing our humanity in the process." Time sickness may sound like a '90s version of Type A behavior. Indeed, many hard-driving Type A's are susceptible to the disorder. But mellower Type B's may be at even greater risk from trying to keep up in a Type A world.

STRESSED BY SUCCESS

Women who juggle the multiple demands of home and business life are particularly prone to time sickness, says stress expert Borysenko, who has just published a new book, *Guilt Is the Teacher, Love Is the Lesson.* Not only are women propelled by the revved-up technology, but they are more likely to try to prove themselves by "doing it all for everyone." Borysenko asks her stressed-out clients three questions: Are you a perfectionist? Are you a compulsive rescuer? Are you afraid of others' anger? "The more you believe that your worth is based on what you can achieve, the worse you'll have time sickness," she explains. "Your life is literally on the line."

Dossey used this simple test on patients who complained of stress: He asked clients to sit quietly and (without counting) tell him when a minute had passed. Most of the stressed execs he studied called "time's up" at about 15 seconds—although one go-getter blew the whistle after only 6.

"It's not like these people were just aggravated or in a hurry," Dossey says. "Most of them were very unhappy."

THE TOLL OF TIME SICKNESS

Experts warn that constantly being in high gear causes the body's "fight or flight" mechanism to kick into action more frequently. This increases the blood levels of adrenaline, noradrenaline and other stress hormones and causes damage to the arteries.

Stress-related diseases—everything from headaches to heart attacks—are the most serious warning signs of time sickness. Other tip-offs include anxiety, depression, insomnia, fatigue, appetite changes and bizarre eating habits. (One time-sick woman drank two gallons of Diet Pepsi before noon every day.) In extreme cases, individuals may abuse amphetamines or barbiturates to speed up or slow down their perception of time.

As the syndrome progresses it can jeopardize family relationships— and even damage careers. One engineer became increasingly impatient with his kids because they didn't respond as fast as his computer could. Another fast-track exec was so anxious that she began sweating at board meetings; embarrassed, she started to avoid meetings altogether.

THE MELLOW '90s

Rifkin warns that humans are hitting their biological speed limit and predicts that the '90s will prove a more easy-going era. The signs. are already here. In avant-garde Berkeley, California, a restaurant offers what it calls "slow" food. A San Francisco social club targets those who want to "start relaxing more and working less in 1990." According to New York trend watcher Faith Popcorn, "cashing out" will become one of the big movements of the decade as baby boomers relocate to small towns and attempt to put the brakes on their fast-paced lifestyles.

We're beginning to discover that spending extra time at the office doesn't always translate into productivity—and cutting out to relax doesn't have to mean cutting down on what gets done. In fact, "studies show that when people have time to relax, they actually are able to achieve more," says stress expert Dossey. West Germans work fewer hours than Americans and most other Europeans, and they take off a month each year. But Germany remains one of the world's top producers.

What's more, pushing to produce without limit ultimately can be destructive from an economic point of view. In Japan, for instance, the government plans to cut about 300 hours out of the average corporate employee's work year; it fears that the economy will be crippled by overproduction.

Despite the obvious benefits of slowing down, the "stress for success" concept has become so ingrained in the American psyche that even mildly time-sick people may have trouble letting go. But as Dossey reminds us, "Lions are mighty, even in repose. After all, they spend half their time sleeping."

LIZ LUFKIN is a feature writer for the "San Francisco Chronicle" who reports frequently on social trends.

HOW TO GET A MELLOW MINDSET

TIRED OF FEELING TRAPPED IN A RACE against time? Time sickness can be cured, say stress experts. Coping with it can be as simple as sitting back in your chair or as involved as biofeedback, hypnosis or meditation. These techniques will help you slow down as well as become more productive.

■**Reset your inner deck.** Does 15 minutes sometimes seem like 15 seconds? Individuals on the fast track often have an accelerated sense of time because of the pressure to get things done—which only adds to their stress level. But your perception of time can be changed, says Robert F. Morgan, Ph.D., vice president of the Pacific Graduate School of Psychology in Palo Alto, California, and author of *Training the Time Sense*. Using a light flashing at 30- and 60-second intervals as well as on the hour, Morgan asked subjects to guess when the next flash would occur. After about 15 attempts, most people got pretty good at "setting themselves," reports Morgan.

■**Take time out.** The first thing many therapists will recommend to a time-sick person is to sit quietly for 15 minutes, four times a week. If you're at home, turn off the TV or radio, turn on the answering machine and dim the lights. If you're at the office, close the door and have your assistant hold all calls. Day One will be the hardest—those 15 minutes will feel like an hour. But the more you do it, the easier it will become.

Faye Wattleton, the controversial president of Planned Parenthood Federation of America, regularly logs marathon 12-hour days. But she keeps her cool when the tension's hot by taking breaks—and occasional ten-minute catnaps over her typewriter when she works late.

■**Set your priorities.** Family is, friends are, perhaps only some parts of your job are. Decide what is possible to accomplish, then be ruthless with time bandits. Cut short endless calls or unimportant office visits with a polite "Thanks for calling" or "I have to prepare for a meeting now."

■**Find small ways to got back in touch with the natural flow of time.** Ditch the digital watch. "All you have are numbers screaming, 'Now! Now! Now!'" observes Jeremy Rifkin, author of *Time Wars*. Wearing a circular timepiece reminds you of the natural cycle of the sun. Getting outdoors during the day also helps.

■**Exercise.** Aerobic workouts can have a calming effect because they cause the body to release natural opiates called endorphins. But don't let your regimen get competitive or compulsive.

■**Cut down on caffeine.** Drinking ten cups of coffee a day sends your system into overdrive and distorts your perception of time. Try to limit your intake to two cups—or, better yet, drink decaf.

■**Take time to linger.** Enjoy the experience of eating a relaxed meal in calm surroundings. When you take a vacation (and do take one), make sure you're not frantically running from place to place. Settle down in one locale and stay there. At work, don't be afraid to let your mind wander occasionally. People are more creative when they're not always pressed for time. Reflection and introspection are good for you— and your company.

■**Adjust your schedule to fit your personality.** Not everyone would be happy dropping out, moving to Tahiti or turning California-mellow. But most of us are more efficient when we take time off once in a while to refuel.

Learn to put things in perspective. As Wattleton says, "The globe doesn't turn upside down if you don't have a problem solved today."

—Liz Lufkin

TRAINING THE TIME SENSE:
HYPNOTIC & CONDITIONING APPROACHES
Robert F. Morgan

TABLE OF CONTENTS

Frontispiece: "Drawing Hands" by N. Escher   v

Acknowledgments   vi

Introduction*   vii

Chapter One — Time, Hypnosis, & Conditioning   1

Chapter Two — Receptor Time for Humans and Others   7

Chapter Three — Hypnotic Expansion of the Present   11

Chapter Four — Hypnotic Time Distortion: Pioneers   33

Chapter Five — Hypnotic Time Distortion: Case Histories   65

Chapter Six — Temporal Conditioning: Theory, Research, Method, History, and Hypotheses   81

Chapter Seven — Temporal Conditioning of Humans I: Pilot Research   91

Chapter Eight — Temporal Conditioning of Humans II: Basic Method   97

Chapter Nine — Temporal Conditioning of Humans III: Twice Over & Out   113

Chapter Ten — Temporal Conditioning of Humans IV: Pavlov's Pause   121

Chapter Eleven — Temporal Conditioning Hypotheses Surviving the Research   129

Bibliography   159

About the Author   171

Name Index   173

*Followed by journalistic comment on this work

CHAPTER ONE

TIME, HYPNOSIS, AND CONDITIONING

A potentially powerful, if often overlooked, factor in facilitating human change is the dimension of time.

As will be illustrated in this section, time can contribute to the etiology of mental distress, to the therapeutic skills needed to alleviate the distress, and even to the enhancement of human potential serving primary prevention of distress.

There are of course anecdotes of those who came close to death and lived years of memories in seconds of time. There are those dying of terminal illness who have expanded hours into centuries by selective use of psychoactive drugs. But: what of normal adults?

Aaronson demonstrated in a classic study (1969) that changing a normal volunteer's time sense hypnotically could:

(1) Create mania when time was sped up

(2) Create depression when slowed

(3) Produce schizophrenic-like episodes when stopped.

Morgan (1965, 1967) found psychogenic senile psychoses based largely on functional suppression of an unsatisfying present and repression of a frightening future.

Dengrove (1973) demonstrated that the hypnotic use of time distortion (more on this later) can shorten treatment time in psychotherapy.

Krauss and colleagues (1974) found that hypnotically induced time distortion could accelerate learning: those volunteers receiving instructions designed to stretch 3 minutes into 10 minutes of nominal time performed as well in a free-recall learning task as those volunteers allotted 10 minutes of nominal time (and better than volunteers allotted 3 minutes nominal time).

We do much to influence our time and space and existence. Thinkers as diverse as Einstein or Vonnegut tell us time is a place, a place with variable geography that may be revisited or anticipated. Psychologically, we may alter our awareness of past, present, or future; we may alter the rate or acceleration of time; we may expand the present to live life more fully; we may even alter our biological time as well as our perception time, accelerating learning and reflex while slowing the processes of aging (Morgan 1977, 1981a, 1981b).

The first selection in this area is a classic but brief excerpt from the work of Jacob von Uexkull (1957). The famous ethologist illustrates the experiential measurable time rate variations in different species (chapter two).

As clinicians, acknowledging species-specific differences, we continue our main interest on individual differences within our own species. A key article by Zimbardo, Marshall, & Maslach (1971) is reproduced to demonstrate the impact of expanding the perception of the present hypnotically on the varied personalities of normal volunteers. Just as von Uexkull suggests interesting measurement/ research techniques, Zimbardo et al offer us what may be a useful technique for clinical practice: psychopathology or primary prevention (chapter three).

Zimbardo's 1971 study demonstrates a competent contemporary approach to research on any hypnotic effects: all the needed controls are in place plus a few for greater 'elegance'. As he suggests, expanding the present hypnotically may retard senility and may even extend longevity. More work is needed here. But hypnotic alteration of time did not begin with Zimbardo.

Quite some time ago, Richardson & Stalnaker (1930) published a study demonstrating that hypnosis can significantly influence the estimation of time. Five years later, Welch (1935) published a study demonstrating this same effect in the context of induced hypnotic dreams. The main figure in this area, however, was Linn Cooper, a physician and hypnotist from Washington, D.C.

In 1948, Cooper published a study entitled "Time distortion in hypnosis". Time distortion, what we now call time acceleration, was the process of experiencing much in short intervals or, less frequently, little in long intervals. Subjects would live an hour in 60 seconds of clock time... if properly hypnotized.

The concept of time distortion created a furor among psychologists and hypnotists. Did the subject *really* live a minute of experiential time for every second of clock time? Or was the subject only hypnotized to think this was so? Was it only experiential time or did the person actually undergo a biological speedup? Could more be accomplished by distorting (accelerating) time: would this give us more time to think? To solve math or personal problems? Would our reflexes speed up or slow down proportionate to how our time was distorted?

In 1950, Cooper teamed up with Milton Erickson, world famous medical hypnotist, to write "Time distortion in hypnosis II". Time distortion was defined as *a marked difference between the seeming duration of a time interval and its actual duration as measured by the clock.* (p. 51) One incident reported a boxer was able to use time distortion to slow (his experience of) his opponent down and better place punches. This is similar to baseball player Henry Aaron's description of how he sees baseballs move 'in slow motion' when he is up to bat. Cooper and Erickson covered a wide variety of case history experiences in time distortion, concluding: "Thought, under time distortion, while apparently proceeding at a normal rate from the subject's point of view, can take place with extreme rapidity relative to world time. Such thought may be superior, in certain respects, to waking thought." (p. 68). They ruled out retrospective falsification (cheating) and found the continuity of experienced events in hypnotically distorted time to be excellent. We hear of the little boy hypnotized for dental work who saw a complete movie in the few minutes of drilling; there is the patient who spends a subjective hour working on personal problems while spending only 60 clock seconds doing so. In this or in later work by the same authors we learn of patients reliving hours of key life experience in just a few minutes of clocked therapy time. We hear of enhanced learning ability (e.g., piano practice) by hours of experienced practice in minutes of hypnotized time. Clearly this mid-century breakthrough offered some intriguing possibilities to time-conscious people.

But: the history of time distortion followed the history of hypnosis. It gained and lost its respectability with the leadership of scientific and medical communities many times over the decades. The 1950s were not high acceptability years for hypnosis. However, time distortion research and practice continued in the hands of a few thick-skinned practitioners. Loomis in 1951 published an article demonstrating the use of hypnosis for better control of time estimation and synchrony with time. Cooper continued to publish in psychology journals: in 1951 he brought a cogent discussion of this topic to the *Journal of Psychology*. In 1953, with D.W. Rodgin, he published a study of the effect of hypnotized time distortion on learning in the prestigious *Science* journal of the American Association for the Advancement of Science. This latter article dealt with non-motor learning but the following year, with C. E. Tuthill, he published another *Journal of Psychology* article on time distortion and motor learning. Time distortion was effective in both. In 1954, Cooper and Erickson published a concise and complete book *TIME DISTORTION IN HYPNOSIS*, a long ignored classic in this area. I recommend the book highly: many libraries carry it although the publisher has not kept it in print.

Cooper had used the term "time distortion" exclusively for incidents where hypnotized subjects sped up experiential time (e.g., see a three hour movie in 10 clocked minutes). In 1958, Erickson published his own article distinguishing incidents where subjective time was slowed from ones where they subjective time was accelerated. When subjective time was slowed, this was "time expansion" and people experienced a lot of living in short intervals. When subjective time was sped up, this was termed "time condensation" and people experienced very little in long intervals. Time expansion could be used to slow down the world when you are on the spot and give yourself longer to think before acting. Time condensation could be used to speed up the (perceived) world and make standing in a long line go very quickly. Perhaps a good analogy is slow motion or speeded photography as shown in a film: the diver can take minutes to reach the water or the building can be built in seconds. . .depending on how fast the real events are filmed. The subjects of Cooper and Erickson could alter the rate of the "filming" of their own life. . .as it occurred, or as it was rerun. Erickson in this article used the technique to deal with a patient's excruciating pain.

The third selection presented here is a reproduction of Cooper & Erickson's second and major contribution (1950) with an excerpt from Erickson's more case-oriented article in 1958 (chapter four).

Among the chief critics of hypnotic research, including time distortion, was T.X. Barber. In 1964, Barber suggested that time distortion could well be produced by direct suggestion without hypnosis. Data did in fact suggest that a simple request to condense or expand time could produce some of the results usually found with hypnosis. There was also the possibility that patients and other subjects were consciously or unconsciously just trying to please the hypnotist but in fact did not really experience time distortion. Further, many subjects produced no time distortion even under hypnosis.

You can see why Zimbardo (1971) used all those control groups. The skeptics were useful in generating better research. But the results confirmed that hypnotized time distortion was a reality; it existed above and beyond compliance, request, or fraud. On the other hand, not every hypnotist could do it nor was every subject equally able to accomplish it. Orme (1962, 1964, 1969) found large individual differences in the ability to distort time under hypnosis. Weitzenhoffer (1964) took on Barber directly, demonstrating that subjects who were *deeply* hypnotized showed significantly better time distortion effects than waking subjects responding to direct suggestion.

The mid—1960s found further scattered investigations of time distortion. Of note was a dissertation (Casey, 1966) at Michigan State University and two articles in hypnosis journals (Aaronson, 1966; Edmunston & Erbeck, 1967). Aaronson investigated time distortion under the name 'altered time rate perception' (1968a, 1968b) and it was his work that first interested Zimbardo in the phenomenon. Another dissertation (Graef, 1969) again used time estimation to chart the effects of time distortion. But probably the most influential presentation of the decade was the chapter by Cooper & Erickson in Les LeCron's 1969 volume *Experimental Hypnosis*. This popular book was used well into the 1980s and did much to bring hypnosis back into credibility for researchers and practitioners. The association of Le-Cron with time distortion was helpful in another way. LeCron and Cheek were pioneers in the use of *auto-hypnosis* (1968) the techniques of hypnosis that subjects learn to use by themselves without the presence of any professional hypnotist. And therein lies the contemporary usage of time distortion or, as it's now called, time acceleration. If we learn the basic techniques of auto-hypnosis we can then use time acceleration on demand as one of the standard benefits. We can choose to speed up or slow down time as it fits our needs. And, possibly, we can choose to speed up or slow down our physical speed (simple & complex reaction time, for example) as needed. Elkind's 1972 study suggests we can even use hypnosis to slow down the aging process itself. These then are skills that can and should be generally available to the public. I can imagine an advanced school curriculum using them, even at the primary school level.

The next chapter in this book reprints an article by Paul Sacerdote illustrating clinical case applications of hypnotically altered space and time perception. He suggests new directions for both organic and functional syndromes unresponsive to more traditional approaches (chapter five).

Do we need to be hypnotized or to be hypnotists to make better use of our time, to accelerate it if we choose? No, there is another way.

It's called temporal conditioning: learning to synchronize yourself with intervals of time.

In 1959, the Soviet research in this area was brought to the attention of American psychology. Dmitriev & Kochigina that year published a review entitled "The importance of time as a stimulus of conditioned reflex activity" in the well-read *Psychological Bulletin*. Not only did they focus our attention on the process, but they had a neurological theory of cortical inhibition (Rozin, 1959) to account for it. What is "it"?

Have you ever known someone who can automatically wake up at exactly any time chosen the night before? Most of us have. This person is setting an internal alarm clock of sorts. Oh, he may also be using external clues (sunrise, birds, traffic, bladder, etc.) but even in isolation subjects can learn to synchronize with nearly any time interval. The Russians believed this learning was accomplished by setting up a rhythm in the brain of alternating excitation and inhibition of electrochemical reactions.

In my own research at Michigan State University (chapters 6-11) I set up a very basic learning situation for training the time sense. Subjects were seated in a dark isolated room with a light bulb which was geared to flash briefly at regular intervals. They were to say "NOW" when they felt the light was about to flash. The game was to come as close as possible without letting the light flash before you could say "NOW". You had 15 tries. Nearly everyone got better at this with practice, demonstrating it could be learned. The most effective way was not to count but rather to relax: your body would tense just before a flash was due (GSR readings confirmed this). Americans had succeeded at short intervals (up to 60 seconds) and Russians at longer intervals (up to 30 minutes). My work demonstrated that temporal conditioning was possible at both short *and* longer intervals with a difficult period in-between. But what is most relevant for this chapter was an accident that occurred.

One of my subjects left the study with his time sense accelerated: He had to be brought back for repairs.

It happened like this: Paid volunteers were needed for the long interval studies. These subjects were paid for a 16 hour day. They showed up expecting a series of experiments, not realizing the entire 16 hours would be spent in a single study. As they entered the experimental room, they noticed a urinal, chicken, and lemonade. . .signs of a long stay. However, when given the instructions (say "NOW" just before the light flashes) they really didn't expect more than a minute or two to be between flashes. In fact, the interval to be tested was *60 minutes*, a full hour, 15 times in a row. As a result, the volunteers all underestimated (after the study) how long the intervals were and how long they had been in the study. Sixty minutes were misperceived to be 5 minutes, for example. One man was so convinced he had only been in the room an hour (rather than 16 hours) that he never used the urinal or ate the food.

This, of course, is classic time distortion technique: the time rate is uniformly off by a constant factor (the hypnotist says each metronome click signifies the passage of a minute but in fact it signifies the passage of a second). One volunteer returned to me weeks after the close of the study: he complained that since his participation, time seemed to be flying by him. He would get in a long line at the bank and before he could get out his checkbook the teller would be waiting for him. People seemed to be whizzing by him. He appeared slow to his wife and friends. He would no sooner sit down and they would point out the passage of an hour. In short, his time rate (experiential) had been accelerated or condensed and he did not like it.

I put him back in the room and applied classical "extinction" techniques. I gradually brought him down to synchrony with shorter and shorter time intervals until we reached 60 seconds. He came back a second day and did 15 trials at 60 second intervals. After this his time rate was normal and remained that way.

I now wondered about accelerating time in the opposite direction. If one learned to synchronize with briefer and briefer intervals would one's reflexes speed up? Would present time expand? And could these different intervals be coded (e.g., different colors) so they could be recalled at will? Could temporal conditioning be used to give us a temporal gear shift?: reverse, forward slow, forward average, forward fast, overdrive. . .Another study that year (Barch, Ratner, & Morgan, 1965) demonstrated that "latent reacquisition" is possible: this means that re-exposure to key elements in a learning situation can bring back the material learned. Hypnotists also use key words or events to key in recalled memories or behaviors.

Research in this area continues. Temporal psychology, via hypnosis or conditioning or standard research, is an important growing area for the 21st century. Ornstein (1972) has well described the temporal dimensions of consciousness. Mo (1975) has demonstrated that experiential passage of time depends on the number of elements within that time unit: you get more time for your money when a lot is happening in it. Von Uexkull (1957) and Fischer (1966) have done much to call attention to the different time rates of differing species of plants and animals. Plants behave much like animals, for example, when their slower time rate is taken into account. Three of the best classic texts in this area were Paul Fraisse's (1963) *The Psychology of Time*; Orme's (1969) *Time, Experience, & Behaviour;* and Henry Still's *Of Time, Tides, and Inner Clocks* (1972) (reprinted 1975). In 1972, the first meeting of the International Society for the Study of Time was held in Europe (Fraser, Haber, & Muller, 1972) as an interdisciplinary effort. Today we have The Association for the Social Studies of Time (ASSET), based in London, England.

Time, clinically, is both problem and solution, pathology treatment, potential and prevention. The following chapters are meant to illustrate, elucidate, and illuminate these aspects; they may be read for enjoyment as well as knowledge: take your time.

CHAPTER TWO

RECEPTOR TIME FOR HUMANS AND OTHERS

Not only do we have differential speeds of perception and response between individuals but we have even more variability between species. Understanding the experiential and physiological bases for this variation may lead us well beyond the early progress in temporal exploration outlined in subsequent chapters.

Perhaps no one has stated this as eloquently as has Jacob von Uexkull (1957) in his classic "Stroll through the world of animals and men: a picture book of individual worlds". While the emphasis of my book must remain with homo sapiens, it seems worthwhile and fitting to begin by a salute to the continued challenge of comparative psychology in tracking down, as major quarry, the impact of time on behavior. To do this, I choose to quote von Uexkull's 1957 piece on the subject of "receptor time":

Karl Ernst von Baer has made it clear that time is the product of a subject. Time as a succession of moments varies from one Umwelt to another, according to the number of moments experienced by different subjects within the same span of time. A moment is the smallest indivisible time vessel, for it is the expressions of an indivisible elementary sensation, the so-called moment sign. As already stated, the duration of a human moment amounts to 1/18 of a second. Furthermore, the moment is identical for all sense modalities, since all sensations are accompanied by the same moment sign.

The human ear does not discriminate eighteen air vibrations in one second, but hears them as one sound.

It has been found that eighteen taps applied to the skin within one second are felt as even pressure.

Kinematography projects environmental motions onto a screen at their accustomed tempo. the single pictures then follow each other in tiny jerks of 1/18 second.

If we wish to observe motions too swift for the human eye, we resort to slow-motion photography. this is a technique by which more than eighteen pictures are taken per second, and then projected at a normal tempo. Motor processes are thus extended over a longer span of time, and processes too swift for our human time-tempo (of 18 per second), such as the wing-beat of birds and insects, can be made visible. As slow-motion photography slows motor processes down, the time contractor speeds them up. If a process is photographed once an hour and them presented at the rate of 1/18 second, it is condensed into a short space of time. In this way, processes too slow for our human tempo, such as the blossoming of a flower, can be brought within the range of our perception.

The question arises whether there are animals whose perceptual time consists of shorter or longer moments than ours, and in whose Unwelt motor processes are consequently enacted more slowly or more quickly than in ours.

The first experiments of this kind were made by a young German scientist. Later, with the collaboration of another, he studied especially the reaction of the fighting fish to its own mirror image. The fighting fish does not recognize its own reflection if it is shown him eighteen times per second. It must be presented to the fighting fish at least thirty times per second. A third student trained the fighting fish to snap toward their food if a gray disc was rotated behind it. On the other hand, if a disc with black and white sectors was turned slowly, it acted as a "warning sign," for in this case the fish received a light shock when they approached their fool. After this training, if the rotation speed of the black and white disc was gradually increased, the avoiding reactions became more uncertain at a certain speed, and soon thereafter they shifted to the opposite. This did not happen until the black sectors followed each other within 1/50 second. At this speed the black-and-white signal had become gray. this proves conclusively that in the world of these fish, who feed on fast-moving prey, all motor processes—as in the case of slow-motion photography—appear at reduced speed.

A vineyard snail is placed on a rubber ball which, carried by water, slides under it without fric-

tion. the snail's shell is held in place by a bracket.   Thus the snail, unhampered in its crawling movements, remains in the same place. If a small stick is then moved up to its foot, the snail will climb up on it. If the snail is given one to three taps with the stick each second, it will turn away, but if four or more taps are administered per second, it will begin to climb onto the stick. In the snail's world a rod that oscillates four times per second has become stationary. We may infer from this that the snail's receptor time moves at a tempo of three to four moments per second. As a result, all motor processes in the snail's world occur much faster than in ours. Nor do its own motions seem slower to the snail than ours do to us.

Having shared these thoughts, we may now move back to the varying of receptor (and other) times for humans alone.

For this we begin with hypnosis.

CHAPTER THREE

HYPNOTIC EXPANSION OF THE PRESENT

Reprinted with permission:

Journal of Applied Social Psychology, 1971, 1, 4. pp. 305—323

Liberating Behavior from Time-Bound Control: Expanding the Present Through Hypnosis[1]

PHILIP G. ZIMBARDO AND GARY MARSHALL
Stanford University

CHRISTINA MASLACH
University of California at Berkeley

Temporal perspective was experimentally manipulated by verbal instructions to expand the present while minimizing the significance of past and future. The reactions of trained hypnotic subjects to this induction were compared with hypnotic simulators and nonsimulating controls. In a fourth group, time sense was made salient but no suggestion given to alter it. Across a variety of tasks, self-report measures, and behavioral observations, this modification of the boundaries between past, present, and future resulted in profound consequences among the hypnotic subjects.

Changes in affect, language, thought processes, sensory awareness, and susceptibility to social-emotional contagion, accompanied an expanded present orientation. Nonreactive measures distinguished simulators from hypnotic subjects who apparently were better able than control subjects to incorporate the induced time distortion and perceive it as a viable alternative to their traditional time perspective. Some implications of time as a pervasive, non-obvious, independent variable in the social control of cognition and behavior are outlined.

"Time is the most undefinable yet paradoxical of things; the past is gone, the future has not come, and the present becomes the past even while we attempt to define it, and like a flash of lightning, at once exists and expires."

(Kugelmass, In Cohen, 1967, p. v)

---

[1] This research was financially supported by an ONR research grant:
N00014-67-A-0112-0041 to Professor P. Zimbardo, and written while the senior author was a fellow at the Center for Advanced Study in the Behavioral Sciences.
[2] Requests for reprints should be sent to Professor P. Zimbardo, Department of Psychology, Stanford University, Stanford, California 94305.

Imagine with us, if you will, that you possess a special kind of psychological calendar watch. What makes it special is that it allows you to set it ahead so that it tells only future time, or back so that past time is all that it measures, or even to capture and hold the present in the imperceptible movement of its mechanism. With such a device, you could be the time keeper of yesterdays or tomorrows, or you might prefer to prevent the present from slipping into past and the future from ever becoming now. How would *you* use it? How would your behavior be affected by the way you chose to operate it?

Such a speculation is more than an intriguing fiction. You already own this special device which has the power of transforming the modes of time, of so readily altering time perspective. It is the human mind.

There is no construct of human imagination that has a more pervasive, yet unappreciated, effect upon our behavior than that of time. We have come to conceive of time as having an external, physical reality independent of its origin and maintenance in the minds of man. While we press time into our service as a constant or a dependent variable measuring and recording events of interest, we ignore the more fundamental role it plays in our lives.

The experience of time makes it possible for us to establish the concepts of causality, consistency, and history out of essentially discrete, isolated, transient, and even random occurrences. Cultural traditions and our sense of individual identity can exist only by implicitly accepting assumptions about temporal continuity. Virtually every social institution that exists to regulate individual behavior does so by forcing a reevaluation of the present within the confines imposed by the conceptual language of the past and future.

In religion, we do penance now for sins of the past, all the while bearing earthly burdens, suffering, and oppression for the promised "pie in the sky when we die." Indeed, Catholics are reminded on Ash Wednesday of their mortal origins in dust and their eventual return to this state of entropy. Justice makes us responsible for keeping not only our past commitments, but those agreed upon by our fellows, as law provides the threats and penalties for failing to do so. Art, as reflected in Keats' Grecian Urn, attempts to impose coherence and a timeless presence on the mutable flux of experience.

It is through the process of socialization that time perspective is created, in order to make communal life possible, and through the emergence of memory that individuals can cope with the challenge of change. Each human being is thereby transformed from an impulsive, ego-centered creature driven by the urgency of biological needs into a more passive, analytical, socially centered citizen able to tolerate frustration and to delay gratification. The actor becomes a reactor, living for the moment becomes living for a purpose, and being is parceled into has been and will be. The past and the future which begin as only cognitive modes of experience, in contrast to the sensory, empirical foundation of present experience, become the reality to which the present is subjugated.

In a later Section of this paper, we shall explore further some of the consequences for behavioral freedom of our usual notions of temporal perspective. Precisely because time is such a central part of our thinking, feeling, and acting, we can only investigate its functioning and impact by disrupting its usual operation. We can theorize about time as an independent variable, but to establish its controlling influence upon behavior, it is necessary to systematically interfere with the temporal process. This methodological strategy is, of course, common to the study of all psychological phenomena which function so efficiently as to go unnoticed by the behaving organism or the observer. Delaying auditory feedback to study the effects of hearing on speech, and distorting the visual field with prisms to study visual-motor coordination, are examples of the effective use of this approach.

Our investigation of time has focused upon altering the perspective of present time by expanding it. How would a person's behavior change if he or she were to alter the perceived relationship between past, present, and future by having the present expand while past and future diminished? Concern with this aspect of "time sense" is in part derived from a model of deindividuation (Zimbardo, 1969). This model attempts to delineate those systems of social and personal control that create a sense of individual identity and self-awareness. It is through these mechanisms that a person's behavior is constrained to make it normal rational, and acceptable. Behavior is liberated from these constraints and allowed to become more irrational, impulsive, chaotic, and uncontrollable as attention to social and self-evaluation is minimized. Controls imposed by guilt, shame, fear, reasoned analysis, past experience, commitment, obligation, responsibility, and liability are shattered once past and future become insignificant. The individual, "living for the moment," should become more sensitive to sensory stimulation and more responsive to arousal cues. Behavior once initiated should be more difficult to terminate, as long as the instigating stimulus remains.

It appears that this kind of disruption of temporal perspective occurs in some people under the influence of psychedelic drugs. It is often a goal of marathon encounter groups and a co-product of states of ecstasy induced by music, dances, and activities associated with "primitive" ceremonial rites.

Following a provocative lead in the work of Aaronson (1968a, b), we decided to induce an expanded present state through hypnosis. Aaronson's intensive work with several selected subjects appeared to indicate that euphoria accompanied induction of an expanded present orientation via hypnotic suggestion, while a schizophrenic-like state followed removal of the present time sense. The validity of these changes unfortunately rests upon such questionable evidence as inferences from paintings made by the subjects and clinical judgments of only a few individuals without benefit of controlled comparisons.

Our study, then, is an exploratory attempt to use hypnosis as a technique for modifying temporal perspective (specifically, expanding the present), while observing the effects of this induction across a range of tasks in experimental and control subjects.

METHOD

Subjects

Thirty undergraduates from Stanford University served as subjects in this research. They were paid volunteers recruited through their introductory psychology course. The equal number of males and females in this sample were selected from among the population of high scorers on a group administration of Form A of the Stanford Hypnotizability Scale (Hilgard, 1965).

Those randomly assigned to the training condition received about 10 hours of experience with hypnotic induction. Those randomly assigned to the no-training condition for this study did, however, receive comparable hypnotic training subsequent to it, and became experimental subjects in some of our other research. There were no differences in either the mean hypnotizability scores or the observed "success" in hypnosis of the four groups of subjects employed in this study.

Hypnotic Training

Our training approach utilizes group inductions in small groups that vary from eight persons in the initial sessions to two in the final ones. We have found this group training to be more efficient than individual sessions and also more effective.

Subjects usually find it more reassuring not to be "one on one" with the hypnotist, especially early in training, and the hypnotist is able to bring to bear additional social pressures upon the occasional subjects who are recalcitrant, "slow," or not confident in their ability to experience hypnosis. The training is permissive in orientation, stressing the subject's choice to follow each suggestion and directed toward getting the subject to achieve self-hypnosis. It also attempts to establish a personal relationship of trust and mutual respect between hypnotist and subject. A variety of induction techniques were used over the course of training (during which time each subject was exposed to each of the three present authors in their capacity as hypnotists). However, common to both the verbal and nonverbal techniques we used was the development of a state of very deep relaxation. Specific training was given in motoric control, perceptual control, fantasy experience, amnesia, posthypnotic suggestions, and analgesia. Underlying these phenomena was the ability, encouraged through training, to concentrate, to dissociate, and to produce vivid images. All subjects reported that it was only after at least several hours of training that they began to believe something special was happening, that they were indeed "hypnotized." Everyone of the subjects was able to alter ischemic pain tolerance significantly more in hypnosis than in a waking, motivated state. On an additional criterion test, all of the subjects successfully carried out a post-hypnotic suggestion and appeared to have amnesia for it. During the final training sessions, general suggestions involving time distortion were given. The subjects were asked to allow the present to expand and then to describe how they felt (without comment by the hypnotist).

Procedure

The research design compared the responses of 12 trained hypnotic subjects given the suggestion to "allow the present to expand and the past and future to become distanced and insignificant" with those of 18 other subjects distributed across three control conditions. In two of them, the same expanded present, time distortion instruction was given (via standardized tape recording). Half of these subjects were hypnotic simulators told to imagine how hypnotized subjects would respond and then to act as if they were hypnotized throughout the study. The nonsimulator controls merely received the time distortion instruction without any mention of hypnosis. The fourth group was a normal-time control informed merely to think of their own conception of time and to describe it in an appropriate metaphor (as the other subjects did before being given the present expanded treatment).

Subjects were tested in pairs within the same condition, although on most tasks they were isolated in separate cubicles. The hypnotic subjects were given a 5-minute relaxation induction at the start of the experimental session, while the simulators were given the same period of time to prepare themselves to be "good" hypnotic simulators.

The first task involved writing projective stories in response to two TAT pictures, one before and the other after the time distortion manipulation. Five minutes' time was allowed for each of the two stories; the order of the two TAT pictures was counterbalanced across subjects in each group. It was predicted that subjects experiencing an expanded present would reveal before-after changes in the language and thematic content of their stories, such as more present tense verbs, greater reference to present events, less emphasis on future goals or antecedent conditions, etc.

A reminder to maintain a sense of the expanded present was repeated before the second and third experimental tasks (except, of course, for the normal-time controls). The second task was designed to thrust the subjects into an unexpected situation that could be humorous or repulsive. Told simply to listen to a tape recording, all subjects heard a 5-minute pirated tape of an abortive radio commercial for an old movie ("The Caddie") by a former comedy team. After committing several bloopers, the comedians begin to criticize, taunt, and curse each other. They become increasingly obscene and vulgar, to the obvious amusement of the recording engineers who could be heard laughing in the background. The overt reactions of the subjects while listening to this tape were recorded by two judges behind a one-way mirror, and their self-reported reactions elicited on a questionnaire. It was predicted that subjects experiencing an expanded present would react more strongly during the recording since they would be able to overcome the normative prohibitions against openly enjoying such material in the sterile confines of a research laboratory.

The final task was designed to get the subjects more directly involved in a sensory experience through physical action. They were told they had 5 minutes to make something out of a large 2-pound mound of clay which was on the floor in front of the room. The subjects left their cubicles and proceeded to work either independently or together, as they chose. A stack of paper towels was available near the moist, sticky clay so that subjects could clean their hands, although this was not explicitly suggested. At the end of 5 minutes, the experimenter entered the room and told the subjects to finish up and return to their cubicles to complete a questionnaire about their reactions to this noncognitive task. Judges observed what the subjects made with the clay, as well as how they handled it, and their reactions to being soiled with it. It was predicted that subjects experiencing an expanded present would be less likely to make an object with a finite form since that would involve planning and a future orientation. In addition, we expected these same subjects to be less concerned, or indeed to enjoy the experience of having their hands coated with the clay. When the first group of hypnotized, expanded present subjects continued to play with the clay, ignoring the request to return to their cubicles, this unanticipated source of behavioral variability was systematically recorded for all subjects (within another 5-minute maximum interval).

After instructing the subjects in the appropriate groups to allow their conception of time to return to normal, and the hypnotized subjects to come out of hypnosis, the experimenter described in detail the purpose and design of the study, answered all queries of the subjects, and solicited any further personal reactions they had.

RESULTS

Overview

Verbal instructions to expand the present appeared to have had a profound effect upon the behavior of hypnotized subjects, who may have been better able than control subjects to incorporate this suggestion into their temporal perspective. Their language changed toward more frequent use of present tense verbs and more references to present events. They were more likely to laugh aloud at funny events and to continue to be physically preoccupied in a sensory experience. They were less concerned with their appearance and had more difficulty answering questions pertaining to memories of their reactions on

TABLE 1

MEAN CHANGES IN TAT RESPONSES BEFORE TO AFTER INDUCTION OF TIME DISTORTION

Treatment	Mean % present tense verbs to total verbs	Mean % total reference to:		
		past	present	future
Present expanded				
Hypnosis (N = 12)	+ 8.5	0.0	+ 3.3	- 3.2
Simulation (N = 6)	+ 12.4	- 10.1	+ 11.3	- 1.3
control (N = 6)	- 14.6	- 1.2	- 8.3	+ 9.6
Normal time (N = 6)	- 20.7	+ 5.9	- 8.8	+ 2.9

prior experimental tasks. Some even got involved in the sensation of writing a questionnaire response and were indifferent to answering the test questions in a socially appropriate manner.

A few of these findings, however, also occurred among subjects simulating hypnosis. Nevertheless, the use of nonreactive response measures relatively insusceptible to experimental demand features or to subject expectation, allowed us to distinguish valid from spurious manifestations of an altered temporal perspective. No sex differences were found on any measures and, thus, only combined analyses are presented.

Temporal Language

The TAT pictures selected for this research rather clearly reflected time themes, since one showed an old woman and a young woman, and the other a farm with a farmer planting crops while a pregnant woman gazed upon the scene. The stories written by the subjects were each scored independently by two "blind" raters, with the average of their ratings being used for analysis. The primary categories analyzed were changes in the use of present tense verbs relative to total use of verbs, and changes in references to events that could be distinguished as taking place in the past, present, or future.

These data, presented in Table 1, indicate that the hypnotic group changed their time perspective in accordance with an expanded present orientation. They used more present tense verbs, more references to present events, fewer to future and no more than previously to the past. However, simulating controls "read" what was the appropriate way for hypnotized subjects to react and outdid the hypnosis group! They used an even greater percentage of present tense verbs, references to the present, and evidenced a marked reduction in concern for past events. These changes cannot be attributed simply to the present expanded instructions since they were absent, or indeed opposite, in the controls given the same induction. These controls and the normal-time controls showed a sharp reduction in their use of present tense and events. These two groups differ significantly from the hypnotized and simulator groups in their use of present tense verbs ($p < .02$. $t = 2.54$, $df = 28$), and differ nearly significantly in their use of present events ($p < .10$). The differences between hypnotized and simulating subjects are not statistically significant.

Perhaps even more revealing of the degree to which the simulators perceived what was expected of them is their consensus across the various measures. Every one of them increased their percentage of present tense verbs while 58% of the hypnotic group. 33% of the neutrals, and only 16% of the normal-time group did so. The simulators thus differed significantly from each of the other three groups beyond the .01 level (by separate ratio analyses). In like manner, five of six simulators decreased their total references to past events and increased their references to present events. Only a third of the hypnosis subjects decreased their references to past events and a half of them increased their concern for present events. On the first measure, the hypnosis group differs from the simulators at the .01 level ($z = 3.52$) while on the second, the difference is at the .05 level ($z = 2.24$). The simulators also differ significantly from the other two groups on these measures, but the latter do not differ from the hypnosis group. None of the differences in references to the future were significant.

If this were our only dependent measure, we would be forced to conclude that the obtained effects of changes in language and thinking in response to the present expanded induction are confounded with consciously controlled expectations about how a hypnotic subject should react to such a suggestion. However, there were important qualitative changes in behavior, such as the dramatic differences in handwriting and language style shown in the two samples of TAT themes written by a hypnotized subject, first in the normal present and then in the expanded present state (Figure 1). On each of the other dependent measures to be reported next, the changes noted between groups were statistically significant.

Affective Reactions

When subjects were exposed to the humorous, obscene taped material, it was assumed that normative influences operating in the laboratory situation would prevent them from reacting strongly to it. However, if they had internalized an expanded present orientation, they then should have been less concerned about how they might be evaluated for their reaction and more able to experience and openly respond to the immediately present situation. This reasoning receives support when we compare the extent to which subjects in the different treatments responded to the comedy material by either smiling or laughing outright. It is evident from the data in Table 2 that the pattern of laughing or simply smiling distinguished the hypnosis group from each of the others.

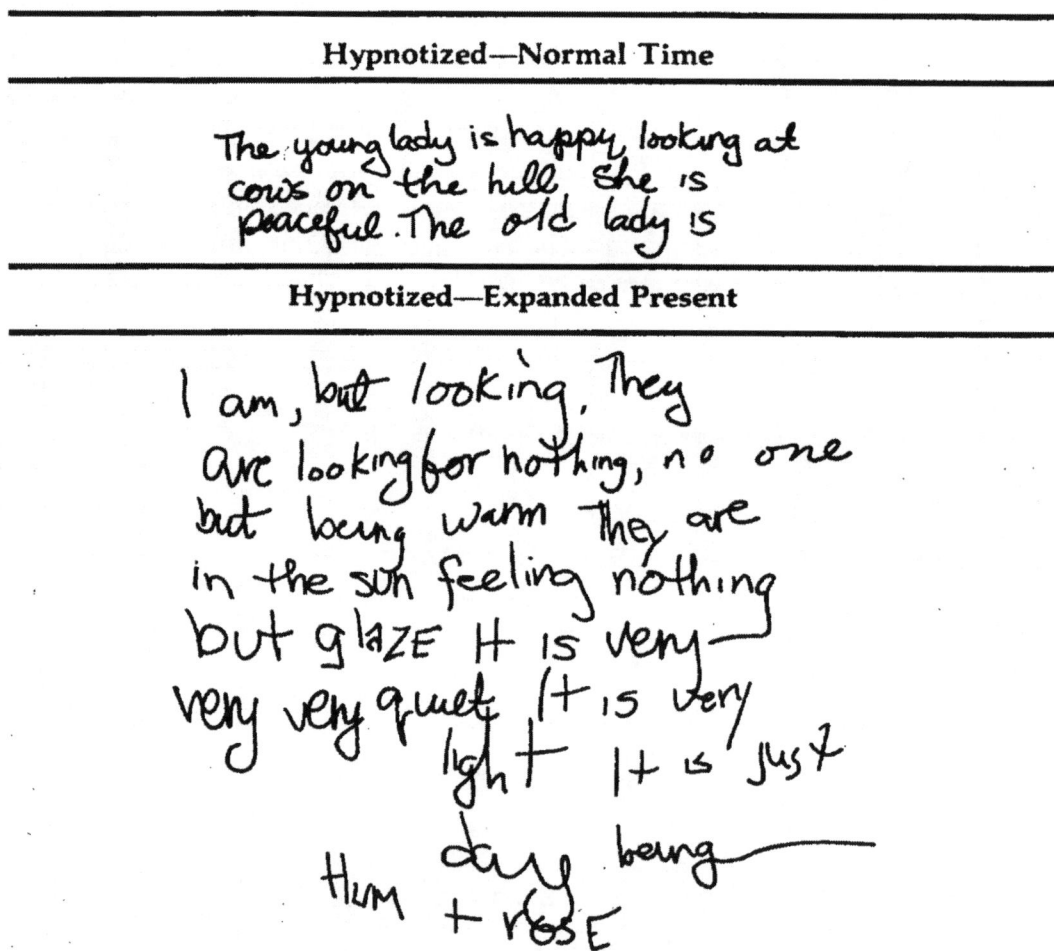

Hypnotized—Normal Time

The young lady is happy, looking at cows on the hill, she is peaceful. The old lady is

---

Hypnotized—Expanded Present

I am, but looking, They are looking for nothing, no one but being warm they are in the sun feeling nothing but glaze It is very — very very quiet It is very light It is just

Hum day being + rose

FIG. 1. Handwriting changes in TAT themes for single hypnotic subject.

These subjects were equally likely to react by openly laughing as by smiling. The simulators smiled as often as the hypnotic group, but they were not observed to react at the more intense level by laughing. Each of the other two groups behaved in a more socially appropriate manner, smiling more frequently, but laughing infrequently. In fact, they smiled significantly more than the hypnosis or simulation groups ($p < .025$, $F = 4.61$, $df = 3,26$). The greater frequency of laughter of the hypnosis group, however, only approaches statistical significance. An analysis of subjects in each group who gave an especially hearty (or "belly") laugh indicated that the only three who did were in the hypnosis group.

TABLE 2

MEAN NUMBER OF SMILES OR LAUGHS OBSERVED IN RESPONSE TO OBSCENE, COMEDY MATERIAL

Treatment	Smiles	Laughs
Present expanded		
Hypnosis	3.0	3.0
Simulation	3.7	.2
Control	5.2	1.0
Normal Time	6.7	.7

This quantitative data is less convincing than some of our qualitative data of the basic changes in time sense and responsiveness to "stimulus immediacy" achieved in many of the hypnotic subjects. Only hypnotized, present expanded subjects expressed the emotional mood of the taped material by themselves using obscenities and jokes in their questionnaire answers. For example,
1. Jerry L. is so f... d up that I got sick and tired of listening to that bastard laugh. At least M. has some class but L. has no class because he's always out to lunch. I think they should lose Jerry L. in a f...g water hazard. Because he is a hazard to humor!!!!"
2. "At first I was rather disgusted, listening to those stupid f...s, but when they started screwing up, it blew my nose."
3. "How in the hell did you get hold of it! I never believed "stars" could swear as much as I do."
4. "Yuk. Yuk and I rate this film ⊗"
A more typical view of the nature of the unusual reactions generated by this alteration of time can be witnessed in the report of one of the hypnotic subjects, written a minute after having heard the tape recording:

> I don't remember much about it now-all I remember is that it was funny and that I'd seen the movie the men were talking about. But actually I don't really care too much about the tape at all right now. I hate writing this. So I'm stopping. Right now. I feel like laughing. But I'd better stop writing this first. Right now."

Another subject in this expanded present condition wrote:

> "Sometimes it was funny-slips of tongue funny obscene-O.K. But sometimes, just two jokes-the situations described weren't funny—not nice. O.K. tape, not great. Not a funny start-sad."

Sensory Involvement

The purpose for having the subjects play with the clay was to provide an occasion for differences in the experience of time perspective to emerge which might not have been apparent on the other, more cognitive tasks. It was expected that those with a sense of expanded present would be less likely to plan ahead and thus, not render the clay into a particular shape or specific figure. The only subjects who did not end up with a distinguishable figure or recognizable "thing" were several pairs of hypnotic, expanded present subjects. They either made many small figures as part of an uncompleted diorama, or continually changed the content of their modeling. However, this measure proved to be unsatisfactory because in the short time period provided, many subjects in all conditions did not make much progress and some hurriedly put their clay into final shape when told to finish up and return to their cubicles for the next task.

The most compelling evidence for the greater involvement of the hypnotic subjects in the "here and now," and their lack of concern with appearance, comes from two rather subtle, nonobvious measures of change in temporal perspective, and also from the subjects' own accounts of the experience.

If the subjects were truly engaged in the ongoing activity of deriving pleasure from manipulating the clay for its own sake (as we would predict for those experiencing an expanded present), then our test situation should elicit two characteristic behaviors. First, when the experimenter said to stop and return to their cubicles to complete the next questionnaire, those who were "stuck in the clay" should have ignored his command once he left and it became a past event. Second, the moist clay (which was chosen because it stuck to the hands) ought to be less disturbing to those with an expanded present orientation since they would continue to enjoy its sensory qualities and not worry about whether to get cleaned up before going on to the next task or how they looked to observers. The data clearly support both of these predictions in demonstrating significant differences in these behaviors between the hypnotic subjects and all others in the three comparison groups.

The mean total time each subject continued to play with the clay after being told to stop is shown in Figure 2. The normal-time subjects tended to complete the task shortly before the allotted 5 minutes. The two expanded present control groups finished up their figures in about a minute after being told to. In sharp contrast, the hypnotic, expanded present subjects continued to play with the clay for nearly 250 seconds more. This value would have been much higher were it not for imposing an arbitrary ceiling of 300 seconds, which five of the subjects reached before being forced to stop. Whether the unit for statistical analysis is the pair of subjects sharing the clay or the individual subject, the results are significant since the shortest time taken by any of the hypnotic subjects was at least 60 seconds longer than the longest continuation recorded for any subject in the other conditions. The significant overall effect ($p = <.0001$, $F = 24.63$, $df = 3, 26$) is primarily due to the large difference between the hypnotic group and each of the others ($p < .001$).

Observers recorded the subject's concern with the mess or being dirty by noting whether they used the readily available paper towels, wiped off their hands on the desk top or on their clothing, or spent time looking at their hands. Two-thirds of the hypnotic group gave no evidence at all of any concern for the fact that their hands were coated with the residue of the clay. This is compared with the almost universal reaction of all (but two) other subjects to clean up immediately after completing the task. The proportion of subjects revealing such concern was significantly less for the hypnotic, present expanded group than the others ($p < .001$, $z = 3.52$).

In addition to these observed behavioral differences In hand wiping or attempts to clean the clay off, hypnotic present expanded subjects also described their reaction to it much more positively than did the other subjects. Some examples of typical questionnaire reactions for these hypnotic, expanded present subjects are:

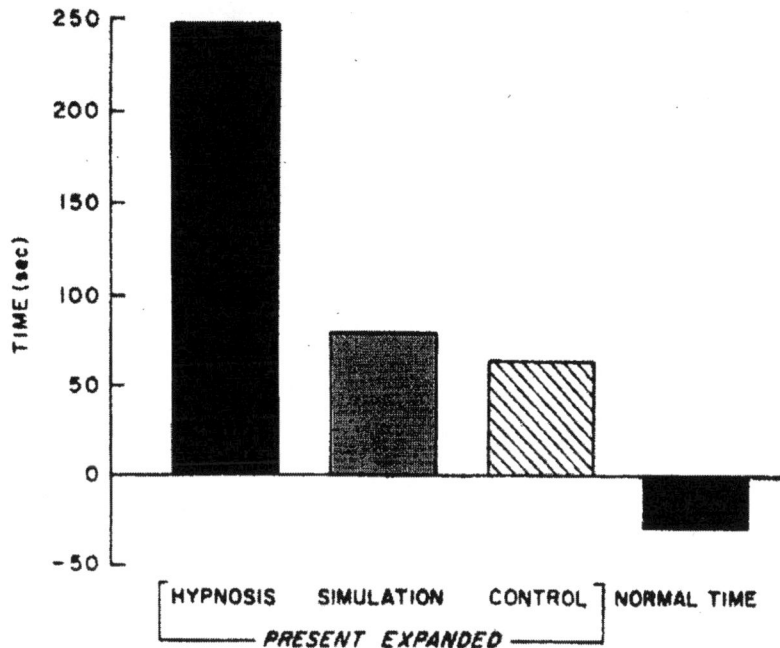

FIG. 2. Mean time spent continuing to play with clay after being instructed to terminate this activity (original 5-minute task period is the zero baseline.

1. "Felt like I was working in the dirt, like the farmer in the picture [the TAT scene]... felt the soil under my fingernails, drying out and becoming like shaving talc."

2. The thing I like *most* about working with the clay is "getting my hands dirty. . . all the clay I've got all over my hands now."

3. The thing I like *least* about working with the clay is "the fact that it stuck to my hands and now I am a clayman;" "my dirty hands afterwards, but that's O.K."

The control subjects across all three conditions, when asked to react to their experience of working with the clay, were rather distressed by the residue on their hands. For example:

1. "My hands are caked with clay, and I got some on my shirt. It's a drag for my hands to feel like this."

2. "I've got all this goddam clay on my hands."

3. "It got my hands dirty as hell."

4. "It got clay under my fingernails and that's probably the most uncomfortable feeling I've had in 2 days."

5. "It leaves your hands filthy."

None of the expanded present, hypnotized subjects reported awareness of being observed during the clay session (through the one-way mirror), but some of the controls in each group spontaneously reported being bothered by the knowledge that they were being watched by the experimenters.

On a 7-point scale of enjoyment with the clay, there were no differences between any of the three expanded present treatment groups. each of which enjoyed it more than did the normal-time control ($p < .02$). The mean ratings were: Normal-time controls, 3.8; present expanded controls, 5.2; present expanded simulators, 6.0; present expanded hypnotized, 6.5.

The final indication of just how profound an effect was created in some subjects by incorporating a present expanded time perspective into their experiential interaction with the environment is evident in their evaluations of the clay task.

For one subject, "The clay was very soft and moist, it felt nice to dig my fingers into it. When I was working with it, the shape just kind of happened. There was very little effort involved. It just kind of worked itself out." Another subject, who really enjoyed working with the clay, was still very much in tune with her immediately present environment when she wrote:

I didn't want to stop. But now I don't care because I'm writing this. I've got clay on my hands. Now I'll move to question #1.

I remember feeling very, very good. But that was clay and now this is pencil and paper. It's amazing how a pencil can make marks on a paper that other people can read and understand. . . I can't really think about working with the clay. These questions interrupt my thought process. That makes me angry. But I don't case because it's all fantastically amazing. I can hear the blood in my ears. . . Now I wonder why that is. No more room. Back in the folder.

None of the control subjects even gave a response that was remotely comparable to these by hypnotized subjects presumably experiencing a present expanded temporal perspective.

DISCUSSION

What is most surprising about the results of this exploratory investigation into alteration of temporal perspective is that such profound effects upon thinking, feeling, and acting could result from mere verbal suggestion to recreate one's perceived boundaries between the present and past and future. On the one hand, it is curious that well-established time-bound controls over behavior could be so readily suspended, and on the other, it is not at all unexpected that an individual's style of interacting with the environment and representation of it will undergo fundamental changes as "becoming," "Here-now" and "eventing" assume new psychological significance. As the present loses its transience by borrowing time from pastness and futurity, the conceptualized awareness of "nowness" apparently changes learned frames of reference for both "objective" stimulus reception and "appropriate" response output.

In pursuing an analysis of what Grunbaum (1967) calls the "mind-dependence of becoming," we wish to consider first the facilitory role played by hypnosis, then present some additional pilot study data relevant to issues of social-emotional contagion under expanded present states, and finally, to outline predicted effects of such states upon a range of basic psychological phenomena not yet investigated.

The Role of Hypnosis

From one point of view, it could be said that the present study shows the effectiveness of simply encouraging people to make salient their personal time perspective and then to allow it to be transformed by expanding the present.

On some measures, subjects in all groups given the expanded present induction reacted differently than those in the normal-time control condition. But across all tasks (and on the basis of our observations, qualitative data, and anecdotal reports), the subjects for whom temporal perspective was most markedly altered were those given hypnotic training and put into an hypnotic state during the experiment.

Why this should be so, we think is understandable as a consequence of the nature of hypnotizability and the reality-distorting experiences characteristic of our training procedures. It is our opinion that the ease with which a person can experience hypnotic phenomena depends, in large part, upon being able to suspend reliance upon "critical reality testing," to be willing to give up objective-subjective differentiations, and to have developed an "imaginative involvement" (Hilgard, 1970) with symbols and words to the extent that they can assume a controlling influence over the individual's behavior.

Given subjects selected on the basis of high hypnotizability scores, we further developed the above characteristics in training sessions, as well as instilling in these subjects an attribution of internal control over experience and behavior. Thus, it is probable that they were preset to accept the viability of the present expanded suggestion, to have confidence they could alter their temporal perspective as suggested, and to be less apprehensive about feeling or acting in nonconventional ways in the experimental situation. The obtained differences between hypnotic subjects and simulators on the nonreactive tasks and in their self-descriptions indicate that something more is operating than subject selection or expectation of behaving like an hypnotic subject or even complying with inferred experimenter demands. That something more is not peculiar to the "mystical" nature of hypnosis, but rather to the combination of learning experiences which increase hypnotizability, and hypnotic training experiences which produce the psychological changes noted above. This is to say that the effects noted are in no way limited to hypnotic subjects but rather to those experimental conditions that facilitate allowing, accepting, and temporarily incorporating such basic changes in one's sense of time. Certain drugs, alcohol, sensory deprivation, intense emotional arousal, and some states of mental illness can lead to changes in temporal perspective; hypnosis merely offers a better methodological strategy for studying the effects of induced changes in time sense on behavior.

Social-Emotional Contagion

Of special interest to social psychologists are some provocative observations we made about "contagion" phenomena in the present expanded state. When hypnotic subjects in groups of three were told to experience the expanded present (not as part of the study reported here), they were quick to move from disposition to act, and to transmit their emotional reaction from one to the other. A subject would report feeling so good, she wanted to scream and laugh and shout—and then would. Or another would describe feeling euphoric and then act euphorically, smiling, singing, laughing, joking, moving. All 12 of the reported hypnotic subjects (and many others we have trained since) described the expanded present experience as very desirable.

When one subject in a group began laughing, the others were quickly "infected" until all were doing likewise. In one group, this erupted laughing of one subject resulted in a kind of group hysteria for a full 15 minutes until we terminated the suggestion. The generally positive nature of the experience does not account for its contagion, as was demonstrated in one group where a subject got angry upon not being able to find a name in a phone book (he was instructed he would not). The other two subjects laughed and joked with each other, oblivious to his plight. One of them kept shouting, because when the present had expanded, the dot on a moving time line (his conception of time) expanded into a huge balloon with him inside it. Any sounds he made were being echoed and reverberated, making him laugh at this unusual state. The angry subject kept flipping through the pages of the phone book, putting so much pressure on the page as his finger scanned the names that the pages began to tear. The other two also were given phone books and began trying to help find the elusive name, but could not remain serious long enough to do so. Then, they started ripping pages from their books, at first slowly, but soon faster and faster. All three were suddenly throwing the pages all around, wadding them up into balls, making paper airplanes of them, and firing the missiles at each other and the experimenters.

It was hard to determine whether their mood was angry or euphoric; it seemed somewhere in between, a kind of affect-laden hysteria without a clear emotional label. The experimenters, frightened by this loss of control, returned the subjects to a deep state of relaxation using a well-conditioned, prearranged, nonverbal cue. When they were awoken, in a room littered with three demolished phone books, their spontaneous "socially appropriate" reaction was to begin cleaning up the mess. They seemed surprised at what they saw and remembered doing. A similar emotional contagion and acting-out also occurred in another group where furniture was overturned and a half-demolished phone book flung at the experimenter before normal time perspective and its controlling influences were invoked.

Temporal Foundation of Psychological Phenomena

Earlier in this paper, we sketched some of the ways in which assumptions about the temporal ordering of experience are essential for establishing self-identity, as well as systems of social and technological control. Here we wish to suggest more specifically how some selected psychological phenomena are or can be shown to be time-bound.

Suggestibility. The contagion effects observed in our small groups of hypnotic subjects under an expanded present orientation may have resulted primarily from a heightened level of suggestibility brought about by a weakened past commitment to socially sanctioned ways of behaving and a lessened concern for future consequences of acting out one's feelings. It should also follow that subjects for whom the past (with its commitments and established "face") is diminished as well as the future (with its apprehension over responsibility for being wrong or inappropriate), will be more perusable and more likely to yield to situational pressures, as in mass hysteria.

Dissonance. This same line of argument leads to the prediction that there would be no cognitive dissonance or attempts at dissonance reduction for those experiencing an expanded present. It becomes obvious that dissonance arises primarily from inconsistency between perception of one's present and past behaviors or from the possibility that present decisions will have negative consequences in the future. It may be possible to separate these two temporal influences on dissonance arousal and reduction by minimizing either past or future and combining the other state with an expanded present.

Catharsis. The experience of feeling a reduction in emotional tension after "getting it off your cheat" by telling another person may be produced by the subtle operation of temporal factors. The act of verbalizing an internal threat puts It into an externalized form that can then be cast out of the present and established as belonging to the reality of the past. "Telling it as it is" automatically tags the content communicated as an event that occurred In a time period prior to any "now," which the person subsequently experiences in thinking about that content. The act of catharsis renders an emotional event which generates anxiety because of its timeless, formless threat into a distanced, analytical event with substance and time coordinates, one which can then be located in memory and subject to recall at the discretion of the individual. Emotional responding in this analysis has a tenseless psychological status, involving a sense of the immediacy of stimulus input and the need to cope with it directly and continually. Thus, emotional arousal becomes both a consequence of an extended present time sense as well as an antecedent inducing it. The dynamic force of repressed thoughts stored in the unconscious therefore derives from the relentlessness of their timeless presence. By not being brought to conscious awareness and given a time-bound location in memory, such cognitions continue to generate the affect originally associated with them, posing a persistently recurring threat. Repression cannot be a totally effective defense against such thoughts because, their contents not being time bound, they continue to exist in the extended present, always potentially available for emergence into conscious awareness, and thus, into an emotional challenge.

No experience, however unpleasant and traumatic, can retain its full emotional impact once it has become labeled as a past event. It should be possible to demonstrate, for example, that emotional reactions used as negative reinforcers in aversion therapy lose their effectiveness over time, because with each repetition they move further into the established, unchanging, and thus unthreatening past. For expanded present subjects, the potency of such negative emotional reinforcers should remain unchanged or even increase with repeated aversive conditioning trials. Such an interaction would show that it was time factors and not sheer repetition that influenced reinforcing strength-

Memory and aging. Amnesia for recent events coupled with memory for more past events attributed to senility and physiological deterioration of the brain may be more profitably thought of as a psychological process initiated by perceived hopelessness. An old person facing a truncated future, who is living a meaningless present existence, "lives" largely in an expanded past temporal state. In such a condition, old stories are retold endlessly, old events given new I significance, and even sad ones are tinged with nostalgia. The present is an impediment to be dealt with and dispatched in order to return to the comfort of the past. However, living in the past often leads to behavior which is situationally inappropriate, then to rejection by younger people, and finally to an old age home. We would expect that techniques (hypnotic and other) which might induce a sense of expanded present or future in old people would be an antidote to retrograde amnesia phenomena and might even increase longevity. A 68-year-old institutionalized patient interviewed by one of the authors said he wished his face were like a shirt which he could wash and starch and put away in a drawer, available whenever he wanted it, but unchanged and still fresh as when it was put there. Perhaps the aged put their memories in such a drawer which preserves their freshness and vigor against the inroads of time.

Memory and mental health. Discrepancies between private time and objective or clock time also occur in some types of mental illness (Cohen, 1967; Lehmann, 1967; Luce, 1970). Some patients experience a temporal claustrophobia in which they are trapped by too many demands in an insufficient amount of time to meet them. Others dread the expanse of unfilled time (a counterpart to agoraphobia). Some obsessives attempt to do away with the flow of time and the threat of change by overstructuring the present. In the characteristic experience of depersonalization, time stands still as the immediate past becomes remote and the present is but a recurrence of what has previously occurred. It must also be that in the psychotic detachment from reality, temporal perspective undergoes transformations necessary to change attributions of causality and reconstitute basic assumptions about behavioral continuities.

But perhaps the most fascinating relation of time orientation to psychopathology centers about concepts of self-identity and self-worth. There is a class of people who are currently attractive, well built, loved and admired, and successful by consensual agreement in their culture, but have come to believe that they are, in fact, the antithesis of one or more of these traits; ugly, too fat or skinny, unloved or a failure. It appears that their present self-evaluation, though inconsistent with presently available positive feedback, nevertheless is congruent with real or imagined negative feedback experienced during their childhood. For example, a father, perhaps fatigued from work, tells his daughter who is eager to embrace him to go away and not bother him. This event, instead of being repressed, is given a salient place of notoriety in memory and comes to be the reality framework into which all subsequent evaluations are distorted. When the present situation becomes subjugated to the sacred reality of the past, neurotic reactions are the inevitable consequence.

Often therapy for such cases attempts to show how the past situation has changed, and the past evaluations, now seen in proper perspective, are no longer relevant. An alternative therapeutic strategy which we have begun to pursue experimentally in our laboratory is called "temporal reconstruction therapy." Under hypnotically induced age regression, the individual's past is cognitively changed to be the way he or she would have wanted it to be. Instead of "now" being woven from the fabric of the past, the past is rewoven from the fabric of the present. Because we all tend to believe in the truth, legitimacy, and ultimate reality of the past, such a proposal seems to be a violation of nature. However, if "experience is the best teacher," and "you knew then what you know now," and "if only it weren't so," and "you had your life to live over," you might be happier and saner through such a therapeutic strategy.

Finally, we conclude with the spontaneous reaction of one of our female subjects (concerned about being overweight) during her experience in the expanded present state. It raises many provocative questions for future research about the interplay between changing temporal perspective, identity, and mechanisms of social control:

> I'm melted, I am so thin, I cover practically everything. In fact. I am sort of falling into everything because I am so thin, and I can hear all the little things vibrating, and I can taste all the different things, like wood and the carpet, and the floor and the chairs. I really can't see any more, though, I mean , it's all different colors, but it's so big you can hardly see it, everything is very confusing, but I've just sort of melted into everything . . .I'm unresponsible! . . . I'm everything! I can keep going. . .I'm not a thing anymore, I'm everything so I can't do anything. There's nobody there, nobody who says to me, "Hey, Everything, you have to do this."

REFERENCES

Aaronson, B. S. Hypnotic alterations of space and time. *International Journal of Parapsychology,* 1968a, 10, 5-36.

Aaronson, B. S. Hypnosis, time rate perception, and personality *Journal of Schizophrenia,* I 968b, 2, 11-41.

Cohen, J. *Psychological time in health and disease.* Springfield, Ill.: Charles C. Thomas, 1967.

Grunbaum, A. The status of temporal becoming. In R. Fisher (Ed,), *Interdisciplinary Perspectives of Time, Annals of the New York Academy of Sciences.* New York: New York Academy of Sciences, 1967, 138, 374-395.

Hilgard, E. R. *Hypnotic susceptibility.* New York: Harcourt, Brace & World, 1965.

Hilgard, J. *Personality and hypnosis.* Chicago, Ill.: University of Chicago Press, 1970.

Lehmann, H. E. Time and psychopathology. In R. Fischer (Ed.), *Interdisciplinary perspectives of time, annals of the New York Academy of Sciences.* New York: New York Academy of Sciences, 1967, 138, 798-821.

Luce, G. G. *Rhythms in psychiatry and medicine.* Public Health Service Publication No. 2088, Washington, D.C., 1970.

Zimbardo, P. G. The human choice: Individuation, reason, and order versus deindividuation, impulse, and chaos. In W. I. Arnold & D. Levine (Eds.), *Nebraska symposium on motivation.* Lincoln. Nebraska: University of Nebraska Press, 1969.

Philip Zimbardo has suggested the inclusion of this important follow-up study. I concur with pleasure.
Reprinted with permission.

Objective Assessment of Hypnotically Induced Time Distortion

Abstract. *The objective precision of operant conditioning methodology validates the power of hypnosis to induce alterations in time perception. Personal tempo was systematically modified by instructions to trained hypnotic subject, with significant behavioral effects observed on a variety of response rate measures.*

Time perception is one of the most important, although least studied, consequences of the socialization process. Infants and children, whose behavior is primarily under the control of biological and situational exigencies, must be taught to develop a temporal perspective in which the immediacy of the experienced reality of the present is constrained by the hypothetical constructs of past and future. Society thereby transforms idiosyncratic, impulsive, and potentially disruptive behavior into approved, predictable, controllable reactions through the time-bound mechanisms of responsibility, obligation, guilt, incentive, and delayed gratification *(1)*. The social acceptability of such reactions often depends on their rate of emission as much as upon other qualitative aspects. Thus, we develop, in addition to a sense of temporal perspective, a time sense of personal tempo, which involves both the estimation of the rate at which events are (or should be) occurring and affective reactions to different rates of stimulus input *(2)*.

The learned correspondence between our subjective time sense and objective clock time can be disrupted by the physiological and psychological changes that accompany some types of mental illness, emotional arousal, body temperature variations, and drug-induced reactions *(3)*. However, it is possible to modify either temporal perspective or tempo within a controlled experimental paradigm by means of hypnosis. Our previous research demonstrates the marked changes in cognition, affect, and action that result when hypnotized subjects internalize the instruction to experience a sense of "expanded present" *(4)*. However, the data used to document such changes

Table 1. Tempo modification. Data are mean devIations In ths rate from baidlms performance.

Treatment	N	No feedback	Objective feedback	Combined
Hypnotized	12	.534	.233	.38*
Role players	12	.299	.004	.15†
Waking controlA	12	.023	.043	.03
		P<.025	*P<.005*	*P<.001*

*P<.01 for comparison with role players; P<.001 for comparison with waking controls.
†Comparison with waking control not significant.

in this and related studies *(5)* have been too subjective and gross. In the present study we attempted to alter personal tempo and measure the behavioral consequences with precise, objective techniques.

The experience of tempo was systematically varied (speeded up or slowed down) by time-distorting instructions administered to hypnotic subjects and controls. If effective, such a manipulation should generate asynchronicity between clock time and the subjective passage of time. This asynchronous responding was assessed by means of the objective precision of a specially designed operant conditioning and recording apparatus. As predicted, the operant behavior of these hypnotized subjects was significantly altered relative to their own normal baseline and also to chat of subjects in two control conditions.

The volunteer subjects were 36 Stanford University undergraduates of both sexes, who were selected from among the high scorers on a modified version of the Harvard group scale of hypnotic susceptibility (6) administered in their introductory psychology class. They were each randomly assigned to one of three treatments: hypnosis, hypnosis role-playing, and waking nonhypnotized controls. Before the experiment, the hypnosis group underwent a 10-hour training program designed to teach them to relax deeply; to concentrate; to experience distortions in perception, memory, and causal attribution; and to induce autohypnosis. The other subjects received no prior training. During the experiment, the testing procedure was identical for all subjects; an experimenter who was unaware of the experimental treatment delivered the standardized instructions to the subject, who sat isolated in an acoustic chamber. A second experimenter induced a state of hypnotic relaxation in the hypnosis group and instructed the hypnotic role-playing subjects to try their best to simulate the reactions of hypnotic subjects, to behave as if they were really hypnotized throughout the study. The waking controls were told only to relax for a period of time equivalent to that given to subjects in the other two treatments.

Subjects were taught to press a telegraph key at different rates In order to illuminate various target lights in an array of ten colored lights. In the first of five 2-minute trials, a comfortable operant rate of responding was established, and it became obvious to the subject that the sequential onset and offset of the lights was controlled by response rate. The functional relationship between response rate and change in the light stimulus was determined by relay circuits in the apparatus and can be characterized as a "conjugate" schedule of reinforcement (7). This schedule creates a dynamic interplay between behavior and a selected environmental event—the stimulus event changing continually as response rate varies. Pressing the key at a faster or slower rate than that required to illuminate the target stimulus light turned on one of the other lights in the array. It was only by empirically determining the rate appropriate to reach a particular target and then by maintaining that rate consistently that a subject could satisfy the task demand, "to keep light X illuminated as long as possible."

Of the remaining four trials, the first and third were baseline and the second and fourth were experimental. On one baseline trial, each subject was instructed to keep the red light illuminated, which required three presses per second. On the other baseline trial a faster rate of six responses per second was required to maintain the illumination of a blue light. Interspersed between these baseline trials and the experimental trials were the instructions to modify personal tempo. After being told about the differences between clock and subjective time, all subjects were instructed to alter their perception of tempo, by experiencing time as slowing down ("so that a second will seem like a minute, and a minute will seem like an hour"), and also by experiencing time as speeding up. Between these two tempo modification instructions, subjects were told to normalize their experience of time. The order in which these two tempo instructions (slower and faster) were given to each subject was counterbalanced across conditions (and did not have a significant effect upon the task behavior). A cumulative recorder provided an ongoing display of the subject's response rate and indicated whether responding was on-or off-target. In addition, an event recorder and electronic timers indicated to the experimenter the sequence and duration of the stimulus light levels being activated by variations in rate of responding.

The reinforcer for maintaining a particular target light level is probably the sense of competence a subject feels in being able to satisfy the experimenter's demand to do so. Knowledge of being off-target should serve as a negative reinforcer and guide efforts to modify responding to achieve the positive consequences of on-target performance. Such performance depends primarily upon two variables: a stable, veridical sense of personal tempo and the environmental feedback necessary for monitoring the effects of different response rates. Our tempo instructions, in conjunction with hypnosis, were designed to alter the first or these, and variation in feedback was introduced to alter the second. Within our repeated-measurements factorial design, the array of lights remained functional during the experimental periods for half the subjects (objective feedback), and they were extinguished during the experimental periods for the other subjects in each of the three conditions (no feedback). Those in the no feedback condition had to rely entirely on their memory of the previously appropriate baseline rates that they were asked to reproduce in the experimental periods, while objective feedback subjects had direct access to the external information provided by the illuminated array.

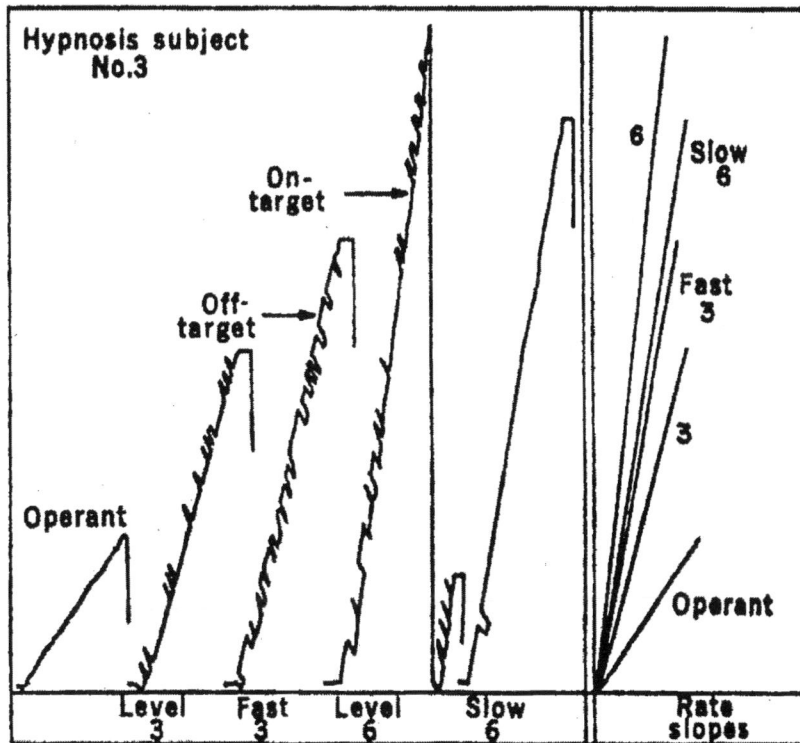

Fig. 1. Cumulative records of representative hypnotized subject during each of five 2-minute test periods. The slope of the curve indicates rate of responding. Superimposed on this curve are upward and downward deflections; downward deflections signify when response rate is synchronized with target stimulus rate *(on-target* arrow), and upward deflections indicate asynchmroy (off-target arrow).

Since the electronic relay circuits in the apparatus function on fixed, real-time parameters, a subject operating on a subjective time dimension not in synchrony with clock time would have difficulty satisfying the task demand of achieving and maintaining a particular state or the apparatus. The absence of feedback frees task behavior from reality demands, thereby generating considerable asynchronous responding. But off-target responding can result from either intentionally altering response rate (without changing time sense) or altering personal tempo and thus indirectly affecting response rate. Feedback serves as a reality monitor to create a conflict only in subjects motivated to change their response rate voluntarily while also being motivated to maintain the target light level. For those who have internalized an altered sense of tempo, there is not a conflict between two competing motivations but rather an inability to successfully perform the task because of their altered cognitive state. They should continue to respond asynchronously even in the presence of feedback; the intentional responders should resolve their conflict in the direction of the most salient reinforcer—being on-target.

Only the hypnotic subjects were reliably able to translate the verbal suggestion of asynchronicity between clock time and personal time into behavioral "reality." This is shown in comparisons of mean rates of response, percentage of total time on- and off-target, mean deviation in individual response rates from baseline to experimental response levels, and in even the more subtle measures of variability—in displacement of the response distribution.

The sequence of responding for a typical hypnotic subject is shown in the cumulative response curves in Fig. 1. From an initially low operant level, the subject responds appropriately to the rate demands imposed by target levels 3 and 6, being on target most of the time. Instructions to speed up time result in a steeper slope, while instructions to slow tempo lower the response rate. In this case, the slopes of the response curves for the two altered time periods almost converge. The substantial percentage of time the subject is responding at off-target rate levels reveals the extent of asynchronicity between his altered experience of tempo and the constant rate requirements programmed into the apparatus.

Our research design permits both within- and between-subject comparisons. During baseline trials, there were no reliable differences on any measure between groups. An analysis of variance performed on the mean deviation in operant rate from baseline to experimental responding (Table 1) demonstrates a highly significant treatment effect $(P < .001)$, and also a feedback effect $(P<.001)$ (8). Deviation from target level (combined across feedback conditions) significantly differentiated between the hypnotized subjects and those in the other two conditions. The marked deviations from target levels in the no feedback condition were attenuated by providing external feedback. However, as predicted, this feedback served primarily to differentiate between the hypnotized and role-playing subjects. It totally eliminated the asynchrony in responding among the role-players, but the reduced asynchrony of the hypnotized subjects was still substantially different from the other two controls $(P < .005)$. Any volitional effect of responding to the tempo instructions as if they were direct suggestions to vary response rate thus appears limited to the no feedback condition. When confronted with information about the consequences of one's behavior, the controls responded with appropriate synchrony, the hypnotized subjects did not. Neither direction of tempo modification (slower or faster) nor target light response level (low or high) was significant.

Perhaps the most convincing data of the extent to which hypnotic subjects altered their sense of personal tempo come from analyses of the pattern of off-target response variability. This measure of variability is the frequency of recorded shifts from one stimulus level to another. The underlying variability in response rate could lead to shifts either around the target level or to shifts around off-target levels. For example, if the target level were 6, shifts to levels 5 or 7 or from them back to 6 would represent around-target shifts. Off-target shifts would be between 7 and higher levels (faster tempo) and between 5 and lower levels (slower tempo). There are no overall differences in total variation between treatments. However, there are significant differences between the hypnotized subjects and controls in the specific pattern of variability $(P < .001$, by Scheff* multiple t-test comparisons). The response distribution for the hypnotized subjects was displaced to off-target stimulus levels (in the experimentally appropriate direction), while that of the controls stabilized around the target levels. Thus, in the no feedback condition in which response variability was greatest, subtracting each subject's frequency of off-target shifts from baseline trials to experimental trials resulted in a group mean of +31.0 for the hypnosis condition, but only + 1.5 for role-players and -5.0 for nonhypnotized waking controls.

To underscore the critical role of hypnosis in creating a cognitive state receptive to this time distortion manipulation, a subgroup of the role-playing subjects was subsequently given our program of hypnotic training and retested with the hypnotic induction. Four of the five subjects showed sizable changes in the suggested direction. While there were no differences in their standard baseline performance between earlier role-playing trials and these hypnosis trials, there were significant experimental trial differences due to the greater effectiveness of the time-distorting instructions when they were hypnotized (mean deviation in rate: +5.1 for level 6, $P < .05$; and +.38 for level 3, $P < .10$).

Interviews and questionnaire responses of the hypnotic subjects indicated that they indeed tried to satisfy the experimenter's demand to keep the target light illuminated, but found they were unable to do so effectively. Their modified sense of personal tempo became a stable reference against which they judged environmental changes. As a result, they believed that the experimenters were covertly altering the apparatus to make their task more difficult (a situational error). By contrast, in an earlier study *(9)* in which clock time had been covertly altered by thc researchers, subjects attributed discrepancies between clock and personal time to their own lack of ability in time estimation (a dispositional error).

We believe that a wide range of behaviors and physiological reactions which are under temporal control, such as drug addiction, depression, emotional arousal, and hypertension, may be modified by altering one's sense of personal tempo.

PHILIP G. ZIMUARDO
GARY MARSHALL.
GREG WHITE
Psychology Department, Stanford University, Stanford, California 94305

CHRISTINA MASLACH
Psychology Department University of California, Berkeley 94720

References and Notes

1. W. Mischel. Progr. Exp. Pers. Res. 3. 85 (1966).
2. R. E. Ornstein. *On the Experience of Time* (Penguin, Baltimore, 1970): W. Durr. in *The Voices of Time,* J. T. Fraser, Ed. (Braziller, New York. 1966). pp. 180-200.
3. R. Fischer, In "Interdisciplinary perspectives of time," R. Fisher. Ed. *(A.m. N.Y. Acad. Sci.* 136, 440-488 [1967])1; *J.* Cohen. *Psychological Time, in Health and Disease* (Thomas, Springfield. Ill., 1967); S. Newell, In *the Future of Time.* H. Yaker,. H. Osmond. P. Cheek, Eds. (Doubleday. New Yort.1971, *pp.* 351—388.
4. P. G. Zimbardo, G. Marshall, C. Maslach, *J. Appl. Soc. Psychol.* 1, 305 (1972); B.S. Aaronson, in

The Future of Time. H. Yaker. H. Osmond. F. Cheek. Eds. (Doubleday. New York. 1971), pp. 405-436.

5. L. F. Cooper and M. H. Erickson. Bull. *Georgetown Univ. Med. Cent.* 4, 50 (1950): T.X. Barber and D. S. Calverly, *Arch. Gen. Psychiat.* 10, 209 (1964); W.E. Edmonston, Jr., and J.R. Erbeck. *Amer. J. Clin. Hypn.* 10, 79 (1967).

6. R.E. Shor and E. C. Orne, *The Harvard Group Scale Of Hypnotic Susceptibility. Form A* (Consulting Psychologists, Palo Alto. Calif., 1962).

7. 0. R. Lindsley. *Science* 126. 1290 (1957); P.G. Zimbardo, E.B. Ebbesen, S. C. Fraser, *J.Pers. Soc. Psychol.* in press.

6. Analysis of this data was performed by Perry Gluckman of the Center for Advanced Study in the Behavioral Science (CASBS) by using Anovar BMDO 6V and 2V computer programs. The statistical advice of Lincoln Moses is also gratefully acknowledged.

9. K. H. Cralk and T. R. Sarbin, *Percept. Mot. Skills* 16, 597 (1963).

10. This study was supported by Office of Naval Research grant N00014-67-A-0112-0041, and was completed while P.G.Z. was a fellow at CASBS.

11. January 1973; revised 13 April 1973.

CHAPTER FOUR

HYPNOTIC TIME DISTORTION: PIONEERS

Cooper and Erickson, more than any other investigators, have pioneered and maintained hypnotic explorations in temporal psychology. The early terminology and techniques were all theirs. Here is a reprinted sample of their pace—setting work:

TIME DISTORTION IN HYPNOSIS II

LINN F. COOPER, M. D.
MILTON H. ERICKSON. M. D.

Reprinted from
THE BULLETIN. GEORGETOWN UNIVERSITY MEDICAL CENTER
1950, IV, No. 3, October and November, pp. 50—68
with permission.

TIME DISTORTION IN HYPNOSIS II

LINN F. COOPER. M.D.
MILTON H. ERICKSON, M.D.

GENERAL INTRODUCTION

In a previous communication,[1] findings were presented which indicated that time sense can be deliberately altered by hypnotic suggestion. Thus a ten-second interval by the clock might seem to be one of ten minutes to the hypnotized subject. Furthermore, the individual concerned might report that he had had an amount of subjective experience in the form of hallucinated activities, thought, feeling, and the like— all proceeding at a normal rate—that was more nearly appropriate to the subjective ten minutes than to the brief ten seconds recorded by the clock. One of the inferences from these results is that mental activity, under the conditions described, can take place at extremely rapid rates while appearing, to the subject, to progress at customary speeds. In the present paper a further inquiry is made into this phenomenon. After a brief consideration of time, it proceeds to the presentation of experimental results, followed by an analysis of the findings and a discussion of their significance.

Notes on Time and the Concept of Time Distortion

Einstein has made the following statement:

"The experiences of an individual appear to us arranged in a series of events; in this series the single events which we remember appear to be ordered according to the criterion of 'earlier' and 'later.' There exists, therefore, for the individual, an I-time, or subjective time. This in itself is not measurable. I can, indeed, associate numbers with the events, in such a way that a greater number is associated with the later event than with an earlier one. This association I can define by means of a clock by comparing the order of events furnished by the clock with the order of the given series of events. We understand by a clock something which provides a series of events which can be counted." [2]

While the hands of a clock move from one position to another, an infinite number of other changes take place in the cosmos. And wherever that phenomenon which we call awareness exists, there is probably a sense of the passage of time, and a sense of sequence. In other words, subjective experience seems to be inseparably interwoven with time sense which, as is true of other primary experiences, is indefinable. Yet we all know what it is, and we apparently conceive of it as a magnitude, for we speak of a long or a short time, and readily compare intervals one with another. And our perception of it as a magnitude differs from that of another magnitude — space — in a strange way. Time seems to be of us, and inseparable from our very existence. Furthermore, one is tempted to think of subjective time as extending from future to past in a direction at right angles, so to speak, to all other experience.

Although we cannot at present measure subjective time, we can gain some idea of the seeming duration of an event or interval by asking a person, "How long did it seem?" He may then reply, "It seemed like ten minutes," meaning, of course, that his sense of the passage of time was approximately that which he generally experiences when the clock hands advance a certain distance—i.e. ten minutes. Were we to inform him that actually the clock had advanced by only five minutes, he might reply, "It seemed longer than it was (by the clock)." Thus we all come to associate a certain quantity of subjective time with a given amount of movement of the clock hands. Exactly how we do this is not known, but certainly we are aided by observed changes in the physical world. At any rate, it is common experience that a given world time interval may seem longer or shorter, depending upon the circumstances. When the difference between the seeming duration of an interval and its actual duration is great, we say that time distortion is present.

Time distortion is most commonly seen in the dream, where many hours of dream-life may be experienced in but a few minutes by physical time. Furthermore, the phenomenon is not infrequently encountered in times of danger or narrow escape, where intervals of but a few seconds may seem to be greatly prolonged. In such cases the long subjective interval may be filled with thoughts and images proceeding at an apparently normal rate, and movement in the physical world, actually often very rapid, may appear to be in "slow motion." It is by no means rare for the individual involved to report that in the emergency his performance was improved because he seemed to have more time for decisions. There are numerous other conditions under which time distortion occurs. Thus, a given interval may seem to be prolonged in the presence of pain, discomfort, anxiety, anticipation, or boredom. On the other hand, it may seem shortened during pleasure, amusement, or interest.

The perception of time may be altered also by organic brain lesions, certain drugs, the psychoses and psychoneuroses, delirium, amid toxic states. In general, time seems to pass more rapidly for the aging than for the young.

Welch' has made a study of time distortion in hypnotically induced dreams, and Erickson[4] has reported the phenomenon in a hypnotized subject who was reliving past events. Ingli[5] had a subject who claimed to be able to bring about an apparent slowing of observed physical phenomena at will, and to have employed 'this ability to advantage while boxing, when it aided him in placing blows.

Finally, time sense can be deliberately altered by hypnotic suggestion and a predetermined degree of distortion thus effected, as reported in an earlier communication.

Depending upon the circumstances, certain changes in subjective experience may accompany time distortion. The following outline presents some of the more important of these:

The Narrow Escape.

A given world time interval seems prolonged.

Sensory experience.

All sensory experience may seem to be slowed down, action appearing to occur in "slow motion."
Actually, high speeds in the physical world are often involved.

Non-sensory experience.

Thought, imagery, etc. are often much increased in amount per unit of world time. As far as the person involved is concerned, the activity seems to proceed at a normal rate.

The Dream.

A given world time interval may seem much prolonged.

Sensory experience.

Physical stimuli are usually not experienced as such.

Non-sensory experience.

Much dream activity may take place in a short world time interval.

This activity appears, to the dreamer to proceed at the normal rate.

Hypnosis (with "slowed" time).

A   given world time interval may seem much prolonged.

Sensory experience.

In the few cases 'where sounds have been "injected" into hallucinatory experiences, their apparent duration was increased.

Non-sensory experience.

Much activity may take place in a very short world time interval.

This activity appears, to the subject, to proceed at a normal rate.

Boredom.

A given interval seems prolonged. Sensory experience.

No change.

Non-sensory experience.

No change.

DEFINITIONS AND ABBREVIATIONS

W.T.—world time—solar time as measured by watch or metronome.

P.T.—personal time — I-time — subjective, experiential, or psychological time.

E.P.T.—estimated personal time—estimate, by the subject, of the length of an interval of his experiential time.

S.P.T.—suggested personal time—a time interval suggested to the subject under hypnosis. In these experiments the subjects came to think of this as "special time." Hence such expressions as "You're going to spend twenty minutes of your special time . . ." were frequently used.

A.T.—allotted time—the time, in world time, that is allotted to a test by the operator. It is not told to the subject. Thus, it may be suggested to the subject that he will have ten minutes for a problem, while the actual interval between signals is only ten seconds.

D.R.—demonstrated rate-in the counting experiments the subject was frequently asked to demonstrate, by counting aloud, the rate at which he counted hallucinated objects. This was done both during trance and posthypnotically. In the former instances the subject had finished the test and was presumably not in a phase of response to suggestion.

(D.R.) (E.P.T.)—demonstrated rate multiplied by estimated personal time—a product- used in the counting tests. It indicates the count that would be reached if the subject counted at the demonstrated rate for a period equal to the estimated personal time.

(D.R.) (W.T.)-.—demonstrated rate multiplied by world time—the count that would be reached if the subject counted at the demonstrated rate for a period equal to the world time.

Time Distortion—a marked difference between the seeming duration of a time interval and its actual duration as measured by the clock.

A description of a test will illustrate the use of these terms:

"You now see a large bag full of jelly-beans on a table. ... Now tell me what you see."

The subject describes the scene.

"Stay there, please, and listen to me. When I give you the starting signal by saying 'Now,' you're going to spend at least ten minutes (of your special time) taking them out of the bag one at a time, counting them as you do so, and placing them on the table in piles according to color. Please don't hurry. At the end of ten minutes I'll give you the signal to stop."

"Here comes the starting signal. 'Now.' "

Ten seconds later—"Now make your mind a blank please. Your mind is now a blank. Tell me about it, please."

The subject reports that he counted 401 candies and gives the approximate number in the black, white, and red piles.

Others were blue, yellow, green, and pink. He tells how the piles were located, and notes that some of the black ones fell on the floor. He tells of wondering whether the spotted white ones, which he used to know as "bird's eggs," are still flavored with banana. He counted "one by one," without hurrying, counting for what seemed to be about eight minutes. There were no omissions. When asked to demonstrate, by counting aloud, the rate which he worked, he counts to fifty-nine in one minute.

In this example then, the world time (W.T.) and the allotted time (A.T.) was 10 seconds, the suggested personal time (S.P.T.) 10 minutes, the estimated personal time (E.P.T.) 8 minutes, and the demonstrated rate (D.R.) 59 per minute.

SUBJECTS

The subjects were divided into two groups, an earlier one of four, which worked for a period of seven weeks, and a later one of two, which worked a little over a week. All except one had had a college education. All were much interested in the experiments, cooperative, and eager to improve their performance. They were paid by the hour.

Subjects A, B, C, D were not informed concerning the nature of the problem until the end. With subjects E and F, on the other hand, this was discussed at the start.

TABLE 1

Table 1 gives further information about them.

Subject	Age	Sex	Marital	Education	Occupation	Interest	Number of tests	Experimental hrs.	Prev. hypnosis
A	25	M	M	College	Student	Psychology	213	39½	Some
B	23	F	M	College	Student	Psychology	202	31	None
C	23	F	S	College	Student	Psychology	184	32	5 hrs.
D	32	F	M	College	Teacher	Music	139	35	None
E	18	F	M	High Sch.	Housewife		41	12	None
F	28	M	M	College	Student	Psychology	29	7	Some

METHODS

In essence, the experiments consisted in suggesting to the hypnotized subjects that they perform certain hallucinated activities, and in studying the relationship between the experiential and the physical time involved. In the majority of tests an allotted time (A.T.) was used. In a few instances the hallucinated activity was explored by means of injected sound signals.

There follows a partial list of the activities used:

Buying various things.
Counseling.
Counting various objects.
Dancing.
Dreaming.
Free association.
Group discussion.
Housework.
Listening to a metronome.
Listening to music.

Making decisions.
Mathematics.
Painting.
Sewing.
Seeing movies and plays.
Thinking.
Walking and riding.
Watching games.
Writing letters.

Induction of a simple trance state was effected by suggestions of sleep. Post-hypnotic amnesia was routinely suggested with the earlier group of subjects, but was only partially successful. The later group was told that they could remember the trance experiences if they so desired.

As a rule, the suggestions were read from cards to insure uniformity. Timing was done with a stopwatch. There were two kinds of sound signals used, one the striking of a (damped) tumbler with a metal knife; the other a note on a pitch instrument.

The work was done in the afternoon, the usual session lasting an hour. During trance the subjects lay supine on a bed with their eyes closed.

Notes on Suggestions

In the following discussion a completed activity is one which progresses to the fulfillment of certain stipulated or implied conditions (none of them concerning the duration), at which point it reaches completion. Examples are drawing a picture, making some toast. counting a given number of objects, walking a certain distance, etc.

Incomplete, or continuous, activities are those which do not progress to such a limit.

It will be noted that we have defined the completed activity as being limited by considerations other than duration. This is done in order to permit a special treatment of the time factor.

The degree of time distortion and the amount of subjective experience occurring within the experiential time interval depends upon various factors. Important among these are the absence or presence of an allotted time (A.T.) and its duration, the assigning of an incomplete or a completed activity, and the absence or presence of a suggested personal time (S.P.T) and its magnitude. A classification of suggestions according to these considerations will be given below.

Suggestions were introduced by the expression, "Now give me your attention please. When I give you the starting signal by saying 'Now,' you are going to . . ." The activity itself was then suggested. If it was felt advisable to "clear" the subject's mind of residual scenes before the above introductory statement, he was told, "Now any scenes that you've been witnessing are disappearing from view. They have now disappeared, and your mind is now a blank."

The method of termination of an activity depended upon the absence or presence of an allotted time.

(a) In the absence of an allotted time (A.T.), and when the suggested activity was a completed one, the subject was instructed to notify the operator when he had finished the assignment. He was told, "When you've finished, you'll let me know by saying 'Now.'" This was also done with incomplete activities without an allotted time (A.T.), which were always given a suggested personal time (S.P.T.) in these experiments.

(b) In the presence of an allotted time (A.T.) the termination of the activity was, of course, brought about by the operator. It was our practice to say nothing to the subject concerning the fact that he would be told when to stop. One may, if one wishes, say, "After a while I'll tell you to stop." Or, in those cases where a suggested personal time (S.P.T.) is used, "At the end of so many minutes (constituting the S.P.T.), I shall tell you to stop." The actual terminating suggestion, given when the allotted time (A. T.) had expired, was "Now make your mind a blank. Your mind is now a blank." No mention of the allotted time (A.T.) as such was ever made to the subject while in trance.

In assigning a suggested personal time (S.P.T.) to an activity the following form was used: "— you're going to spend (at least) ten minutes (of your special time) watching a baseball game." The phrases in parentheses were used frequently in the later experiments. The "at least" gives a certain leeway to the subject, and the "special time" gives expression to the uniqueness of distorted personal time, a concept which the subjects came to appreciate of themselves.

In the classification of activity suggestions, code designations are built upon the following symbols:

A.T.0 ——no allotted time was used.

A.T.+ ——an allotted time was used.

A ——an incomplete activity.

B ——a completed activity.

1 ——no mention is made concerning the duration of the activity.

2 ——subject is told, "You'll have plenty of time," or, "There'll be plenty of time."

3 ——a definite suggested personal time (S.P.T.) is assigned.

Thus A.T.0, A1 means that no allotted time was used, that the activity was incomplete, and that no stipulation was made concerning its duration.

Classification of Suggestion Types

I. Without Allotted Time.

Incomplete Activity.

Without suggested personal time. (Code A.T.0, A1.)

"——you're going to go walking."

With suggested personal time. (Code A.T.0,A3.)

"——you're going to walk for 10 minutes."

Completed Activity.

Without suggested personal time. (Code A.T.0,B1.)

"——you're going to draw a picture."

With suggested personal time. (Code A.T.0,B3.)

"——you're going to spend ten minutes drawing a picture."

II. With Allotted Time.

Incomplete Activity.

Without suggested personal time. (Code A.T.+,A1.)

"——you're going to go walking."

With suggested personal time. (Code A.T.+,A3.)

"——you're going to spend 10 minutes walking."

Completed Activity.

Without suggested personal time. (Code A.T.+,B1.)

"——you're going to draw a picture."

With suggested personal time. (Code A.T.+ ,B3.)

"——you're going to spend ten minutes drawing a picture."

Termination suggestions.

I—as in paragraph (a) above.

II—as in paragraph (b) above.

After a test activity was finished, the subject was asked to report on his experience. The following form of request was used: "Now tell me about it please," or, "Now tell me what you did."

Other questions were then asked, such as the following:

"Was it real?"

"Were there any omissions or gaps?"

"Did you hurry?"

"How long was it?"—"How long did it take?"—"How long did it seem?"

"Were you aware of the sound signal?"

"How high did you count?"

"Did you enjoy it?"

RESULTS

Introduction

In these experiments the results consist of the reports of our subjects plus the actual time observations by the experimenter. The reports, in turn, are descriptions of subjective experiences while responding to suggestions in hypnosis. So amazing are they when their time relations are considered, that the opinion has been expressed in connection with previous similar work that the subjects, in reporting, probably resort to retrospective falsification, elaborating on a very meager original experience in order to please the operator.

Thus we are faced at the start with the question—"Did these subjects really have the experiences they say they had?" The question is one of the utmost importance, and is, by its very nature, most difficult to answer. The difficulty arises from the fact that purely subjective phenomena cannot be shown to another person and thus proven to exist by demonstration. It is true that, because we all claim to have such experiences as dreams, emotion, thought, sensation, and the like, we readily grant that our neighbors also have them. Consequently these phenomena have come to be accepted as realities that are experienced by mankind as a whole. However, the sort of experience reported in this and in a previous paper has been had by too small a group to attain acceptance in this manner. Moreover, we cannot, at present, know these alleged phenomena "by their fruits," for they have not yet been correlated sufficiently with behavior, nor has "operational" mental activity yet been demonstrated to occur more rapidly in "prolonged" time than normally.

The best we can do under the circumstances is to give an account of our subjects' reports, which are fairly numerous and uniform, and to hope that the reader will find them interesting, and will speculate upon their significance. Indeed, our ignorance of the nature of subjective phenomena per se is abysmal. Yet, in a sense, these are the most "real" part of existence. Our relatively great knowledge of the physical world has been won largely as the result of our ability to apply to it the process of measurement. This process, unfortunately, can be used only indirectly in the study of the subjective world. Yet many of us feel subjective time to be in the nature of a magnitude—.which won't stand still long enough to be measured. It is obvious that we need some other tool for our work, possibly at tool of new and strange design.

Table 2 gives some of the significant data on certain tests. These were selected because they show the performance of the subjects at their maximum proficiency after adequate training.

TABLE 2

Subject	Code	Activity	W.T.	A.T.	S.P.T.	E.P.T.	Count	D.R.
A	A.T.O. B1	Walking one mile	59"			13'		
A	A.T.O. B1	Watching movie short	1' 35"†			12'		
A	A.T.O. B1	Walking to school	1' 6"			20'		
B	A.T.O. B1	Walking to school	1' 53"			20'		
B	A.T.O. B2	Painting a picture	43"			15'		
B	A.T.O. B1	Counting 200 flowers	3' 26"			15'	200	
C	A.T.O. B1	Listening to music (piece)	2' 45"			10'		
C	A.T.O. B1	Walking to school	2' 17"			30'		

TABLE 2 (continued)

Sub-ject	Code	Activity	W.T.	A.T.	S.P.T.	E.P.T.	Count	D.R.
A	A.T.+ A1	Group discussion		1'		13'		
A	A.T.+ A1	Reliving		1'		1 hr. 35'		
A	A.T.+ A1	Reliving		20"		15'		
B	A.T.+ A1	Group discussion		1'		10'		
B	A.T.+ A1	Free association		1'		15'		
B	A.T.+ A1	Picnic		2'		20'		
C	A.T.+ A1	Group discussion		20"		14'		
C	A.T.+ A1	Shopping		20"		10'		
D	A.T.+ A1	Watching races		10"		5'		
A	A.T.+ B1	Considering problem		1'		20'		
A	A.T.+ B1	Counseling		10"		12'		
B	A.T.+ B1	Morning routine		10"		10'		
B	A.T.+ B1	Making a pie		1'		15'		
B	A.T.+ B2	Swim		1'		25'		
C	A.T.+ B1	Counseling		20"		10'		
C	A.T.+ B1	Counseling		10"		10'		
D	A.T.+ B1	Listening to music (piece)		20"		5'		
D	A.T.+ B1	Watching ballet (scene)		20"		10'		
D	A.T.+ B1	Problem		1'		15'		
A	A.T.+ A3	Watching football game		10"	10'	10'		
A	A.T.+ A3	Counting candies		10"	10'	8'	402	60
B	A.T.+ A3	Visiting friends		10"	10'	5—10'		
C	A.T.+ A3	Counting candies		10"	10'	10'	127	
D	A.T.+ A3	Watching races		10"	10'	10'		
D	A.T.+ A3	Swimming		10"	10'	8'†		
D	A.T.+ A3	Dancing		10"	10'	10'		
A	A.T.+ B3	Counting pennies (50)§		10"	10'	3'	28	19
A	A.T.+ B3	Considering a decision		30"	1 hr.	1 hr.		
C	A.T.+ B3	Counting flowers (150) §		10"	10'	10'	145	
C	A.T.+ B3	Counting pearls (200)§		10"	10'	10'	100	

† — indicates correction of error in previous printing.
§ — subject to count at least this number.
W.T. — world time
E.P.T. — estimated personal time.
A.T. — allotted time
D.R. — demonstrated rate, in terms of items
S.P.T. — suggested personal time
       counted per minute

Generalizations from Results

The following generalizations can be made on the basis of our results.

There is a marked difference between subjects as regards their ability to produce the various phenomena under study. This is to be expected, and it is mentioned here in order to call attention to the fact that the amount of training required is variable within wide limits. Thus one subject may require only three hours training while another may require twenty.

In all cases the reports were simple narrative accounts of a recent experience, given in much the same way as any waking person might go about answering the request, "Tell me what you did this morning?" The amount of detail varied with the individual. Because of the time required for complete reporting, the subjects were usually asked to be brief.

All subjects showed the phenomenon of time distortion, and all were able to engage in mental activity during the prolonged subjective time intervals. This activity proceeded at a rate considered normal or usual so far as the subject was concerned, yet its amount was greatly in excess of what the world time interval would ordinarily permit.

In all cases performance improved with practice.

All four subjects who worked with the metronome were able to effect marked slowing of the instrument. With two of these, practice was required.

Four out of the five subjects who practiced counting activities during time distortion achieved satisfactory results. The fifth had difficulty but showed progressive improvement, and there is reason to believe that she would succeed with further training.

All subjects were astonished by the things they did, some of them strikingly so, when informed of the facts.

Sound signals could be introduced into hallucinated experiences in all cases in which this was tried with sufficient care. Their position in the experiential time interval corresponded fairly well to that in the world time interval.

Individual Reports

The following two case reports are presented:

(1) "What would you like to do now?"

"My husband molds bullets for his gun. I could be counting them as he makes them."

"For how long do you want to do this?"

"For ten minutes."

The following suggestions were then given:

"When I give you the starting signal by saying 'Now,' you're going to spend at least ten minutes of your special time counting bullets as your husband makes them."

"If the sound signal is given, you will be aware of it."

"Here comes the starting signal—'Now.'"

The pitch instrument was sounded from the fourth to the seventh second.

At the end of ten seconds—"Now make your mind a blank. Your mind is now a blank."

"Now tell me about it."

"It was at a molding party of the club. There was quite a crowd there. I counted for maybe six minutes and ran out of bullets, so I waited for more. I didn't count the full ten minutes. While I was counting them this other boy walked up—he was talking and waving his arms. The pot of lead tipped over. It burned his foot rather badly. I got up but then sat down again and continued counting. The others were running all over the place. The remainder of the lead we put back on the stove. I counted 493. That's when J stopped and waited. Then later I got up to 546."

"Did you hurry 7"

"I didn't hurry too much as I was counting, but I kept busy."

"Was it real 7"

"Yes."

"When I give you the signal to start, please show me, by counting aloud, how you counted the bullets. Now."

Subject counted at a rate of 54 per minute.

"Were you aware of the sound signal 7"

"When they spilt the lead it sizzled a lot."

"How long was the sizzling?"

"It seemed like three or four minutes."

(This interpolation of the sound signal into the hallucinated activity will be discussed later.)

(2) "What would you like to do now?"

"To package some cookies. I used to do this."

"For how long?"

"Twenty minutes."

The following suggestions were then given. "When I give you the starting signal by saying 'Now', you're going to spend at least twenty minutes of your special time packaging cookies. As you do this, you'll count them. If the sound signal is given, you will be aware of it. Here comes the starting signal—'Now'."

The pitch instrument was sounded from the fifth to the eighth second.

At the end of ten seconds—"Now make your mind a blank. Your mind is now a blank."

"Now tell me about it please."

"I was down in the basement. There were work tables. I was counting. I counted them as I put them in the smaller sacks. I counted 1003. That was all I got. In the middle the telephone outside rang on and on. Just after that there was so much cookie dust all over that I started to sneeze. I sneezed ten or twelve times. I just couldn't stop. I dropped one package. I didn't answer the phone."

"When I give you the signal to start, please show me, by counting aloud, how you counted the cookies. 'Now'."

Subject counted at a rate of sixty per minute.

"How long did the telephone ring?"

It must have been five or six minutes. No one answered it outside."

"When I say 'Now', please recall parts of the scene and see if you can tell me what the count was when the phone started ringing and when it stopped."

"It was about 498 when it started, and 889 when it stopped."

"Was it real?"

"Yes."

"Were there any omissions?"

"None."

"How long was it?"

"Probably 23 minutes."

The code designation for the two above tests, and for the one below, is A.T.+, A3.

The following account gives one an idea of the richness of these subjective experiences:

Having said that she would like to spend a half hour riding in an automobile, the subject told how she and her sister, both children at the time, sat on the back seat of the car and counted cows seen along the way. Her sister won the game, counting 45 to her 42. Then they decided to count license numbers bearing the letter C. This was slow, for there was but little traffic. They both saw the same ones, 14 in all. Then they stopped at a roadside stand to buy lemonade from a little girl with pigtails and several missing teeth because they "felt sorry for her." The experience was continuous, without omissions of any kind, and seemed to last "a half hour easy." Asked if she enjoyed it, she replied, "Oh yes!"

Actually this elaborate response to the simple suggestion "You're going to spend at least a half hour of your special time riding in an automobile, and it's going to be a nice ride," took place in an allotted time of 10 seconds.

TABLE 3

Subject	Code	Counting	A.T.	S.P.T.	E.P.T.	Count	D.R.	D.R.x E.P.T.
A	A.T.+ A3	Flowers	10"	10'	8'	140		
A	A.T.+ A3	Flowers	10"	10'	7'	41	48	336
A	A.T.+ A3	Flowers	10"	10'	10'	35	42	420
A	A.T.+ B3	Pennies (50) §	10"	10'	3'	28	19	300
A	A.T.+ A3	Potatoes	10"	10'	5'	165	60	300
A	A.T.+ A3	Candies	10"	10'	5'	140	60	300
A	A.T.+ A3	Candies	10"	10'	8'	402	60	480
A	A.T.+ A3	Candies	10"	10'	3'	75	60	180
C	A.T.+ B3	Flowers (150) §	10"	10'*	10'	145		
C	A.T.+ B3	Pearls (200) §	10"	10'	10'	100		
C	A.T.+ A3	Candies	10"	10'	10'	127		
C	A.T.+ A3	Candies	10"	10'	8'	49		
C	A.T.+ A3	Candies	10"	10'	10'	127		
E	A.T.+ A3	Flowers	20"	20'*	20'	115	54	1080
E	A.T.+ A3	Flowers	20"	20'*	20'	40	35†	700†
E	A.T.+ A3	Strawberries	20"	60'*	50'	600		
E	A.T.+ A3	Tomatoes	20"	60'*	40'	225		
E	A.T.+ A3	Bullets	10"	10'*	10'	516	54	540
E	A.T.+ A3	Flowers	10"	15'*	15'	973	60	900
E	A.T.+ A3	Cookies	10"	20'*	23'	1003	60	1380
F	A.T.+ A3	Nuts	20"	20'*	20'	400	66	1320
F	A.T.+ B3	Candies (200) §	10"	10'*	60'	2500	72	4320
F	A.T.+ A3	Flowers	10"	10'*	10'	60		

* — time suggestion preceded by the phrase "at least"
§ — subject to count at least this number.
W.T. — world time
E.P.T. — estimated personal time.
A.T. — allotted time
D.R. — demonstrated rate, in terms of items
S.P.T. — suggested personal time
counted per minute

Counting

By far the most dramatic results were those obtained in the counting experiments. These were usually run as incomplete activities, with a short allotted time (A.T.) and a moderately long suggested personal time (S.P.T.) In a few instances, however, the suggestion was put in the completed form by saying. "Since you can easily count 30 in a minute, you will have no difficulty counting at least 300 in ten minutes. Please take your time and don't hurry." This was generally done during training, in an attempt to utilize the performance-increasing value of the completed activity.

Generally the subject was given a "preview" of his surroundings in the following manner:

"You now see several large bags of gum drops on a table. Please tell me what you see."

Then, after a brief description by the subject, "Stay there now, and listen to me."

The activity suggestion was then given.

Table 3 shows the more important data on the counting tests done after proficiency had been attained.

It will be noted that the count, although much greater than the product (I).l{.)(W.T.), is almost invariably less than (RR.)(E.P.T.).

Sometimes the subjects had no explanation for this. At other times they ascribed the discrepancy to the fact that part of the time was occupied otherwise than by counting.

Sound Signals

The idea of exploring hallucinatory activities by means of injected sound signals was suggested to us by Dr. J. B. Rhine[6].

In one group of tests the subjects were told to take a familiar walk—from house to school. No allotted time (A.T.), or suggested personal time (S.P.T.), was used. Thus the code designation is A.T.0, BI. A single short sound signal, produced by striking a damped glass with a metal knife, was employed at various intervals from the start. The subject was then asked to estimate, at the end of the test, the personal time of the entire experience and the approximate location of the sound signal. The latter they usually did by considering where, in their walk, they were when they heard the signal. The accompanying figure shows the relation of the signal to world and experiential times.

In other cases a pitch instrument was sounded for a known length of time during an activity with an allotted time. The subject was later asked to estimate its duration. Some of the results are shown in table 4.

Subject A

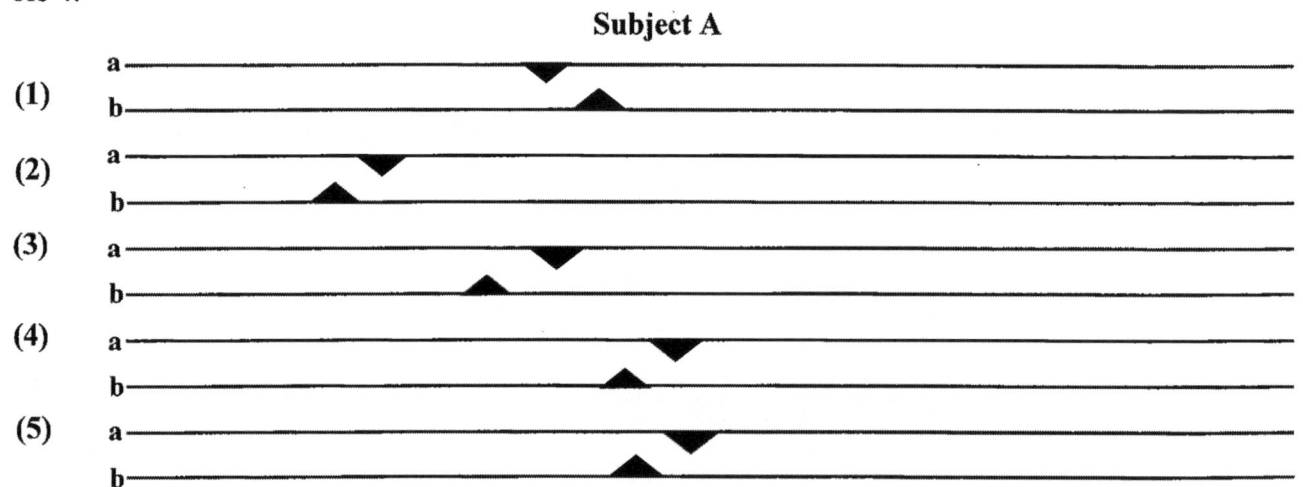

Subject B

Subject A

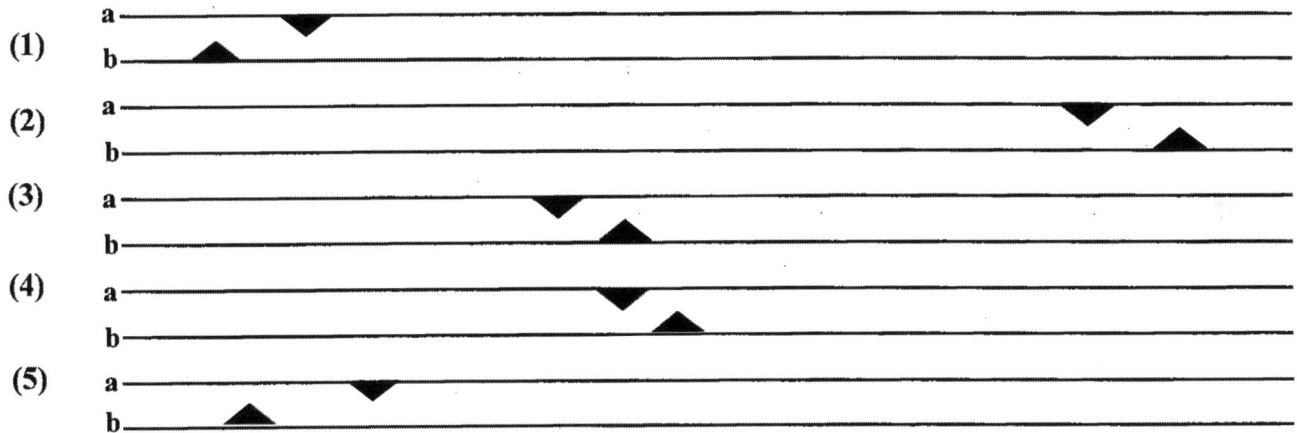

The pairs of lines represent the world time interval (a), and the personal time interval (b), for a given test.

The markers show where the sound signal actually occurred in relation to the world time interval (on lines a), and its location in the personal time interval (on lines b), as determined by asking the subject how long it seemed from the beginning of the activity to the signal.

Note that the subject locates the signals with fair accuracy.

The above chart is based on the following data:

	World Time (secs.)		Estimated Personal Time (min.)	
	Signal	Total	Signal	Total
Subject A				
(1)	60	155	5	12
(2)	20	105	1.5	10
(3)	60	164	3.5	12
(4)	90	192	5	12
(5)	120	252	5	12
Subject B				
(1)	60	133	10	20
(2)	90	135	14	20
(3)	110	133	17	20
(4)	30	107	4	20
Subject C				
(1)	30	163	3	30 †
(2)	120	137	28.5	30
(3)	60	159	13	30
(4)	90	210	17	37
(5)	46	196	4	30

47

TABLE 4

Subject	Activity	Code	A.T.	S.P.T.	E.P.T.	Time	Sound Signal Appearance Form	Est. Duration
E	Baking cake	A.T.+ B3	15"	15'	10'	5th to 10th sec.	Auto horn stuck	3 or 4'
E	Mowing lawn	A.T.+ A3	10"	10'	10'	3rd to 5th sec.	Squeaking	2'
E	Counting bullets	A.T.+ A3	10	10'	10'	4th to 7th sec.	Sizzling lead	3 or 4'
E	Picking flowers	A.T.+ A3	10	15'	15'	5th to 8th sec.	Bird singing	5'
E	Embroidering	A.T.+ A3	10	15'	15'	4th to 7th sec.	Radio static	3 or 4'
E	Counting cookies	A.T.+ A3	10	20'	23'	5th to 8th sec.	Telephone ring	5 or 6'
F	Watching basketball	A.T.+ A3	10	10'	5'	5th to 6th sec.	"Funny noise"	1'
F	Picnic	A.T.+ A1	20"†		20'	10th to 15th sec.	"Like a train"	"Quite a while"

The subjects, even though forewarned, were not always aware of the sound signal, and when they were, it was experienced in various forms.

Striking the glass, to some subjects, sounded exactly as it does normally, and did not take on any significance in the hypnotic scene. More often, however, it was heard as a somewhat similar sound, such as a tumbler dropping on the floor, ice striking the side of the pitcher, an object falling on a hard surface, etc. Sometimes, however, the actual sound signal acquired an entirely different significance, e. g. the sizzling of the lead and the ringing of the telephone noted above.

Since the subject had been led to expect a sound signal, he quite possibly anticipated it and included appropriate "properties" in his hallucination. Thus, in three successive counseling scenes, glass was present either as a tumbler or a pitcher.

Even so, there is much food for thought here, for an object must fall before it can strike the floor and make a noise, and there must be some cause for the fall. Somehow or other, all this is arranged in a most skillful way. Interestingly enough, to one subject the sound signal came just as he struck a pole with a stick. After telling about it he added, "I had anticipated hitting the pole, for I saw it in the distance." It may be that there is a definite lag between the communication of the signal to the brain and its entry into the hallucinated world as an appropriate part of the picture.

Similarly with the pitch instrument, at times it was unchanged, but more often it was altered.

The presence in our group of two musicians, one with "absolute pitch", gave us the opportunity of determining whether a sound, coming into the hallucinated world of altered time sense, would itself be altered in tone, i.e., lowered, by virtue of the new time relations (;). The answer apparently depends upon the degree to which the sound is disguised. In hallucinations where it was heard as a horn and an air-raid "all clear", the pitch was recognized as C. Usually, however, there was little resemblance to the original, the pitch instrument being heard variously as a bird, a fan, a squeaky lawn-mower, the buzzing of a crowd of people, etc.

Of considerable significance is the fact that almost always the duration of the sound seemed much longer than it actually was. This is what we would expect in the presence of time distortion and, in a way, confirms the reports of the subjects. Here too we have the awareness of a physical phenomenon during time distortion, and the event seems to be slowed. Compare this with reports from persons following a narrow escape, who may say that world events appeared to be in "slow motion."

Not always was the intruder welcome, for on several occasions the hallucination was completely destroyed. On others the subject would become "nervous", irritated, or apprehensive.

In fact, one subject reported that in subsequent walks, whenever he passed the spot at which he had previously been "jolted" by the sound signal, he had a sense of impending trouble. Here, apparently, we have an instance of conditioning to a hallucinated environment. This is evidence of the subjective reality of the experience.

Metronome

Initially, a metronome was started at 130 strokes per minute and the following suggestion then given: "You now hear a special variable speed electric metronome striking at 60 strokes per minute. Please listen to it.
- - - -I'm soon going to slow it down gradually. When it's going very slowly, please let me know by saying 'Now'."

At varying intervals thereafter this suggestion might be given,—"It's going slower and slower, slower and slower—."

The metronome, of course, continued at its initial rate of 60. Three of the four subjects who were thus tested reported marked slowing. However, for one of these, the slowing did not always occur.

Next, four subjects were trained to "imagine" that they were listening to a metronome. This was accomplished with little difficulty. The following suggestions were then used:

"When I give you the starting signal by saying 'Now', you're going to imagine that you hear that metronome beating at 60 strokes a minute. As you listen, it will go slower and slower. It will slow down fairly rapidly. When it's going very slowly, you'll let me know by saying 'Now'. As you listen, you will count the strokes to yourself."

All four subjects reported marked slowing, usually after an interval of less than two minutes. Along with this they almost always had visual hallucinations, generally involving a metronome. In the case of some subjects these were bizarre and elaborate, and included pendulums with sliding weights, large and small hammers striking in counterpoint, flexible and adjustable shafts, men swinging hammers or beams, airplanes looping, etc. The subjects were asked to state the count, and to demonstrate the initial rate and the rate during the last five or ten beats. The count generally averaged much less than 60 per minute.

Finally, all four subjects were again allowed to listen to the real metronome and were given the suggestion noted in the first paragraph of this section, plus instructions to count the strokes to themselves. No further "slowing" suggestions were given. All reported slowing, and there was usually an appropriately low count. Actually the rate was unchanged.

There were, however, occasional reports in the last two exercise described above where the subject reported marked slowing although the count was not proportionately reduced. In view of the fact that these subjects could very closely approximate a rate of 60 per minute, the conclusion is inescapable that there was a purely subjective lengthening of the interval between sounds, whether real or hallucinated. Two of the subjects studied in previous experiments, incidentally, showed the same phenomenon.

A few pilot experiments were run in an effort to learn whether our subjects could review for a history examination in distorted time. The results were inconclusive, but it led one of them, a professional violinist, to attempt to review certain pieces and to practice these while in a self-induced trance, using her "special time" for this purpose. Her own account of the procedure follows.

"I put myself into a trance and then practiced in several different ways. I might see the music before me and mark the spots that needed extra practice. I would then play the different spots over and over until I got them—which helped my finger memory because I was actually playing in the trance." (This was hallucinated activity only. In other words, she was "actually playing" only in the hallucinated world and not in the physical world.)

"I did 'passage practice' picking hard passages and playing them in several ways to facilitate speed and accuracy."

"Then I went through the whole composition for continuity. In doing this in 'special time' I seemed to get an immediate grasp of the composition as a whole."

Thus she was able to practice and review long pieces over and over in very brief world time periods, and she found that not only did her memory improve strikingly, but also her technical performance. This remarkable result is attested to by her husband, himself a musician. In other words, she felt that hallucinated practice of these pieces, learned years ago, improved her subsequent performance.

It is impossible at present to evaluate these reports which, if confirmed, carry important implications for facilitation of the learning process. They suggest at least two possibilities for making use of distorted time in the hypnotized subject.

The first is that the memorizing of new material might be speeded up by hallucinating the frequent repetition, either in visual or auditory form, of whatever is to be learned. The second, of course, is that hallucinated practice and review be used to aid in the acquiring of new motor skills. So important are these considerations that we feel obliged to mention them, however far fetched they may be, for their experimental investigation is fairly simple.

Coincidental Happenings

Not infrequently certain fortuitous and sometimes unwelcome things occurred and were reported. They are listed here because they so convincingly bespeak the reality of these **experiences**, all of which occurred during time distortion.

While rowing a boat, the subject lost an oarlock.

While picking up shells, he stepped on a jelly-fish.

While getting out of the way of an automobile, he tripped over the curb.

"Mother helped me on with my coat. It wouldn't button. Dad buttoned the vest."

In changing a tire, he found only 3 lugs in place. Later he found the fourth one in the huh-cap.

"I hurried to get past a hayfield which was irritating my nose."

In changing electric light bulbs, the one he threw into the scrap-basket broke.

While drilling, the man next to him "passed out" from heat prostration.

Asked to sing a hymn in church, "I stood on the platform and announced to the Baptists that I was going to sing a Jewish chant. I sang it all the way through." (In an allotted time of 10 seconds!)

While burning trash, he watched the match burn down, after striking it on his pants.

"I shaved but I didn't wash my face afterwards. I didn't have authority to do that."

(Suggestion "You're going to shave." A.T., 10 seconds.)

"The barn door stuck because it had been raining."

"While getting shaved, the barber spent so much time talking to the other barber that the lather began to set."

While pulling up and counting iris, "the reason it took so long was because I had to get the dirt off them."

While watching a football game, his attention was drawn away from the play by a fight in the stands.

In counting potatoes, as he removed them from a basket and placed them in a sack, some fell back into the basket and hit the rim. "I had to count them over again."

While counting candies as he removed them from a box, "there was a strawberry cream that had mashed and cracked and had run a little bit. What to do with it passed through my mind."

In counting gum-drops, he noticed that some were stuck together. "I pulled out the whole bunch and broke them off and put them in separate piles."

While picking berries, the carton got so full that they kept falling out.

While riding the waves during a swim, she hit the bottom.

While washing the baby, she spilled all the water.

In making sandwiches, she cut her finger with the knife, and it bled.

In counting chickens, she noticed that one had started sprouting wing feathers, and one was sick.

In playing truth and consequences, "they blindfolded me and a fellow kissed me and embarrassed me."

"The Victrola started slowly. I had to wind it again."

While roller-skating, she fell down.

While crocheting, the thread broke.

In buying shoes, she tried on four pairs first.

A student who came for counseling said, "I want you to know that I'm not here because I'm crazy."

While counting chickens, the first one defecated in his hand. Asked what he then did, he replied. "I wiped it off on the second chicken."

Special Inquiry

After a subject had completed his report, various questions were asked of him, designed to clarify certain aspects of his experiences. The following section is devoted to a presentation of the knowledge thus acquired.

Falsification

One who hears a number of these accounts soon becomes convinced, intuitively, of their truth and of the actual existence, for the subject, of the alleged experiences. The subjects were honest individuals, interested in the research, and their waking reports agreed with those given under hypnosis. They all insisted that the reporting was an entirely different event from the original experience, and that they did not elaborate. They repeatedly resented the implications of questions directed to the discovery of possible retrospective falsification. Incidentally, during the reporting, they saw scenes from the activity, but they were generally "stills." Questions directed to the "subconscious" concerning the presence of falsification were invariably answered in the negative. Finally, the locating of the sound signals, the coincidental happenings, the apparent conditioning, the spontaneous expression of emotion during reporting, and the subsequent amazement on learning the true time relations, all render retrospective falsification unlikely.

Realness

In the accomplished subject the hallucinations possess a high degree of "realness", which is fairly consistent. At times, however, reports will mention a lack of clearness in the imagery. Such instances are, on the whole infrequent. Often, however, the definition and clarity will be confined to those things which occupy the immediate attention, the background remaining vague.

As training develops the ability to hallucinate, so also it aids in the production of scenes that are real and true to life. Thus, with practice, there comes an increase in detail and in color. To encourage this, we daily gave our subjects the following suggestion—"In this trance any scenes you see will be very clear and any experiences you have will be very real, so that you will actually live them."

One very striking evidence of the realness of the activities is the frequent reporting of accidental or coincidental happenings. For instance, the subject who is crocheting breaks her thread, and later cuts her finger while making sandwiches or spills the water in which she is bathing her child. Another one, asked to burn some rubbish, strikes the match on his pants and watches it as it burns, or, while walking past a hayfield, begins to sneeze. The chalk that the angry teacher throws strikes the blackboard and breaks, and the little boy, who's ears stand out so far, scratches his head as he strives to find the answer to his problem. Such telltale details were frequently mentioned, and a partial list of them is given elsewhere.

It was not uncommon for the subjects to say how much they enjoyed an activity and how much they regretted its termination. At other times they would get tired or become bored. In one case, a subject who had been waked was telling about an activity in which he seemed to be quite young. After telling how rough the ground was over which he had been dragging a bushel basket of apples, he asked, "Did I breathe hard?" When answered in the negative he replied, "Then I guess I must have just imagined it." Thus, the subjective reality of the experience was so great that even in the waking state he expected physical manifestations of it.

Continuity

Action was continuous in all but a very few hypnotically suggested experiences. This was ascertained by frequent questioning. In fact, the subject himself would usually volunteer information concerning an omission or a skip. When these occurred, there was generally a shifting of scene without apparent transit from one location to the other. Another form would be a "floating" from one place to another instead of walking. One subject did this when she became bored.

In several instances a shift of scene apparently represented an amnesia, for on being asked to relive the action, the subject reported the missing experience.

The hearing of rather long pieces of music without omission by musicians is most suggestive of true continuity. One of our subjects was a skilled professional violinist, and another an accomplished amateur. They frequently reported that there were no omissions in the familiar pieces they heard or played in trance. Other subjects gave similar testimony concerning familiar popular music.

Another point that bespeaks continuity is that injected sound signals invariably arrived during hallucinatory action. In other words, this type of exploration revealed no action-free intervals.

The counting experiments also support the view that continuity is present.

Time Sense

For successful "utilization" of experiential time by increased mental activity it is probably mandatory that the subject be totally unaware of his surroundings and of world time. With some subjects this is difficult at first; with others it is easy. Three of our subjects were apparently helped by a brief talk on the relation between subjective and physical time, the dream being cited as the most familiar example of the variability or the former. The transition period which preceded the full acceptance of "special time" in these subjects was most interesting, as the following accounts will show.

The efforts of these subjects to get away from world time are worthy of note. One of them, who said she seemed always to be aware of world time, would hallucinate a weird cellophane covering for herself, into which to "escape." With this pulled down over her, she was able to hear several minutes of music, in normal tempo, during but a few seconds of world time. Her difficulties disappeared one day, and with them the necessity for these odd creations, while she was counting silently the strokes of an hallucinated metronome. She counted 27 metronome strokes in 55 seconds, and as she did so, found herself watching a "sky-writing" pilot in the air. She was much impressed with what she saw. "Here I am counting by myself in one kind of time and watching an airplane do fancy loops, and it seemed to me that he had so much time to kill between strokes. He had time to do all kinds of fancy loops and things, and it didn't seem strange at all. If he had been writing a word, which he wasn't, there were enough loops to take care of a 6 or 7 letter word." Later she said, "I think the thing that convinced me most (of the reality of another sort of time) was seeing the airplane, and noting how easily, effortlessly, or unhurriedly it was looping in between strokes. He seemed to have so much time to kill. Now I really realize that the thing to do is to relax and accept the fact that there is more than one kind of time."

Another remark that is worthy of record was made by a subject who, while in trance, refused to demonstrate the rate at which she picked flowers. When asked why she couldn't do so, she said. "I'll try, but I tell you I picked 145 in 10 minutes and I can't repeat it now because I don't have a time limit right now—neither a time limit nor a limit on the flowers I might pick. It doesn't coincide. But there I'm in a certain frame of mind—and it can't be repeated here. I can't do it incomplete—in a fragment. It's impossible. I can do it again too!"

Then, after waking, she said, "Well, I consider this a unique experience with a certain time limit and a certain amount of work to be accomplished. If the time limit or the amount of work or both are eliminated, it is not the same experience any more, so I can't show you in a fragment how it went, or how it was."

Some weeks later she was crystal-gazing in a trance and was asked to see herself picking the same flowers, and to count them aloud as she did so. Under these circumstances she readily complied. The demonstrated rate was 42 per minute.

Another subject, in the transition period, once tried to escape world time by "going off from the main shaft of a mine." His difficulties were further revealed in the following remarks:

"Here's a funny thing now. I was conscious that the physical time was perhaps 11 seconds, but the hallucinated time seemed to be about 2 minutes."

"And I was able to move these marbles, one at a time, without taking a handful or anything like that and without hurrying."

"Were you aware then of two time factors?"

"Yes—I was aware of the consciousness of physical time and also of hallucinated time."

"Would it be fair to say that you weren't completely lost in the hallucinated experience?"

"No—I was engrossed in the hallucinated experience but yet some other factor seemed to indicate that it was merely 10 or 11 seconds."

"Were you aware of that while you were counting marbles?"

"No—but when I said (while reporting) 'two minutes,' the other factor came into play and gave a quiver—a physical shock—to my body, and then the idea of 11 or 10 seconds came."

In some of the tests the subjects spontaneously hallucinated a watch or a clock. In others, these instruments were suggested to them. Usually, but not always, the time indicated by the hallucinated timepieces was appropriate to the subjects' experience.

Thought

All our subjects felt that the thought processes they employed in their hallucinations were comparable to those of the waking state. In fact, some of them felt that they were possibly of a superior type, there being an increased ability to consider situations as a whole. One said, "Considerations are weighed out mentally instead of verbally." We were, unfortunately, unable to give this matter the attention it deserved.

We feel that this is true thought. If such indeed be the case, then it is obvious that this all-important mental activity, at least a form of it, can take place at very rapid rates, while appearing to proceed normally. It is obvious also that such thought can deal only with concepts available through memory. Yet it is possible that the increased accessibility of material from the unconscious might be advantageous under certain circumstances. Creative thinking likewise might be aided.

To date, the ability to perform mathematical thought more rapidly while time sense is distorted under hypnosis has not been demonstrated.

Hallucinations and Dreams

We do not consider these hypnotically induced experiences to be identical with dreams, and have never used the word dream in a suggestion unless we wish to produce such an entity. That our subjects were, in most cases, aware of a difference is evidenced by the fact that they occasionally, while resting, would say, "I went to sleep and had a dream." Howvever, these dreams had no connection with the experimental work. Between assignments it was customary to give the suggestion, "Now let your mind wander whither it will—to pleasant scenes," in response to which they usually engaged in desultory hallucinated activity, which they did not consider the same as dreaming.

Five of our subjects were asked to compare these two types of activity, and all felt that there were differences. Their remarks follow.

Concerning hallucinated activities in hypnosis.

Hallucinations are,

—"better organized."

—"more real than dreams."

—"directed dreams."

—"very true to life, and the experiences carry on as if they were really happening."

"You are conscious of what you are doing and can control the situation better."

"They make sense whereas dreams are often silly and impossible."

Concerning dreams.

Dreams are,

—"less meaningful."

—"often far-fetched."

"They contain nonsense and extraneous things."

"They show less continuity."

"They contain something impossible or unreal."

"In dreams the mind jumps from one subject to another and it is as if the dreamer were looking on instead of participating in it."

"Most dreams are next to impossible."

Awareness of Surroundings

The subjects with the best performance all reported that while engaged in an assignment they were completely unaware of their surroundings. The ones who were unable to lose touch completely with the physical world had difficulties with time distortion.

Miscellaneous

The subjects all said that the hallucinated activity never started before the starting signal, and that it invariably ended abruptly at the termination signal.

As an example of the sudden cessation of action, one subject told how the signal came as he was reaching for something, and his hand was in mid-air as the hallucination disappeared.

Aside from their intrinsic significance, these findings speak against retrospective falsification.

ANALYSIS OF' RESULTS

Experiential Time

If we simply assign a completed type of activity to a subject and ask him to let us know when he has finished it, we shall find the following to be true:

    a)   He will complete the activity.

    b)   It will appear to proceed at the usual rate.

    c)   It will probably take less than 3 minutes by world time.

    d)   It will seem, to the subject, to take much longer.

In other words, there will be definite time distortion even though the suggestion made no stipulation whatever concerning time.

These relations are shown in an analysis of 55 tests in which the activity was a completed one, and in which there was no allotted time (A.T.) or suggested personal time (S.P.T.).

World Time.

Average	127 secs.
Maximum	270 secs.
Minimum	35 secs.

E.P.T.

Average	17 min.
Maximum	45 min.
Minimum	3 min.

E.P.T. was invariably longer than W.T.

It is thus seen that, in hallucinatory activity in hypnosis, there is apparently an inherent tendency for time distortion to occur.

Another basic consideration is the fact that the subject will try his best to carry out whatever is suggested,—to "obey orders" in other words. Thus if, with a given activity, we use an allotted time and gradually decrease this in repeated tests, assuring the subject that he will not have to hurry and will have plenty of time, he will learn somehow to adjust his hallucinated action to the short world time interval. He will "fit it in," so to speak. Yet he will continue to complete the assignment without hurrying, it will appear to be real in every way, and the experiential time will be appropriate. Use is made of this in training subjects, and it is of considerable importance for this reason.

A little reflection will reveal that in assigning a completed activity we not only assign a definite amount of action, but also, in effect, an appropriate amount of experiential time. This is especially true if we tell the subject not to hurry. The reason for this, of course, is that the awareness of action or change is invariably accompanied by a sense of the passage of time.

On the other hand, time sense itself may be prolonged without the awareness of an equivalent amount of action. This is seen in the dream, where there is often a relative poverty of action. It is also true in those hypnotically induced hallucinations where, on occasions generally involving a suggested personal time' (S.P.T.), the amount of activity, though large, is still much *less* than would he expected when one considers the estimated personal time (E.P.T.).

We can see from the above that, in hypnotically induced hallucinations, the experiential time is influenced by some inherent factor, and by the assigned activity itself.

A third consideration, and a most effective one, is the direct suggestion of a subjective time interval—the use of a suggested personal time (S.P.T.).

Amount of Action

Where an incomplete activity is used, and there is no suggested personal time (S.P.T.), the accomplishment depends upon the rate at which the subject chooses to carry out his hallucinated action and the allotted time (A.T.) or world time (W.T.).

On the other hand, where an incomplete activity is used and a suggested personal time (S.P.T.) given, the subject will strive to fill up his suggested interval with action. Most of our counting experiments are of this type and are indeed remarkable.

With a completed activity, the most important factor determining the amount of action is, of course, the assignment itself. Within undetermined limits, a proficient subject will complete activities as requested.

Summary

The essential points in the above discussion of the relation between type of activity, S.P.T., amount of activity, and E.P.T. are recapitulated below.

I.   Incomplete activity.
1. Without S.P.T.
Amount of action depends upon subject's chosen speed of hallucinatory action, and upon A.T. or W.T.
E.P.T. will be appropriate to the action.
2. With S.P.T.
Amount of action will be consistent with S.P.T. where the subject is proficient.
E.P.T.   will equal S.P.T.
II Completed Activity.
1. Without S.P.T.
Amount of action is determined by the suggested activity.
E.P.T.   is appropriate to the suggested activity.
2. With S.P.T.
Amount of action is determined by the suggested activity.
E.P.T.   equals S.P.T.

It is understood, of course, that the subject has had enough training to have become proficient. Thus, in a sense, the above statements apply to the "ideal" subject. The commonest short-coming is an inability fully to accept a suggested personal time (S.P.T.) It is important to note, furthermore, that in these experiments the allotted time (A.T.) was never less than 10 seconds and only rarely was the suggested personal time (S.P.T.) over 30 minutes. No attempt was made to explore the limits of performance.

It is clear from the above that hallucinated action and subjective time are, to a certain degree, interrelated.

Time distortion, as effected in these experiments, is accompanied by a marked increase in the ratio E.P.T./W.T. It is usually accompanied by an appropriate increase in hallucinated activity. In order to produce these results, then, the following conditions should be fulfilled:

For an incomplete activity.
A familiar activity.
S.P.T.—long.
A.T.—short.

For a completed activity.
A familiar activity the completion of which requires a relatively long period of time.
S.P.T.—not of primary importance. If used, it should be appropriate.
A.T.—short.

In general.
Subjects often find that the suggestion "Please don't hurry, you'll have plenty of time," reassures them and helps them to relax.

TRAINING

The following suggestions may be helpful in the training of new subjects.

Keep concurrent reporting, that is, reporting while a hallucination is actually in progress, to a minimum. This will give the subject an opportunity to become accustomed to dissociating himself from his physical surroundings and becoming wholly engrossed in the hallucinated world. Without the ability to do this, satisfactory time distortion cannot be obtained. We used concurrent reporting only in the "previews" to the counting experiments.

In teaching a subject to hallucinate, a good expression to use is, "I now want you to imagine that you're in such and such a place." After a brief interval—"Now make your mind a blank. Your mind is now a blank. Now tell me what you saw."

After the ability to hallucinate has been acquired, it is best to start with either simple incomplete or continuous activities, such as looking in shop windows, with a long allotted time (A.T.), or with a simple completed activity without A.T. By a long allotted time (A.T.) we mean one or two minutes. An estimated personal time (E.P.T.) should he asked for after each activity. It will almost invariably show distortion fairly early during training. It might help to point out this distortion to the subject, who will then realize that there is nothing amiss in experiencing a subjective time interval that is out of proportion to world time.

We have usually postponed the suggestion of a personal time until the subject has acquired some proficiency with simpler procedures, on the theory that failure might discourage him.

Throughout the training, advantage is taken of the following:

a. The inherent tendency toward spontaneous time distortion in hallucinated activities.
b. The effort and the need on the part of the hypnotized subject to carry out suggestions, especially to finish a completed activity.
c. The fact that, at the beginning at least, familiar activities are more readily hallucinated than unfamiliar ones.
d. The fact that the interest and curiosity of the subject, and his feeling of being productive, tend to improve cooperation and performance. Advantage can be taken of this by giving him sufficient understanding of what he is doing so that he accepts and does not reject it.
e. The tendency to improve with practice.

As training progresses, a series of tests are run with completed activities, and a gradually decreasing allotted time (A.T), but without a suggested personal time (S.P.T.). As mentioned elsewhere, it is not necessary, and is possibly not desirable, to give the subject any notice to the effect that the operator is going to tell him when to stop. We generally began with an allotted time of one or two minutes, and cut it down by 10 to 30 seconds at each step. The subject, "caught short" at first, will soon learn to adjust to the shorter allotted time (A.T.), and will fit his hallucinatory experiences into the interval allowed him, without hurrying or compromising in any way. In this way he learns to work with short allotted times. How far this process can be carried is not known at present.

The next step is the giving of a suggested personal time (S.P.T.). This is of special importance with incomplete activities. Some subjects readily accept this early in their training; others have difficulty doing so. The difficulty seems to arise from at least two factors,—a residual awareness of surroundings and consequently of world time, and a deep conviction that it "just ain't so." Practice, and use of a deeper trance, will help overcome the first difficulty. With the second, it may help to point out to the subject that he has on many occasions during his training himself experienced the variability of subjective tune in relation to world time. The results of some of his earlier tests will convince him of this, when shown to him. In addition, it may help to give him some such explanation as the following, which proved to he of definite assistance with sonic of our subjects.

"There are two kinds of time, one, the time the clock tells us, the other, our own sense of the passage of time. The first of these is known as physical, or solar, or world time. It is the time used by the physicists and the astronomers in their measurements, and by all of us in our work-a-day life. The second is called personal, or subjective time. Einstein refers to this as 'I—time.'

"It is this subjective time that we are most interested in here. One of the most important things about it is that it is very variable. Thus, if several persons are asked to judge the length of a five minute interval as measured by a clock, they may have very different ideas as to the duration of the interval, depending upon the circumstances in which each person finds himself. To those who were enjoying themselves, or who were absorbed in some interesting activity, the interval might well seem shorter. On the other, hand, to those in pain or discomfort, or anxiety, the five minutes would seem much longer. We call this time distortion, and the most familiar example of it is found in the dream. You yourself have probably often noticed that you can experience many hours of dream life in a very short time by the clock."

"Now, it has been repeatedly demonstrated that subjective time appreciation can be hallucinated just as you can hallucinate visual or auditory sensations, in response to suggestion during hypnosis. The subject thus actually experiences the amount of subjective time that is suggested to him. So, in a sense, you have a 'special time' of your own, which you can call on as you wish. Moreover, you have an unlimited supply of it. It is the time of the dream world and of the hallucinated world, and since it is readily available, you will never have to hurry in these tests. Furthermore, it bears no relation whatever to the time of my watch, which, consequently, you will ignore."

"Knowing these things, you can now relax and take your time."

CONTROLS

As a control, our subjects were asked-to estimate both short and long world-time intervals while engaged in various activities. With the short intervals, which varied from 10 to 30 seconds, the activities were counting small objects, sorting cards, talking, and reading. The instructions, incidentally, were patterned after those used under hypnosis in assigning activities. With the longer intervals, ranging from 15 minutes to several hours, ordinary daily occupations were engaged in.

It is quite obvious from the results in Table 5 that the estimated times are in far closer agreement with the actual world-time intervals than under the type of time distortion studied in this report.

TABLE 5
Controls

Estimation of Short Intervals (10-30 seconds).

Subject	Maximum Error (%)
A	120
B	85
C	100
D.	150
E	100
F	66

Estimation of Long Intervals (15 minutes to several hours).

Subject	Maximum Error (%)
A	80
B	30
C	—
D	25
E	25
F	25

SPECIAL DISCUSSION OF PSYCHOLOGICAL AND PSYCHIATRIC IMPLICATIONS
MILTON H. ERICKSON, M.D. Phoenix, Arizona

The discovery or development of every new concept in science poses the difficult question of what will be its eventual significance and application. The publication of the senior author's first experimental study of time distortion impressed this writer with the possibility of new and better understanding of certain psychological functionings and, consequently, of different and more searching procedures and methodologies in dealing with psychological problems. Long experience in the fields of experimental and clinical psychology, and in psychotherapy, has repeatedly demonstrated the tremendous importance of experiential realities in human living and, at the same time, the laboriousness and often futility of any attempt at reaching a measurable understanding of them. Certainly, the findings made in the original study and confirmed by this second report suggest the definite possibility of new readily available avenues for the examination of those inner experiences that constitute so large a part of life, and which are so difficult to study in a rigorously scientific manner. However, no attempt will be made to offer an elaborate discussion of the psychological and psychiatric implications of these two studies. Rather, a number of them will be mentioned briefly with the hope that the reader will accept the task of considering for himself those implications bearing upon fields of special interest to him.

Foremost to this writer are the implications of time distortion in the field of psychotherapy. Certainly no one questions the importance of the subjective experiential life of the individual, nor the present unsatisfactory, laborious, time-consuming, and unscientific methods of studying it.

What constitutes a subjective reality? Of what seemingly pertinent and irrelevant elements is it comprised? In what way is it integrated into the total life of the person? What self-expressive purposes does it serve for the personality? What determines its validity? How does it differ from a memory, a dream, a fantasy and from retrospective falsification? In what way is it distorted present methods of concurrent or retrospective reporting, and how much time does it require? All of these considerations are touched upon either directly or indirectly in this study and each of them constitutes a significant problem in psychotherapy, to say nothing of psychology in general.

The girl who, in an allotted 10 seconds, subjectively experienced in voluminous detail a 30 minute automobile ride upon which a report could be made with "stills" of the scenes, demonstrated a challenging possibility of a new approach to the exploration of the experiential past of the individual.

The subject who found it impossible to demonstrate in the waking state her experiential behavior in picking flowers because it was under a "different" time limit and work limit, and yet, weeks later in a trance state was able to demonstrate in actual accord with the previous findings, discloses the possibility of controlled studies of subjective realities.

Delusions and hallucinations have long constituted intriguing problems. They are subjective realities accepted by the person as objective realities. Yet, one of our experimental subjects experienced dragging a basket of apples with such vividness that he expected the experimenter to note his forced respirations, which, similar to the basket, were only subjectively real. Nevertheless, he recognized the total experience as entirely subjective but did so without it losing the experiential feeling of its objective reality. Experimental studies patterned from this and the other similar findings above might lead to a better understanding of pathological delusions and hallucinations.

Theories of learning and memory are constantly in need of revision with each new development in experimental studies in those fields. In this regard, the findings on the subject who, in an allotted 10 seconds, took a long walk and developed a conditioned response reaction by being "jolted" by an interjected sound signal, pose definite problems for research on learning, memory, and conditioning.

Similar is the instance of the violinist who, in allotted 10 second periods, subjectively experienced playing various compositions with practice effects as attested by a competent critic. Subsequent to this study, she made use of her "special personal time" to experience subjectively practicing a difficult long forgotten composition, and then to play it successfully in reality from memory without having seen the written music for years.

In this same connection, one may speculate upon the role of motor functioning in mental learning since this violinist subjectively experienced the total process of playing the violin, studying the written music, and memorizing it, while lying supine and inactive, and yet demonstrated the actual effects of reality practice.

A tempting experimental study based on these findings would he the exhibition of a form board to naive subjects and having them in special personal time, at an hallucinatory level, practice assembling it. The findings of this study warrant the assumption that, even as motor activity facilitates learning in every day reality, subjective motor activity, as contrasted to objective, is an effective aid to memory and learning.

Another interesting, actually significant finding bears upon the validity of the experiential realities to the subjects, negates assumptions of retrospective falsification, and serves to confirm the findings of various competent experimenters that hypnosis cannot be used to induce anti-social behavior. This was the discovery, in several instances, that suggested hallucinatory activities were unexpectedly regarded as objectionable by the subjects. The reactions were essentially the same in all cases and can be illustrated by the following example.

The subject was instructed to experience herself in the role of a psychologist counseling a client relative to a problem involving epilepsy. Although willing to serve as a counselor, the experiential reality of the situation was so great that she could not tolerate the task of dealing with the problem because she felt that epilepsy was beyond the rightful scope of a psychologist and that any counseling she might offer would be unethical. Accordingly, she referred her hallucinatory client to a medical man and developed intense resentment and hostility toward the experimenter for calling upon her to violate, even at a subjective level, her personal code of ethics.

While much could be said about the implications of time distortion and the experimental findings reported here in relation to concepts of gestalt psychology, the molar psychology of Tolman, Hull's modern behaviorism and Freudian psychology, this will be left to the special interests of the reader. Time and its relationships constitutes a significant element in all psychological functioning no matter from what school of thought it is viewed. Hence, any study dealing with the element of time itself in psychological functioning must necessarily have important bearing upon every school of thought, and this concept of time distortion offers a new approach to many psychological problems.

A final item of special interest to this writer centers around the problem so pertinent in research in clinical psychology and psychotherapy, namely, the problem of how to create for a subject or a patient a situation in which to respond with valid subjective reality. Certainly, this study indicates the possibility of much more rigorous controlled research with time as aid rather than a barrier.

To conclude, this writer, in all modesty, since the conception, plan, and organization of this study was entirely original with the senior author, can express the opinion that the experimental findings reported in this paper offer a wealth of highly significant ideas and concepts for extensive psychological research and clinical psychiatric application.

SUMMARY

The relation between experiential time and world time during hallucinated activity in hypnotized subjects was studied.

Various hallucinated activities were suggested, and were carried out by the subjects, a record being made of their duration. In activities which did not involve a completed act, a personal time interval was often suggested to the subject. The hallucination was terminated either by the subject himself, or by the experimenter. In some instances the period of action was explored by injecting sound signals into the hallucination. In another group of tests the suggestion was given that a metronome, either real or hallucinated, would slow down. A brief study was made to determine the value of hallucinated review of previously learned material. An interesting attempt to improve motor function by hallucinated practice is reported.

The most important findings were that the investigator can control, within limits, the subject's sense of the passage of time, and that, in a prolonged experiential time interval, an appropriate amount of subjective experience, hallucinatory or otherwise, may take place. The suggested slowing of the metronome was accepted. Thus the findings of our initial report were confirmed. The sound signals often were apparent in the hallucination, their position in the subjective interval roughly corresponding to that in the world-time interval. Continuous sounds were definitely prolonged, as was to be expected. In one case, the sound signals set up a conditioned stimulus in the hallucinated environment.

Inquiry was made into various aspects of the hallucinatory, experiences. They were found to possess both realness and continuity. Time sense was strikingly altered. Thought seemed quite natural in distorted time. Subjects felt that their hallucinated activities in these experiments differed from nocturnal dreams. Subjects were unaware of their surroundings during their hallucinations.

The findings as a whole are analyzed.

Suggestions are given concerning the training of new subjects.

The experiments are discussed from a psychological and psychiatric point of view.

CONCLUSION

In view of these findings, the following statements are probably true:

1) The results reported in an earlier communication on time distortion in hypnosis "'can be duplicated in the majority of subjects. Time sense can be deliberately altered to a predetermined degree by hypnotic suggestion, and subjects can have an amount of subjective experience under these conditions that is more nearly commensurate with the subjective time involved than with the world time. This ac-

tivity, while seeming to proceed at a natural rate as far as the subject is concerned, actually takes place with great rapidity.

2) Retrospective falsification does not enter into the subject's reports.

3) The continuity of these subjective experiences during distorted time is good.

4) Thought, under time distortion, while apparently proceeding at a normal rate from the subject's point of view, can take place with extreme rapidity relative to world time. Such thought may be superior, in certain respects, to waking thought.

BIBLIOGRAPHY

1.Cooper, L. F. Time distortion in hypnosis, Bull., Georgetown Univ. M. Center. 1:214-221, April-May 48.
2.Barnett, L. The Universe and Dr. Einstein. William Sloane Associates. New York. 1950, page 40.
3.Welch, L. The space and time of induced hypnotic dreams, J. Psychol. 1:171-178. 1935-6.
4.Erickson, M. H. Development of apparent unconsciousness during hypnotic reliving of traumatic experience, Arch. Neurol. & Psychiat. 38:1282-1288. Dec. 37.
5.Inglis, N. R. Interview.
6.Rhine, J. B. Interview.
7.Suggested by P. F. Cooper. Jr.

Acknowledgement

We wish to thank our subjects for their generous cooperation and their interest throughout these experiments.

CHAPTER FIVE

HYPNOTIC TIME DISTORTION: CASE HISTORIES

Subsequent to the research, the Ericksons pioneered application of temporal hypnosis to human problems experienced by their clients. One such study is reprinted here, followed by later examples in a reprint by Paul Sacerdote.

(Reprinted from THE **AMERICAN JOURNAL OF** CLINICAL HYPNOSIS, *Vol. 1, No. 2, Oct. 1958)* with permission.

FURTHER CONSIDERATIONS OF TIME DISTORTION: SUBJECTIVE
TIME CONDENSATION AS DISTINCT FROM TIME EXPANSION[1]

by Milton H. Erickson, M.D., and Elizabeth M. Erickson, B.A.

Shortly after the publication of the first edition of this book, one of the authors of this new section (E.M.E.) noted a definite oversight in the development and explication of the concept of time distortion and its clinical applications. This new section is intended to correct that omission and to clarify, from a slightly different angle, the concept of time distortion and other aspects of its clinical application.

In both the experimental and the clinical sections of this book, the concept of time distortion has been developed unilaterally in relationship to the "lengthening" or "expansion" of subjective time. The converse manifestation, that is, the "shortening," "contraction," or "condensation" of subjective time has received no direct recognition or elaboration, except for brief mention in discussions to establish contrast values. However, the implications to be derived from, and the deductions warranted by, the experimental and the clinical sections of this book make apparent that time distortion as an experiential phenomenon may be either in the nature of subjective "time expansion" or its converse, "time condensation."

Though not then recognized as such, the first experimentally and clinically significant instance of hypnotic time condensation known to these writers occurred some years previous to the initial work basic to the first edition of this book. The situation was that of a young woman trained as a hypnotic subject for the delivery of her first child. No suggestions of any sort had been given her concerning her perception of time except that she would "have a good time" and would "enjoy having her baby."

Nevertheless, spontaneously she experienced the following subjective phenomena:

1. The twenty mile automobile ride to the hospital seemed to be remarkably rapid, despite her repeated checkings of the speedometer, which always disclosed a speed. within established limits.

2. The elevator ascent to the maternity floor seemed to be unduly rapid and in marked contrast to the definite slowness of subsequent rides in that elevator.

3. The delivery room preparation of the patient seemed barely to begin before it was completed.

4. Nurses seemingly dashed in and out of the hospital room, orderlies appeared to run rapidly up and down the corridor, and everybody apparently spoke with the utmost rapidity. She expressed mild wonderment at their "hurried" behavior.

5. The obstetrician "darted in and out" of the room, "hastily" checking the progress of her labor, and he seemed scarcely to complete one examination before beginning the next.

This article is being published simultaneously as an additional section in the' second edition *of Time Distortion in Hypnosis* by Linn V. Cooper and M.H. Erickson, which is published by The Williams and Wilkins Company, Baltimore. The first edition of this book was published in 1954.

6. The minute hand of the bedside clock appeared to move with the speed of a second hand, an item of bewilderment on which she commented at the time.

7. Finally, she was transferred to the delivery room cart and was "raced" down the corridor to the delivery room, where the minute hand on the wall clock was also "moving with the speed of a second hand."

8. Once in the delivery room, the transfer to the delivery table, the draping of her body, and the actual birth of the baby seemed to occur with almost bewildering rapidity.

Actually the labor lasted a total of three hours and ten minutes and had been remarkably easy and unhurried. Detailed inquiries to the mother subsequent to delivery, supplemented by various pertinent comments she had made during labor, served to furnish an adequate account of the greatly increased subjective tempo of all the activities comprising her total experience. All of this, she explained, had "interested" her "mildly," but she had been much more interested in the arrival of her baby. The interpretation offered at that time of her subjective experience was the simple jocular statement that she "obviously just couldn't wait for the baby."

Cooper's development of the concept of time distortion, however, makes apparent the fact that the patient, in her eagerness to achieve motherhood, spontaneously employed the process of subjective time condensation, thereby experientially hastening a desired goal.

The above case report is a strikingly illustrative example of spontaneous experiential condensation of subjective time. However, this phenomenon is one of common experience in everyday living. We all readily recognize how pleasures vanish on fleeting wings, but, to date, it has been primarily the poet who has best described time values, as witness: "Time travels in divers paces with divers persons. I'll tell you who Time ambles withal, who Time trots withal, who Time gallops withal, and who he stands still withal." (Shakespeare, *As You Like It,* Act III, Sc. 2, lines 328 ff.)

A common general recognition is easily given to time condensation in daily living. The vacation is so much shorter than the calendar time, the happy visit of hours' duration seems to be of only a few minutes' length,—indeed, too many pleasures seem to be much too brief. Unfortunately, in the very intensity of our desire to continue to enjoy, we subjectively shorten time; and conversely, in our unwillingness to suffer, we subjectively lengthen time, and thus pain and distress travel on leaden feet.

These spontaneous untutored learnings from everyday experiences suggest the importance of a continued and even more extensive study of time distortion in both of its aspects of subjective expansion and condensation.

In our experience as well as the experience of various colleagues the ready reversal of the usual or ordinary learnings of subjective time distortions seems to be limited primarily to learnings achieved in relation to hypnosis. In this regard, a wealth of observations has been made on hypnotic subjects in both experimental and clinical situations.

To cite an example, a dental patient, who had an extensive knowledge of hypnosis and who was definitely interested in subjective time expansion, sought hypnotic training for dental purposes. The results achieved did not derive from the actual hypnotic instructions given but were expressive of the patient's own wishes for subjective experiences. Dental anesthesia and comfort were achieved by a process of dissociation and regression, by which she subjectively became a "little girl again and played all afternoon on the lawn." As for the dental experience itself, as she remembered experiencing it subjectively, she adjusted herself in the dental chair, relaxed, opened her mouth and was astonished to hear the dentist say, "And that will be all today." She surreptitiously checked her watch with his clock and then another clock before she could believe that an hour had elapsed. Yet, at the same time she was aware of the prolonged dissociative regressive subjective experience she had had as a child for an entire afternoon.

Thus, within the framework of a single total experience, both subjective time expansion and time condensation were achieved to further entirely separate but simultaneous experiences, that is, simultaneous as nearly as the writers can judge.

Another subject, untrained in time distortion, was employed repeatedly to demonstrate hypnotic phenomena at the close of an hour long lecture. After the first few occasions, the subject developed a trance state at the beginning of the lecture which persisted until the demonstration was concluded. By chance it was discovered that there-after the subject inevitably misjudged the lapse of time by approximately the duration of the lecture. After repeated observation of this manifestation, inquiry elicited the significant explanation from the subject, "Oh, I just stopped the clock. I didn't want to wait all that time while you lectured." By this she meant that she did not wish to experience the long wait for the close of the lecture. Instead, she had arrested subjectively the passage of time and thereby reduced it to a momentary duration. Or, as she expressed it in her own words, "You see, that way, you start the lecture, I go into a trance and stop the clock, and right away the lecture is over and it is time for the demonstration. That way I don't have to wait." In other words, she had subjectively arrested the passage of time and thereby had reduced the duration of the lecture to a seeming moment.

That report is but one of many similar accounts that could be cited. One of us (M.H.E.) has repeatedly encountered over a period of years, while assisting in conducting post-graduate seminars on hypnosis, volunteer subjects, themselves physicians, dentists or psychologists, who have spontaneously developed time condensation. Furthermore, they have done this without previous training in hypnosis or in time distortion.

Usually the situation in which this manifestation developed was one wherein the teaching needs of the lecture period required the repeated withdrawal of the instructor's attention from the volunteer subject.

One such subject, in a post-trance review of his hypnotic activities in an effort to develop a more adequate understanding of hypnotic phenomena, inquired at length about the nature and genesis of his apparently altered visual perception of the lecture room clock. He explained that, during his trance state, he had been distracted and fascinated by his discovery of a repeated sporadic movement of the minute hand of that clock. This hand, he explained, did not consistently move slowly and regularly. Some of the t time it did, specifically, during those periods when the instructor kept him busy at various tasks. When left to his own devices because the instructor's attention was directed to the classroom, he noted that the minute hand "would stand still for a while, then jerk ahead for maybe *five* minutes, pause, and then perhaps jerk ahead for another fifteen minutes. Once it just slid around a full thirty minutes in about three seconds' time. That was when you were busy using the other subject (a second volunteer). It annoyed me when you kept demanding- my attention when I wanted to watch that clock." Inquiry disclosed that his awareness of the passage of time had greatly decreased. In other words, he, too, had "stopped the clock."

Reprinted with permission.
The International Journal of Clinical and Expermental Hypnosis
1977. Vol. XXV, No. 4, 3O9-324

APPLICATIONS OF HYPNOTICALLY ELICITED MYSTICAL STATES TO THE TREATMENT OF PHYSICAL AND EMOTIONAL PAIN[1]

PAUL SACERDOTE[2]

Montefiore Hospital and Medical Center, New York. New York

Abstract: Mystical states by-pass usual sensory perception and log. cal thinking. They often represent the ultimate goal of long apprenticeships in Eastern or Western monastic practices which stress self. discipline and meditation; or they correlate with sudden religious conversions. While interest has also been revived in mystical experiences stimulated by hallucinogens within the appropriate physical, intellectual, and emotional environment, less attention has been paid to those mystical experiences which appear spontaneously during hypnosis and Transcendental Meditation. The present author facilitates the unleashing of mystical experiences by using hypnotic approaches specifically aimed at altering space and time perceptions. Case presentations illustrate the methodologies for guiding receptive subjects to mystical states with the aim of relieving or correcting organic and functional painful syndromes unresponsive to other interventions. The probable biopsychological processes are discussed.

The use of hypnosis in medicine, clinical psychiatry, and psychology has gradually extended from simple approaches aimed at reducing symptoms through direct or indirect suggestions, to the introduction of hypnoanalytic techniques (e.g., age regression, dreams, etc.), to the application of ego-psychology and of transactional analysis, to the facilitation or reinforcement of behavior modification techniques, and to the utilization of abreaction. Valuable results obtained through these various approaches to hypnotherapy have at least one common denominator: intensified transference and countertransference which almost invariably develop with successful hypnotization and continued hypnotherapy. Few clinicians, however, have utilized those perceptual alterations that are such an integral part of

Manuscript submitted December 12. 1975, final revision received December 20, 1976.

[1]An earlier version of the paper was presented in Erika Fromm (Chm.), Altered states of consciousness and hypnosis Symposium presented at the 27th annual meeting of the Society for Clinical and Experimental Hypnosis. Chicago. October 1975.

[2]Reprint requests should be addressed to Paul Sacerdole, 4465 Douglas Avenue, Riverdale, New York 10471.

subjective hypnotic experience. This may seem incongruous, since the patient himself often spontaneously reports such experiences: his body or part of his body feels very heavy or very light or larger or smaller, or he has lost awareness of part or all of his body. Similarly, he may report having lost track of time, having his mind go blank, having lost touch with spatial reality, or having experienced floating or sinking sensations. Often he may simply recognize a relaxation more profound than any experienced before.

These and other changes, whether spontaneous or unwittingly stimulated by suggestions leading to sensory isolation, are enough to suggest that perceptual distortion may be an integral part of hypnosis (see Gill & Brenman, 1959). The modifications of ego-image, mood, and attitude which often accompany the changes in perception would appear to be potentially useful in therapy. Many therapists, however, are probably incapable of subjectively experiencing such phenomena because their own upbringing has emphasized "reality" and discouraged the recognition of "abnormal" experiences; they have become deaf and blind to any suggestion of unreality. I find it natural that behavioral therapists, trained and indoctrinated in the use of the systematic techniques of experimental psychology, tend, when using hypnosis, to avoid the unfamiliar seas of unusual perceptions and of mystical experiences. But even psychoanalysts, so thoroughly trained to understand how dreams distort or translate reality, often fail to recognize or utilize spontaneous mystical experiences. They refuse to resonate effectively with their patients' parataxic distortions and with corresponding parts of their own egos. Generally, we all have become accustomed, since childhood, to feeling comfortable in the awareness of the "passage of time"; in the concepts of past, present, and future; in the position of our bodies within space. We function as if our existence and the relationships and dimensions of things and creatures within space and time were independent of subjective personal experience. Thus, when, as therapists, we avoid involvement with anything that cannot be understood in logical terms within a well-organized experiential world, we put ourselves out of reach of those patients who have needs for at least temporary respite from a world that overwhelms them physically, intellectually, socially, and emotionally.

Traditional religious and para-religious movements (including American versions of Zen Buddhism, Transcendental Meditation, etc.), drug-cults, and psychotherapies that emphasize sensory awareness have been offering to the multitudes expectations of religious, mystical, or magical discoveries, often tinted with a strong touch of the mysterious wisdom of the Orient.

If we compare subjective experiences of people trained in Transcendental Meditation, with the experiences spontaneously reported by good hypnotic Ss, we find similarities if not identity: only individual idiosyncrasies or different atmospheres and expectations within which the experiences occur seem to differentiate one from the other. This is hardly surprising, as the methodologies often used for eliciting states of Transcendental Meditation differ little from the progressive relaxation and eye-fixation techniques often used for hypnotic induction. Even the *mantra* looks suspiciously similar to that not-too-well-defined sound which Meares (1960) teaches subjects or patients in the induction of individual or group hypnosis. Meares reports that patients exposed to such simple experiences spontaneously recover from emotional illnesses without suggestions, systematic catharsis, hypnoanalytic insights, or behavioral manipulations. It is possible that some patients need to experience — even if for only a limited period of time — states of feeling and nonthinking which differ from the everyday perception of reality. For every person seeking understanding and relief from emotional stresses through the ministrations of a psychiatrist, clinical psychologist, or psychiatric social worker, there are thousands willing to utilize alcohol, sedatives, tranquilizers, psychedelic substances, stimulants — or the suggestive atmosphere of Transcendental Meditation or massive religious revivals.

Mystical Experiences Through Hypnosis

For the purpose of this paper, mystical states are defined and operationally described as states of ecstasy, rapture, and trance. The experiencing subject finds himself perceptually, emotionally, and cognitively immersed in oceanic, universal feelings; i.e., in direct intuitive or supernatural communion with the universe or with a superior being. Visual (lights, colors, shapes), auditory (music), olfactory, and other sensations are often part of the experience, but the mystical states by-pass ordinary sensory perceptions and logical understanding. Therefore, they cannot easily be described in terms of everyday reality. They are, by definition, ineffable — beyond verbal expression. In spite of these "inborn" difficulties of communication, patients usually attempt and partially succeed in giving some ideas of perceptual, emotional, and cognitive experiences which can only be described as mystical.

As this is a clinical paper, no useful purpose would be served by attempting to catalogue hypnotically elicited, mystical experiences along Fischer's (1971) continuum in his interesting "A cartography of the ecstatic and meditative states: The experimental and experiential feature of a perception-hallucination continuum are considered." (Incidentally, this cartography does not include hypnotic states!) Nor would the methods which I am about to describe or my patients' experiences be clarified if I were to spell them out in terms of Zen Buddhist or other religious or philosophical terminology.

I find it of some use, however, to accept Aaronson's (1971) distinctions between an "introvertive mystical experience" and an "extrovertive mystical experience." The former culminates in the subjective experience of "nothingness" — the absolute void. The latter tends to expand the person's awareness to unlimited, universal experiences. To facilitate introvertive mystical experiences, Aaronson (1971) developed a progression of deepening verbalizations aimed at guiding trained Ss into abandoning identification of the senses, relinquishing ego-identification, and dispensing with usual logical categories of distinction. To achieve extrovertive mystical states, he used techniques aimed at expanding the ego across barriers of space and time.

The techniques which I have evolved and will describe were inspired by the original observations and experiments conducted by Fogel and Hoffer (1962), and by the more recent experiments of Aaronson (1968). In Fogel and Hoffer's experiment, a talented and well-trained S was led into deep hypnosis and made to listen to an oscillator with the belief that its speed was constant. When, unknown to her, the speed was progressively increased, S became progressively more manic. When the speed was gradually decreased, depression set in, until, at speeds near zero, she retreated into a catatonic state. This experiment suggested that a person's behavior, mood, emotion, and cognition can be altered very radically through basic manipulations of the dimensions of time.

Aaronson (1968) gave to his trained, deep-hypnotic Ss various posthypnotic suggestions. For instance, posthypnotic suggestions of a "restricted present" generally produced evidence of depression; suggestions of total absence of the present elicited a schizophrenic-like catatonic state. On the other hand, posthypnotic suggestions of "expanded" time — especially expanded present and expanded future —led his Ss to experiences of supreme serenity, during which the strictures and anxieties connected with passage of time disappeared. Similar suggestions involving "restriction" or "elimination" or "expansion" of space elicited comparable alterations of perception, emotion, mood, and cognition. These changes were dramatically illustrated by one S through drawings and paintings of the same scene, seen under different posthypnotically suggested time-conditions or space-conditions.

I have found it feasible to apply the above observations to the clinical area. The patient's conscious and subconscious needs, as well as our own understanding of such needs and our ability to follow and to guide him, determine the results: a schizophrenic-like experience, or a "conversion" occurrence, or a mystical state. For instance, an excellent S and superb student became belligerently paranoiac when she emerged from hypnosis; the opening of her eyes was the cue for the posthypnotic suggestion that, "upon coming out of hypnosis, distances would seem very short, people and objects would be close, clear, and distinct." Upon opening her eyes to this radically changed space, she had felt terribly closed-in and threatened. The same student was given the posthypnotic suggestion that, upon opening her eyes, she would find herself in a gently expanding space, with people and objects shining in marvelous luminosity. Upon emerging from hypnosis she seemed to radiate ethereal serenity. She later described her experience as soothingly unreal, ineffable, without end or beginning, a wonderful universe without problems.

METHOD

Selection of Patients

It seemed to me that patients suffering from severe protracted or recurrent pain and who were insufficiently or no longer responding to other hypnotic techniques might benefit by achieving mystical experiences. The pain itself and, in patients with incurable illnesses, the known or surmised hopelessness of the diagnosis would be strong motivating forces. The majority of patients to whom I offered the possibility of mystical experiences had had at least two or more sessions of hypnosis. I knew, therefore, with sufficient approximation, their potential hypnotic talent and what resistances they might offer. I knew their ability and their willingness to let go of reality, and I had given them training in primary-process thinking and stimulated their imagination-potential through guided imagery and induced dreams. For their part, they had had the opportunity to test my understanding and my empathy.

Procedure

Before presenting appropriate cases, I will give some of the verbalizations which I currently utilize. It should be kept in mind that these are modifiable according to the patient's capabilities, needs, responses, and degree of hypnotic talent and training. Transference and counter-transference obviously play an important role.

Introvertive mystical experiences. Usually the patient has been previously induced to a medium level of hypnosis by my method of "reversed hand levitation," which is based largely on concentrated attention with detachment. The reversed hand levitation has generally the advantage, when compared with traditional levitation, of implicitly suggesting relaxation, deepening, and "letting go" (Sacerdote, 1970).

The patient who has responded well to previous inductions will already be able to experience dissociative phenomena and deep relaxation. When there is evidence for both, I repeatedly, patiently, and monotonously suggest:

Now, as every word travels from my lips to your ears to reach your brain, your body progressively enjoys more and more complete relaxation in every muscle and cell; and your mind delights in calm, clear, peaceful serenity. . . . You are now surrounded by a soothing atmosphere of absolute calmness . . . , protected from danger, disturbance, and fear. And while relaxation and peaceful serenity penetrate deeper and deeper to every cell of your body, we are safely surrounded in every direction by wider and wider transparent, concentric spheres of luminous serenity, of cheerful calmness. . . .[3] You are safely bathing and comfortably breathing in the center of these transparent spheres, while luminous calmness all around you penetrates even more deeply within your body and permeates your mind. . . . All voluntary and involuntary reactions and responses gradually fade and disappear. . . . Little by little, you become free of fears, of anxieties, of thinking, of feeling.

Extrovertive mystical experiences. The patient who has similarly been led to a state of increasing dissociation and body relaxation is first guided by me through an imaginary climb to the top of a symbolic mountain:

Now finally you are at the top and you are able to look towards the sunny side of the mountain. . . . You notice the blue of the sky and the brightness of the sun. You enjoy the warmth of the sunshine on your shoulders and your back, on your arms and hands, on your legs and feet. You breathe in slowly and deeply the clean, pure, cool air. . . . In front of your eyes under the quiet blue sky you see the beautiful green valley; and beyond the valley a picturesque chain of mountains. . . and beyond that first chain, you distinguish another valley; and beyond it another chain of mountains . . . and then beyond, more and more valleys and more and more mountains and plains, and rivers, and lakes and oceans extending and expanding further and further out in every direction to receding horizons.. . . As the view continues to expand, your ears rejoice in the natural music of the wind, the restling of grasses and leaves and tree branches, the singing of birds, the chirping of crickets, the tolling of bells; your nostrils smell all the fragrances of the trees, and the grasses, and the flowers . . . and your eyes watch in wonderment the continuously "expanding" view of the expanding future. . .

Remarks about Physical and Emotional Pain

It is probably absurd to attempt a totally unequivocal differentiation between physical and emotional pain. However, we accept the conceptual distinction made by Hilgard and Hilgard (1975) between physical pain and suffering. Pain, as a physical condition related to damaging alterations of some organ or tissue, obviously serves the patient as an important, protective alert-system. It also supplies important clues for the physician searching for the correct diagnosis. But after this teleological function is accomplished and appropriate treatment had been instituted, pain often persists because physical and emotional components interact to perpetuate or recreate physiological pain and emotional suffering.

Butler (1954); Crasilneck, Stirman, Wilson, McCraine, and Fogelman (1955); Erickson (1958); Sacerdote (1970); and others have described and explained methodologies for the relief of pain in clinical situations through the use of hypnosis. What I shall present below is how and, hopefully, why the induction of mystical experiences can add new dimensions to the treatment of resistant pain. I shall not repeat here the reasons for my firm belief that hypnotic analgesia and anesthesia have a neurophysiological and neurochemical basis (Sacerdote, 1970), but I must add that I cannot see the basis for the assertion by Davidson and Goleman (1977) that, while Transcendental Meditation acts primarily by eliminating sensory input, hypnosis operates by reducing the experience of suffering through an alteration in the subject's criterion for reporting pain. Their statement, "techniques utilizing a strategy which require the sustained focusing of attention on a single target-percept (T.M.) result . . . in modifications of afferent input which may, in certain instances, take place below the cortical level [p. 299]" seems to imply that hypnosis does not; but is is well known that selected attention to a single target has been

---

[3]The transparency which I explicitly mention communicates to the patient that he can see and be seen; that he is not emotionally isolated.

utilized for hypnotic induction since the time of Braid. In general, our conception of what we are doing and the physical, intellectual, and emotional environment in which "happenings" occur are more important than the label used for classification: in a certain atmosphere and with a certain expectation, something will be called Transcendental Meditation which, in a different environment and with different expectations, would be called hypnosis.

Why and How Should Mystical States Help to Relieve Pain?

The idea of eliciting extrovertive mystical states came to me while I was dealing with advanced cancer patients; they were raked with pain, beyond the reach of any further palliative treatment. I was familiar with the effects that the perception of expanded present, expanded future, and expanded space could have on the mood and reality-perceptions of normal individuals. It seemed worthwhile to see if patients in pain, guided into symbolic, multisensory imagery, could be led to experience perceptions of expanding time and space. Such experiences might "free" them from the limits of time, from the restrictions of activity; death itself could become merely the completion of life, rather than an event to be feared. In the expanded present and future, people and objects could appear to the patients as bathed in luminous reflections. Synesthesias of colors, music, and fragrances would further distance them from the "reality" of pain, desperate illness, dependency, and depression. Mystical states could enable the patient to deal in entirely new ways with problems of guilt and punishment, of life and death. They might also encourage him to come to terms with these problems on a philosophical or theological basis.

The other approach, leading to "introvertive" mystic (a) experiences, is based upon progressively deeper states of muscular relaxation and increasing psychological calm and serenity. The gradual restrictions of perceptions and responses suggested to the patient are also symbolized for him with the image of his body fully relaxed at the quiet center of concentric, luminous, serene spheres of wider and wider radius. Thus, a kind of sensory and emotional isolation is established which, in itself, can facilitate psychological and physiological dissociation of the loci of pathology from the thalamic and cortical centers of pain perception.

CASE REPORTS

Case 1

A 62-year-old woman was referred with complaints of severe headaches, spastic painful contractions of the throat, neck, and back, accompanied by hypertension, depression, insomnia, and dryness of oral mucosa. Years of orthodox analysis and several months of intermittent therapy, including hypnoanalysis, and produced little physical and emotional improvement.

Introvertive mystical experiences were elicited by conducting reversed right-hand levitation, followed by slowly administered suggestions that she would feel herself to be the center of concentric spheres of luminous, transparent calmness where she would feel protected from all disturbances, but without fear of separation or isolation: she would bathe in these transparent, concentric spheres of luminous calm that would penetrate and permeate her body and mind. One month later, somewhat different introvertive mystical experiences were elicited by simply describing to her a gradual reduction of responses to outer or inner stimulations, her brain learning to eliminate all voluntary and autonomic nervous system responses during the state of hypnosis, while, again, wider and wider spheres of transparent calmness developed around her.

Before the induction of mystical states, the patient had been unable to resume a painting career. When I saw her 2 months later, she had completed three paintings, she had become chairman for a series of symphonic concerts, she was feeling less guilty in her relations with her husband, and had achieved improvement in her entire emotional outlook in spite of the recurrence of occasional bouts of headaches and tension. Also, in the middle of a hot summer, thirst and dryness of the mouth, a complaint of longstanding, had disappeared. She now learned to enter self-hypnosis and enjoy excellent mystical states while swimming alone in the pool in the early morning hours. The depression and multiple symptoms almost completely faded away; no further therapy was required. Her feelings were expressed in a letter she wrote several months later: "I feel now that there is a calmness within my grasp. That I have seen it and touched it and that with some more practice it will become easier and easier to keep it at hand when I need it."

Case 2

Mr. H., a bachelor in his late 30's, had been in therapy sporadically for several years. He was constantly struggling with anxiety, depression, and guilt accompanied by very painful physical symptoms. The week which had preceded the first hypnotically induced mystical experience was, in the patient's own words, "pure hell; my back has been killing me constantly, and I have been angry and getting angrier with myself. My neck has been stiff and my head has been awful and my abdominal cramps and diarrhea have not let up."

The patient spontaneously entered hypnosis while talking to me, asked for additional time to become more relaxed, and then permitted me to guide him through an imaginary mountain-climbing. I slowly and monotonously started to describe the climb step-by-step through the last few hundred feet of a difficult and dangerous path to the top. I would let him rest from time-to-time and let him look back and down along the path to notice the many difficult and dangerous places through which he had been: the precipices and crevices into which he had fallen and from which he had been saved with difficulty, and the heavy fog and dark clouds hanging over the lower valleys. Finally, he was led to the very top of the mountain, free to look over to the sunny other side and to take in the "expanding view of the expanding future."

The following is a verbatim transcript of the conversation that occurred at this point:

Pt: I see clouds and clouds and clouds. . . I'm waiting for a break in the clouds. . . my feet are covered by clouds.. . . Way up there, there is a little beautiful corner of blue sky coming out.

Dr: More beautiful and more blue than ever.

Pt: Just nothing but the soft clouds (jerking movements of his head and neck). Way off there is an opening (his hands point forward), then he shakes his head with a disgusted expression). This beautiful white layer is disappearing, destroyed by the blue that's coming over. . . . There is the tip of a triangle right at my feet and I wish I could cover it up again ... the blue is not the sky, it is water and I can feel it on my feet... Now finally I am getting very relaxed, and it is so soothing on my back; so soothing and delightful because I am swimming further out in the triangle of blue water, further and further away from the clouds. . . just between the blue of the sky and the darker blue of the water ... swimming so smoothly without effort and delightfully [laughing aloud at this point]. It is so crazy, but such a delightful idea—I still see the mountain sticking out of the water because I am swimming, but at the same time I am standing on top of the mountain and from the top looking down at me swimming so smoothing and so easily.

Then, spontaneously coming out of hypnosis, he stated,

As the me standing on the mountain was becoming smaller and smaller, I felt some sadness. At the beginning, when the small blue triangle was opening up, it scared me, until I felt the water starting to lap at my feet; then it was natural for me to move gently into the water and to swim gracefully and without effort, like never before.

At the next visit he continued to talk.

All week I tried to recapture the mystical experience of last Saturday. The image of me would pop into my mind unexpectedly, looking from the right side at me on the mountain, at other times from the left, and then I would try to merge the two images.

The experience of last week was real; I was really those two people, with such clarity of feelings and seeing. But even on the much reduced scale of intensity and reality, each time the experience reoccurred during the week I became fully relaxed with disappearance of all pain and suffering.

Then, spontaneously entering hypnosis, he started to describe:

I'm now on top of the mountain, just about to dive in to blend with the me who is swimming. But I am still aching because I'm still struggling so hard, digging in the rock with my fingers, tugging to pull myself to the top of the mountain.

After having accepted my suggestion to let himself go, he described himself as floating without effort on top of the clouds.

One week later, upon entering hypnosis, the patient found himself again climbing toward the top of the mountain and, upon reaching the top, he described "an uninterrupted layer of clouds expanding into the expanding horizon of the expanding future." He then described the beautiful perfection of all the colors extending over the horizon and, following my suggestion that all his senses were becoming involved in the experience, he spontaneously smelled the fragrance of a red rose and then saw red roses growing all over — out of the clouds, for miles and miles, each rose larger than his hand. His eyes closed because they hurt from the profusion of colors. The clouds themselves became an infinite field of roses, and he stepped in to feel and touch the soft velvety petals, enjoying the experience of being, at the same time, in the middle of all those petals and in my office.

When he suddenly became saddened by the appearance of huge black clouds sweeping over the sky and hiding everything he was enjoying, I suggested, "The clouds will soon open up and pour rain on the roots of the rose plants." It is then that he explained how the clouds disappeared and the beautiful and gorgeous rainbow took their place, while he enjoyed the rich smell of fresh rain and became involved with the reflection from diamond-like drops of rain inside the rose petals, and with the colors of the rainbow, and with the perfect blueness of the sky. But the rainbow faded in mid-arch.

The abdominal pain and gastro-intestinal dysfunction, and the stiffness and pain in his head, neck, and back ceased, only to recur a few weeks later. He had understood, experienced, and accepted the emotional basis for his painful and disabling symptoms; he had enjoyed total freedom from them, but had unfortunately concluded that he would neither let himself change, nor be prodded into permanent changes.

Case 3

Mrs. K. M., aged 62, was still very active in a successful, independent career, despite migraines, from which she had suffered since the age of 18, and which had recently become even more disabling. The result of thorough work-ups at well-known headache clinics had resulted only in prescriptions for ergotamine, which, however, did not prevent severe attacks from occurring as often as every 2 or 3 days.

Deeply religious, she felt she had intellectually succeeded in reconciling strong beliefs with independence of judgment. The convent where she had spent a good part of her childhood and adolescence had molded her habits into ones of strict self-discipline and in the use of meditation. More recently, she had sought help in the practice of Yoga.

The first few sessions of hypnotherapy not only reduced the frequency of migraine attacks but also removed the pain of a concurrent severe attack of herpes zoster. She easily accepted the hypnotic experience of feeling in the center of wider and wider spheres of transparent, calm relaxation. She also surprised her physician when the herpetic lesions disappeared in a few days with no after-pain. The migraine attacks also became more manageable as she became able to perceive a kind of "aura" which preceded the attacks and which permitted her to abort them with very small doses of medication. The patient discovered that her migraine attacks were associated with situations in which she was prevented from expressing anger: in the long years of convent training she had felt pushed to attain some kind of sainthood through self-sacrifice, pain, and punishment which she had been taught to consider as ennobling experiences. In her own words:

The main difference between religious meditation and hypnosis is that the latter has permitted me to reach a state where there is almost total exclusion of all thoughts. . . . If thoughts are present they seem to be flowing like water and I feel weightless, protected, and insulated in a kind of Nirvana.

Later in therapy, I guided her—as I had the previous patient—to the top of the mountain to have multisensory experiences involving expansion of space and time. She then became almost free from migraine by utilizing self-hypnosis which brought her additional mystical perceptions, such as those described below:

I saw a beautiful golden light extending all over and permeating everything, and I knew that it was the hereafter and it was very comfortable. . . . Since then I'm free of all preoccupations which had enveloped me since I had lost in close succession my mother and a very close friend of mine.

I found myself trying to reach toward a deep, deep blue, not quite making it, but opening up a conscience that had been so deeply buried. ... I sensed myself a God-like creature on top of the mountain, while many people from every direction were trying to pull me down.

... very earthy experience, with babies sucking at my breasts and little children holding on to me and I feeling just love. The music of another composition had brought me into the waters of luminous caves, where I felt cold and fearful at first, then comfortable and warm while passing beyond an arch. Later on I was looking down from the moon at a small space which surrounded the earth with diminutive trees, animals, and little me's, then gradually feeling that I was passing into the sunshine.

New insights facilitated by these mystical experiences brought her recognition that she could put order in her life; that, while avoiding being tugged in every direction by many people, she could achieve a real rebirth. She now realized she needed more time for herself, for enjoyment of music, for quiet contemplation, while reducing her involvement with her children and grandchildren.

Spontaneous hypnotic mystical experiences elicited by music differed somewhat from the mystical experiences this patient had had in my office or during formally induced self-hypnosis.

It is mostly the control of myself that I've learned with hypnosis: as I go into it I see the very deep blue of the ocean, feel the urge to become submerged into it even if somebody or something is trying to pull me out. Often it is the children who drag me out; and then I feel as a 16-year-old girl out of another time, and the being pulled out of the water is a rebirth to a new way of life which I need and want. What it means is I'm not quite ready to abandon all that I have concretely achieved and what I am: I am not yet able to become one with this blue ocean to which I'm afraid to surrender myself. . . though I look at it as a blessing.

A few months later she underwent the following mystical experience while taking Communion:

I was again in the deep blue sea, surrounded by playful porpoises. Joyful tears were welling up; hundreds of happy children and many people I know were surrounding me, happily clapping hands and smiling at me. Also, penguin-like religious figures were smiling.

A very similar experience during hypnosis in my office marked the final disappearance of all migraine attacks.

Case 4

Mrs. L. L., aged 50, about whom I have reported in greater detail (Sacerdote, in press), was suffering from massive pulmonary metastases from a giant-cell tumor of the right radius. Severe episodes of sudden massive hemoptysis had threatened her life. At the time of her first visit, she suffered from severe pain in her back and chest, with persistent cough and dyspnea. Almost resigned to a progressively more painful and disabling disease and to death within a few months, she, today, attributes the fact that she is active, reasonably well, and comfortable—5 years after her expected demise — to the effects of hypnotherapy.

In this patient's case, the use of mystical experiences was introduced in the therapy shortly after her recovery from a near-fatal hemorrhage. As in Cases 2 and 3, I guided her to the top of the mystical mountain to relax, rest, enjoy, and experience with all of her senses the warmth of the sunshine, the purity of the air, the blue sky, and the expanding view.

The implications of a perceptual expansion of space and time were included in my suggestion that she look "at the expanding view of the expanding future," within which she could gracefully advance, thereby removing the usual limitations of space and time. After her first mystical experience, no specific suggestions for relief or prevention of pain were needed, and, in her words, "the expansion of time and space also became identified with an expansion of the vital capacity of my lungs."

The "trip to the top of the mountain" became a routine conclusion to each of her visits. A talented musician and music-lover, she has been left free to experience the symphonic background of the mystical experience.

DISCUSSION

The two approaches that I have described and illustrated are comparatively simple methods for the induction of mystical experiences. The trip to the top of the mountain appears to facilitate a form of extrovertive mystical experiences, while the experience at the center of transparent, concentric spheres provides the basis for attaining introvertive mystical experiences without eliciting anxiety or panic.

Other approaches can easily be conceived. The therapist must use his own experience and his intimate knowledge of his patient before choosing to guide him through any kind of mystical experience; he must be able to judge who can respond and who cannot and how to induce a positive response. The hypnotic induction of mystical states[4] represents a powerful tool which enables the therapist to further reduce or eliminate unnecessary pain, while usefully and favorably involving his patients in new areas of perception and understanding.

REFERENCES

AARONSON, B. S. Hypnosis, time rate perception and personality. *J. Schizophrenia,* 1968, *2,* 11—41.
AARON5ON, B. S. Time, time stance, and existence. *Studium Generale* (Springer-Verlag), 1971, *24,* 369—387.
BUTLER, B. The use of hypnosis in the care of the cancer patient. *Cancer,* 1954, *1,* 1—14.
CRASILNECK, H. B., STIRMAN, J. A., WILSON, B. **J.,** MCCRANIE, E. J., & FOGELMAN, M. J. Use of hypnosis in the management of patients with burns. *J. Amer. med. Ass.,.* 1955, *158,* 103—106.
DAVIDSON, R. J., & GOLEMAN, D. J. The role of attention in meditation and hypnosis: A psychobiological perspective on transformations of consciousness. *Int. J. clin. exp. Hypnosis,* 1977, *25,* 291—308.
ERICKSON, M. H. Hypnosis in painful terminal illness. *Amer. J. clin. Hypnosis,* 1958, *1,* 117—121.
FISCHER, R. A cartography of the ecstatic and meditative states: The experimental and experiential feature of a perception-hallucination continuum are considered. *Science,* 1971, *174,* 897—904.
FOGEL, S., & HOFFER, A. Perceptual changes induced by hypnotic suggestion for the posthypnotic state: I. General account of the effect on personality. *J. clin. exp. Psychopath. quart. Rev. Psychiat. Neurol.,* 1962, *23,* 24—35.
GILL, M. M., & BRENMAN, M. *Hypnosis and related states: Psychoanalytic studies in regression.* New York: International Universities Press, 1959.
HILGARD, E. R., & HILGARD, J. R. *Hypnosis in the relief of pain.* Los Altos, Calif.: Kaufmann, 1975.
MEARES, A. *A system of medical hypnosis.* Philadelphia: Saunders, 1960.
SACERDOTE, P. Theory and practice of pain control in malignancy and other protracted or recurring painful illnesses. Int. *J. clin. exp. Hypnosis,* 1970, *18,* 160-180.
SACERDOTE, P. Hypnosis in the emotional care of the cancer patient. In A. H. Kutscher (Ed.), *Emotional care of the cancer patient ,* in press.

---

[4]We can also wonder if the hypnotic induction of mystical states could produce the kind of neurochemical changes which occur under the influence of LSD and other psychedelic substances. Incidentally, LSD has been used experimentally to reduce or eliminate pain in terminal cancer patients.

Die Anwendung von hypnotisch hervorgerufenen, mystischen Zustanden in der Behandlung von physischem oder gefuhismassigem Schmerz

Paul Sacerdote

Abstrakt: Mystische Zustände umgehen gewöhnliche, sensorische Perzeption und logiscbes Denken. Sie stellen oft das endliche Ziel einer langen Lehrzeit in östlichem und westlichem, mönchischem Exerzieren dar, das Gewicbt auf Selbstdiszipun und Meditation legt. Es kann auch cine Korrelation mit plötzlichen, religiösen Bekebrungen baben. Wäbrend das Interesse an mystischen Erlebnissen, die durch halluzinatorische Mittel stimuliert werden, unter geeigneten, physischen, intellektuellen und gefühismassigen Konditionen wieder aufgelebt ist, ist doch weniger Aufmerksamkeit soichen mystischen Erlebnissen geschenkt worden, die spontan durch Hypnose oder transzendentales Meditieren auftreten. Der gegenwärtige Author vereinfacht die Befreiung solcher mystischen Erlebnisse, indem er hypnotische Annaherungsverfahren gebraucht, die speziell darauf gerichtet sind, die Perzeption von Raum und Zeit zu ändern. Die Darbietung von Fällen illustriert die Methodologien, durch die rezeptive Subjekte in mystische Zustande versetzt werden, wobei das Ziel verfolgt wird, organiscbe oder funktionelle, scbmerzvolle Syndrome zu lindern, die andern Interventionen unzugänglich waren. Die möglichen, biophysiologischen Prozesse werden bier diskutiert.

Les applications d'états mystiques suscités par l'hypnose au traitement de Ia douleur physique et émotionnelle

Paul Sacerdote

Résumé: Les états mystiques court-circuitent la perception sensorielle habituelle et la pensée logique. Ils représentent souvent le but ultime des longs apprentissages des pratiques monastiquec orientales ou occidentales qul mettent l'emphase stir la discipline personnelle et la méditation; ou bien, ile entreat en corrélation avec des conversions religietses subites. Alors qu'un intérêt s'est également développé poor les expériences mystiques stimulées par les hallucinogénes à l'intérieur d'un environnement physique, intellectuel et émotionnel approprié, peu d'attention, a été accordée aux expériences mystiques qui surgissent spontanément pendant l'hypnose et la méditation transcendantale. Le présent auteur facilite le déclenchement d'expériences mystiques en utilisant des techniques hypnotiques spécifiquement ceatrées sur la modification des perceptions spatie-temporelles. Des histoires de cas illustrent lee méthodologies utilisées pour guider lee sujets réceptifs dane des états mystiques et dent le but est d'apaieer on de corriger des syndromes de douleur organique et fonctionnelle qui ne répondent pas a d'autres interventions. Les proceseus biopsychologiques prohablement impliqués sont discutés.

Aplicaciones de los estados místicos obtenidos bajo hipnosis al tratamiento del dolor fisico y moral

Paul Sacerdote

Resumen: Los estados místicos sobrepasan la percepción censorial y el pensamiento lógico habituales. A menudo representan el objetivo último de largos aprendizajes inscritos en practicas monásticas orientales u occidentales, que ponen el acento en la autodisciplina y Ia meditación; o están en relación con conversiones religiosas subitas. Mientras que se ha mostrado un renovado interés por las experiencias provocadas por drogas alucinógenas dentro de un entorno fisico, intelectual y emotivo apropiado, se ha prestado menos atención a aquellas experiencias místicas que se producen espontáneamente durante la hipnosis y la meditación transcendental. Este autor facilita la liberación de experiencias místicas utilizando procedimientos hipnóticos específicamente destinados a alterar la percepción del tiempo y del espaclo. Las presentaciones de casos ilustran los métodos empleados para llevar a sujetos receptivos a estados místicos, con el fin de aliviar o corregir sindromes dolorosos, orgánicos y funcionales, refractarios a otras intervenciones. Se discuten los procesos biopsicológicos probables.

CHAPTER SIX

TEMPORAL CONDITIONING: THEORY, RESEARCH, METHOD, HISTORY, & HYPOTHESES

Time was one of experimental psychology's first independent variables. Subsequent decades of research have not diminished this central role. Temporal discrimination has been shown to be critical to operant avoidance learning (Anger, 1963) and to response latency in repetitive vigilance tasks (Hardesty and Bevan, 1965). This section focuses on this ubiquitous variable importance as a stimulus in the context of classical conditioning.

An important summary, translated from the Russian, reviewed over half a century of such temporal conditioning research (Dmitriev and Kochigina, 1959). Beginning in 1907 with Zelenyi, a student of Pavlov, 68 studies were completed. Subjects ranged from bats to hedgehogs to collies to humans; unconditional stimuli varied from shock to food powder to temperature; measured responses included salivation, leg flexion, ear temperature, and even white blood cell count. Thus, over a wide range of species and techniques the Russian investigators demonstrated respondent conditioning to a time interval to be an accomplished fact.

North American psychology in the same period of time, however, barely acknowledged the phenomenon of temporal conditioning. Learning texts listed it in a sentence or two but usually without discussion. Conditioning studies varied their intertrial intervals (ITIs) or otherwise control for temporal conditioning but typically without much conviction or overt rationale. By the mid—1960s, only two temporal conditioning studies could be located in North American psychology journals.[1] Brown (1939) shocked rats at 12 second intervals, measuring the force of the jump response on a postage scale. After 35 trials, rats were shocked at 3, 6, 9, 12, 15, 18, 21, or 24 seconds after the last shock. Rats jumped with most force at the 12 second test shock with decreasing force as the interval grew smaller or slightly larger. Bugelski and Coyer (1950) trained rats to jump a barrier in response to periodic shock and found quicker temporal conditioning at a 15 second ITI than at a 60 second ITI.

On the other hand, North American psychology dealt more fully with temporal response in the context of fixed interval schedules in operant learning (Ferster and Skinner, 1957). Nevertheless, of 79 studies classically conditioning a response to a temporal CS (as located in Psychol. Abstracts up to August 1965), 72 originated in the USSR with others in France, West Germany, and Japan.

The Russian studies were generally strong on detailed observation and imagination but too often weak on experimental controls and statistics even of descriptive nature. Number of subjects (Ss) rarely exceeded five, often with one S per condition. Furthermore, these very Ss were traditionally passed down over the years from experiment to experiment much as precision timers might be in North America. A final drawback prevalent until very recently has been a relatively rigid adherence to only those areas of exploration the early Pavlovians demonstrated as viable. Within this ground there was much imagination, but beyond it studies never reached the printed page. One case in point was the long exclusive Russian ITI range of five to 30 minutes, below or above which no Pavlovian went.

One of Kochigina's later studies (Dmitriev and Kochigina, 1959) is a good example of the Russian technique. Conditioning the leg flexion of dogs to periodic shock, she observed three successive stages of temporal anticipation. Stage 1, the "generalized reflex to time," was characterized by increasing, then decreasing, intersignal errors throughout the ITI. (The intersignal error refers to premature leg flexions anticipating the shock.) Stage 2, the "differentiated reflex to time," begins when intersignal errors occur only during the last half of the ITI. Over further trials errors converge in time on the end

---

[1]This does not include Grant, McFarling, and Gormezano (1960) or Prokasy and Chambliss (1960) since an external CS remained in their "Temporal conditioning" studies. Neither human eye—blink study found fixed ITIs (15 and 25 sec.) to excel variable ITIs but Prokasy (1965) later cited unpublished data supporting significant temporal cue effects with an alternate measure.

point of the ITI. Stage 3, the successfully conditioned temporal response, is operationally defined as occurring when any and all intersignal errors fall within the last 20% of the ITI or to a criterion of 80% accuracy. Kochigina's ITI in this case was the current Russian mode of 5 minutes; four dogs took from 90 to 135 trials to reach criterion.

Temporal conditioning in its classical framework has much relevance for North American psychology today. Research is needed, if for nothing else, than to justify controls against it[2] as well as to explain "sensitization" effects where periodic US presentations elicit an enhanced response level. Russians used this latter effect to increase livestock yield: optimal periodic feeding and milking rhythms were determined experimentally and universally applied (Dmitriev and Kochigina, 1959). Some of the aspects of temporal conditioning demanding basic well controlled research are the effects of ITI, stimulus intensity (Int.), concurrent temporal estimation, concurrent interoceptive process or methods of synchrony, and the role of inhibition.

When Russian psychologists had first determined that a fixed rhythm of stimulation enhanced response magnitude over that elicited by random or haphazard stimulation, animal husbandry specialists set up immediate searches for optimal species—specific ITIs. Unfortunately, the academic temporal conditioners did not follow suit so extensively. The differential effect of ITI length on level of conditioning had not yet been broadly investigated. Bugelski (1956) was among the first to acknowledge this need: "The area of temporal intervals is still largely unexplored. We do not as yet know the most effective intervals for such conditioning." (p. 131)

The findings on this point were, at first glance, among the most directly contradictory of all the explored aspects of temporal conditioning. There was what might be called a Washington—Moscow ITI controversy. Bugelski and Coyer (1950) in the study already cited found conditioning in rats at the 15 second ITI to be faster than at the 60 second ITI. Bugelski concluded that temporal conditioning became more difficult with increasing ITI length. The other American study operated at a 12 second ITI (Brown, 1939) while the French contribution (Fraisse & Jampolsky, 1952) successfully conditioned human gsrs to shock at an ITI of 8 seconds. On this side of the globe then, ITIs had been in terms of seconds backed by the cited opinion that intervals beyond a minute would yield diminishing or non—existent returns. The Russians came to the opposite conclusion.

Zelenyi (1907) launched temporal conditioning in Pavlov's laboratories with a 10 minute ITI. The following year it was replicated at an ITI of 20 minutes (Krzhishkovskii, 1908). Four years later came the much discussed work of Feokritova (1912) with an ITI of 30 minutes. Under Pavlov's supervision (Pavlov, 1927) she brought salivary conditioning well within Kochigina's third stage at this ITI with no canine salivation until the last minute before stimulation. But with the 1930's came moderation. From then up to the present, Soviet ITIs have clustered about five minutes with a general range of three to seven minutes. Nevertheless, there was a consensus that no upper ITI length limit need apply. Pavlov decreed:

"...any length of time interval can be employed. No experiments, however, were made with intervals longer than half an hour" (Pavlov, 1927, p. 42). On the other hand, a lower limit soon crept in. In 1937 Baiandurov found it impossible to condition pigeon activity to periodic shock at ITIs of from 5 to

---

[2] ...Whether fixed or varied, the time functions adopted can influence behavior (i.e., can produce some form of temporal conditioning) and are worthy of analysis in their own right." (p. 121, Prokasy, 1965) An illustrative "pseudo—conditioning" study is Kimble, Mann, and Dufort (1955). Prokasy rejected temporal influence as critical to "pseudo—conditioning" in 1960 but reversed himself in 1965 on the basis of new data.

15 minutes. He had to push as far as 300 trials before 'even' a 30 minute ITI allowed criterion to be reached. Dogs, regarded as capable of conditioning at a somewhat lower ITI than pigeons, still seemed to have a lower limit of their own. A good illustrative study is that of Bolotine (1952a) who conditioned canine time flexion to either a 10 minute or 3 minute ITI. All Ss conditioned at 10 minutes with a mean 180 trials to criterion. Only 1/3 of his dogs were able to condition at the 3 minute ITI and these Ss needed a mean of 520 trials to criterion. Testing the possibility that this finding was a function of his choice of species, he replicated his study with monkeys (1952b) achieving substantially the same results. Bolotina concluded that ITIs of 3 minutes or less were nearly impossible for temporal conditioning since neural excitation was too arhythmic at short intervals to allow the neural traces of inhibition to concentrate. The next year Bolotina (1953) attempted to artificially set aside this neural difficulty by administering bromides to both his dogs and his monkeys. The relaxed animals were able to go as low as ITIs of 2 minutes with level of conditioning improving with increasing bromide strength. A possibility of course was that the bromides were aided by continued use of the same Ss from experiment to experiment. Dmitriev and Grebenkina (1959) demonstrated this possibility when, unable to temporally condition leg flexion in any of six dogs <u>directly</u> to ITIs of 1 or 2 minutes, they trained down Ss at successively lower ITIs (starting with 5 minutes) and eased their dogs into the difficult ITIs. The moral was clear: temporal conditioning became more difficult with decreasing ITI length; any ITI at 3 minutes or less would yield diminishing or nonexistent returns.

Bugelski (1956), aware of these conflicting perspectives, recommended further research. The Soviet—oriented and Washington— oriented studies were standing on different geographical ranges of ITI: perhaps there was something involved in the exposure of complex mammals such as dogs and humans to that 1 to 3 minute range that depresses performance. Or perhaps the two ranges reflected the dominance of separate methods of temporal synchrony. What was needed was a comparative ITI study to explore the gap.

Among the Russians only a few crossed that gap at all (Dmitriev and Kochigina, 1959; Elkin, 1964). With Kochigina, Dmitriev temporally conditioned a verbal anticipatory response to an auditory stimulus in children aged 8 to 14. The ITI was 30 seconds. Elkin conditioned humans to ITIs as low as 3 to 10 seconds. His study will be discussed more fully in another section.

The intensity of the unconditional stimulus has special implications for temporal conditioning although it has been a central variable in classical conditioning since its inception.

Pavlov (1927) reported the speed of conditioning as well as resistance to extinction to vary with the intensity of the unconditional stimulus. American research supported this over subsequent years. Passey (1948), for example, found that conditioning the eye—blink reflex to an air puff varied significantly with the pressure of the puff: both rate and final level of conditioning increased with increasing air puff intensity (cf. Spence, Haggard, and Ross, 1958; Ratner and Denny, 1964). In general it has been found that performance in the learning situation improves with increasing amount of positive or negative reinforcement (Kimble, 1961). Therefore, in that temporal conditioning is a member of the category of classical conditioning, similar results were expected. But not necessarily.

Temporal conditioning has a property which at the same time distinguishes it from the other more complex forms of conditioning (of which it often is a basic component) and which leads to opposite predictions. That property is the <u>internal</u> nature of the CS; interoceptive rhythms must be set up as cues to achieve the CR. It is relatively easy to set up a range of US intensities which does not prohibit the S's discrimination of an external CS. In temporal conditioning, however, a stimulus intense enough to disturb the <u>S</u> disturbs both the discrimination of internal rhythms as well as the regularity of these rhythms. Pavlovians have long demonstrated level of temporal conditioning to be inversely related to S's level of arousal. Feokritova (1912) noted that somnolent dogs excelled normal animals. Stukova (1914) found "excitable" dogs to be more prone to distraction from extraneous stimuli than dogs with "well developed inhibition processes." The tranquilizing effect of bromide injections has, as previously mentioned, been used to facilitate temporal conditioning (Stukova, 1914; Deriabin, 1916; Bolotina, 1953; Dmitriev and Kochigina, 1959) while the excitant of caffeine retarded the process (Dmitriev and Kochigina, 1959). Presumably, the increased arousal somehow interfered with the production and/or discrimination of the interoceptive CS. Pavlovians prefer to discuss this effect in inhibition terminology; the discrimination interpretation was my own.

It might be expected then that increasing intensity would retard level of temporal conditioning where the ITIs are so short as to allow S insufficient recuperation or relaxation time before the next ITI occurs. On the other hand, when ITIs are quite long enough for relaxation to occur in spite of a strongly arousing US, one would expect the traditional superiority of the more intense US to emerge.

Data from fixed interval studies in operant conditioning contexts support this prediction. While stronger reinforcement at moderate or long ITIs has excelled performance at weaker reinforcements (Collier and Myers, 1961; Guttman, 1953; Collier, Knarr, and Marx, 1961; Dufort and Kimble, 1956), the opposite was found at very short ITIs (Collier and Myers, 1961; Conrad and Sidman, 1956).

One final aspect of the intensity variable worth mentioning is the too often neglected obligation of the researcher to demonstrate that cranking up physical intensity produces any substantial subjective increment as well. Often a Russian study would designate a certain acid dosage on a dog's tongue as noxious without any proof; without appropriate and controlled avoidance measures the US might well only have been "tangy." Temporal conditioning with humans, especially, offers an easy opportunity for S to vocally identify the intensity as to pleasantness or unpleasantness.

The interaction of US intensity and ITI was once predicted and observed (ITIs of 15, 45, 135 sec.), but not significantly supported, in a human eyelid conditioning study where photic CS overlapped air puff US (Prokasy, W., Grant, D., and Myers, N., 1958). The simpler temporal conditioning procedure, omitting the external CS~, looked as though it would clarify the issue.

Temporal research with humans had been well cultivated along another area parallel to our interests: temporal estimation. Taking advantage of the unique phylogenetic link between E and S, humans for nearly a century have been asked to produce, reproduce, estimate, and describe intervals of time. During temporal conditioning, human Ss maintain some conscious impression of the magnitude of the ITI. That this process, if not directly related to the conditioning process, is at least affected by it has been shown by Elkin (1964). Elkin temporally conditioned 11 human Ss to ITIs of 3, 5, or 10 seconds. A temporal estimation of all 3 ITIs was made before and after training. Each S showed improvement at estimating the ITI he had been conditioned to with no generalization in increment of estimation accuracy at the other ITIs. This was the only study to ever tie together the two processes of temporal estimation and conditioning. Further investigation of the aspects of their inter—relations is needed.

American, French, and German psychologists have turned out volumes of temporal research when it comes to estimation. Among the best current review sources are Fraisse (1963), Woodrow (1951), and Wallace and Rabin (1960). Some of the aspects of estimation might well be investigated in a temporal conditioning context since the large body of research, despite its bulk, is contradictory on many points. Many studies associate over estimation with high stress and arousal (Gulliksen, 1927; Cutler, 1952; Eson and Kafka, 1952; Anliker, 1963) while many others associate over estimation with low stress and relaxation (Rosenzweig and Koht, 1933; Bakan, 1955; Hare, 1963; Geiwitz, 1964). Johnson

(1962) found no relationship between over estimation and stress concluding that "available methods in time perception experiments do not provide an adequate test." Less pessimistically, Zelkind and Spilka (1965) found over estimation to correlate positively with an optimistic outlook for the future. Even general non—directional accuracy of estimate has been found to increase with high anxiety (Burns and Gifford, 1961) as well as decrease with high anxiety (Weybrew, 1963). But if the literature is far from clear as to arousal effects, the influence of ITI length is generally clear. Accuracy of estimation has been found to increase as the interval increases. Furthermore, the ranges of interval tested have been quite broad. Gilliland and Humphreys (1943), for example, found Ss estimated a 14 second interval at a mean accuracy of 72% as opposed to a mean accuracy of 82% for a 117 second interval. Stimulus intensity ties in to estimation in so far as it heightens anxiety or arousal. Yet, as has been mentioned, the consequences of this were far from clear. If Benussi (1907), using an auditory stimulus, was any guide, increasing intensity shortens the perceived interval. A final point of temporal estimation worth exploring was that of S's retrospective opinion of that estimation; an estimation of the estimation. Bakan (1962) found this retrospection to add information or accuracy to the estimate. Ss in a temporal conditioning context then might be generally expected to identify the direction and possibly the magnitude of the error of their estimate of the ITI. All these S reports seemed worth investigation.

Verbal reports also offered a look at some of the ongoing interoceptive processes used to accomplish temporal synchrony. The question of which process or processes are basic to time perception has long teased psychology. Long range process change (blood sugar count, white blood cell count, and hormonal secretions) were linked to circadian rhythms (Kayser, 1952) and even have been conditioned (Dmitriev and Kochigina, 1959). Along these lines, Kleitman (1939) determined the existence of a diurnal temperature cycle in humans and conditioned it to different cycle lengths in an assistant (Kleitman, Titelbaum, and Hoffman, 1937). This kind of approach with slow moving processes demonstrated the relative ease with which interoceptive rhythms can be made to synchronize with exogenous ones. Waking at a specific time each morning, for example, has been traced to individual empathy with degree of bladder distension (Fraisse, 1963).

But when synchrony with intervals of minutes or seconds is involved, some more immediately periodic processes must be examined. Fraisse (1963) lists breathing, pulse, and EEG activity as the three most important such rhythms, giving priority to the last. In the area of temporal estimation, choice of the critical interoceptive rhythm again led to a wide variety of findings. Schaefer and Gilliland (1938) ruled out pulse rate, breathing rate, and blood pressure change as reliable indicators of estimation accuracy for intervals of 4 to 27 seconds. Bell and Provins (1963) also ruled out pulse and changes in room temperature as well. However, body temperature was shown to be related to temporal estimation and production (Francois, 1927, 1928; Hoagland, 1933, 1934, 1936a, 1936b, 1936c, 1936d, 1943). As to EEG activity, Adrian (1934) demonstrated that the alpha rhythm can be synchronized with intermittent light. Werboff (1957) brought EEF into the estimation of short intervals and found alpha activity highly related. With brain activity as a possible cue rhythm, one might then have expected research designed to locate its physiological source. Dimond (1964) concisely summarized the ablation approaches to locating a temporal center in the cortex. For three decades, parietal lobes, prefrontal lobes, dorsomedial thalamus, mammallary bodies, and other slices of cortex were removed in this search (Ehrenwald, 1931; Harrison, 1940; Remy, 1942; Hyde and Wood, 1949; Spiegel and Wysis, 1949; Partridge, 1950; Spiegel, Wysis, Orchinik, and Freed, 1955) with "temporal confusions" (as Dimond put it) occurring in all cases. Dimond himself preferred the prefrontal areas as the most likely suspects.

Theory had not lagged behind research in attempts at pinning down this internal programming. Popov (1948, 1950a, 1950b), taking off from Adrian's EEG work of 1934 evolved the general temporal theory of "cyclochronism."

"Cyclochronism" bases itself on the nervous system which at all levels supposedly reproduces external excitations in the same order and at the same temporal intervals as when they first acted on the organism (cf. Fraisse, 1963). This theory of nervous mimicry, currently accepted by French psychology (Fraisse, 1963), does not directly oppose Pavlovian doctrine since Pavlov (1927, 1928) insisted that all interoceptive processes had their effects on the cortex. However, Popov de-emphasizes the role of the middle man: the interoceptive processes relaying the periodicities to the cortex. Pavlov, for example, attributed temporal conditioning of the salivary reflex primarily to the slow rhythms of the digestive organs. Thus, ITIs were long to allow for the substantial latencies of digestion; it was not until the 1930's, when motor reactions were first investigated (Beritov, 1932), that Soviet ITIs dropped to the 5 minute range. Furthermore, Pavlov felt that excitations were not immediately reproduced internally but rather gradually took on this form with repeated exposures. The process which ultimately separated responses from one another for the correct time interval was, according to Pavlov, inhibition.

Before discussing inhibition, a final word might be said about the search for critical methods of synchrony. Human Ss were asked to identify their methods of time judgement in a well controlled study. Spivack and Levine (1964) identified "visual clock" (S sees an imaginary clock and judges time by it) and "feel" (S has a strong intuition) methods as well as some form of counting when short intervals of 1 to 64 seconds were estimated. An inventory of the conscious methods used by human Ss as well as their differential effectiveness should always be done for temporal conditioning. Recent evidence suggests that breathing rate, for example may be as important as Munsterberg (1889) once thought it was. Stolz (1965) found vasomotor conditioning impossible when breathing was "controlled" by synchronizing it to a metronome. The relative frequency and effectiveness of methods of choice for a large number of humans temporally conditioned would, if nothing else, say something about human species behavior in a temporal situation.

Whatever the rhythm, another process is needed to hook up the external stimulus with an internal response specific in time. To Pavlov (1927, 1928, 1957) this process was the concentration of cortical inhibition in the right temporal areas. Extinction or unlearning involved irradiation of this inhibition such that concentration was destroyed. Although Pavlov thought of inhibition as a strictly cortical event, it was analogized with other physiological events from the beginning. Frolov (1937), for example, said:

> ... since nearly all activity of the musculature consists in the alternating flexion and extension of the extremities at the joints the... fact of reciprocal excitation and inhibition by means of reflex action acquires almost universal significance. All interfering movements are inhibited as soon as they become unnecessary. (p. 107)

Although Inhibition retained Its central role for Pavlovian conditioning (Prokasy, 1965), Its definition broadened over the years. Inhibition soon came to include relaxation of the musculature in any form up to and including sleep. Rather than demonstrating nervous tissues' concentration or irradiation of inhibition, Russian studies only differentially manipulated observable relaxation. Operationally this approach had been quite productive, especially in the area of temporal conditioning. Feokritova, as far back as 1912, noted that her dogs took better account of the passage of time during sleep than during a period of activity (Frolov, 1937). Bromide and caffeine studies, manipulating relaxation by drug, have found temporal conditioning superior for those Ss best able to inhibit their responses at the right time:

those relaxed artificially by drug (Stukova, 1914; Deriabin, 1916; Bolotina, 1953; Dmitriev and Kochigina, 1959). Pavlovian theory rests on the assumption that conditioning is learning when (and being able) to relax or (see Denny and Adelman, 1955, for "Secondary Elicitation," a similar emphasis on relaxation in a North American learning theory) learning when not to respond. Naturally, it was represented in other more complex terminology:

> *It appears that in the establishment of a conditioned reflex to time, internal inhibition becomes stronger, as a result of which it can at some point and under certain conditioning become prepotent over the stimulation of the dominant response and delay the...reaction ...From this point of view, the conditioned reflex to time is the result of the imminent relative insufficiency of internal inhibition during interaction of the dominant response. (Rozin, 1959)*

Inhibition supposedly grows from the midpoint of the ITI, since that is the farthest point in time from stimulation, expanding to concentrate over the entire non-stimulted interval with sufficient trials (Pavlov, 1927; Dmitriev and Kochigina, 1959). How could this be measured?

Birman (1953) classified human Ss as "excitables" and "relaxeds" on the basis of their observed waiting room behavior before the experiment began. Trace conditioning was far superior for the "relaxeds." I felt that a better way to get at pre-treatment arousal as well as the development of relaxation during conditioning was by gsr recording. A good deal was known about this measure (Woodworth and Schlosberg, 1954) and gsr changes have been found to be associated with CRs in a human operant learning situation (Doehring, Helmer, and Fuller, 1964) and URs in an earthworm responding situation (Morgan, Ratner, and Denny, 1965).

In summary, the literature had delineated the independent variables of ITI, stimulus intensity, and prior relaxation as potentially important to temporal conditioning. The concurrent dependent variables of temporal estimation, interoceptive process or methods of synchrony, and relaxation during the ITI also seemed relevant for inclusion in any parametric study of temporal conditioning. It was decided to attempt such an investigation of these variables through a series of temporal conditioning experiments with humans in a common methodological context.

Pilot research, including a variety of conditioning methodologies, ultimately led to the adoption of Dmitriev's (1959) vocal anticipation of the periodic stimulus as most fruitful method for pursuing the temporal variables suggested by the literature. Human Ss selected for the pilot research performed well in the vocal anticipation paradigm of temporal conditioning.

A photic flash in a dark room was adopted as the periodic US this reduced the problem of manipulating stimulus intensity to switching light bulbs of differential wattage. Theoretically, US intensity might also have been changed by varying the intensity level during the ITI with absence of light as the US. In either case, the change in photic intensity should have subsequent unconditional response consequences for S if such a change can in fact be taken as a US. Pilot work indicated that both high and low wattage flashes, at ITIs of 30 seconds or more, elicited consistent gsr arousal in humans. This gsr arousal had not habituated after 20 successive flashes. The gsr drops were only part of a generalized response complex including slight head withdrawals, eye blinks, and general skeletal movement. Thus the US consistently produced a UR or URs. However, in the pursuit of a discrete and more readily identifiable response, the vocal anticipation was chosen. This choice departed from most North American classical conditioning research in that the vocal response, in the absence of prior instructions, would not be a consistent (unconditional) response to the photic flash. The prior instructions, however, allow the vocal response to function as such a UR within the specific experimental context of the temporal conditioning situation. Since its significance as a consistent stimulus is thus acquired, we are really dealing here with a higher order conditioning of the temporal response. Fortunately, through the use of the human "second signaling system" of language, such conditioning is eminently feasible. One objection that might have been raised by North American psychologists of an earlier era would be to the "voluntary" nature of the response in what is purported to be a classical conditioning paradigm. However, since in subsequent years "involuntary[1]" responses have been conditioned in operant situations and even controlled by voluntary procedures (Stolz, 1965; Kimble, 1961), North American definitions of the classical procedure were somewhat liberalized. Kimble (1961) said:

> *The original distinction between instrumental and classical conditioning is made purely on operational grounds. The two designations refer respectively to training procedures in which the response of the subject does and does not determine whether the US appears (p. 78). ...the conditioned response is a combination of voluntary and involuntary processes.* (p. 108)

Pavlov was sensitive to the controversy of volition, which he regarded a pseudo—controversy, and for years the word "voluntary" was forbidden in the Pavlov laboratories (Frolov, 1937).

Pilot research led to the establishment of experimental conditions designed to reduce, as much as plausible, all competing or distracting extraneous stimuli from the environment to maximize the chance of temporal conditioning's occurrence. Since such conditioning at the ITI range contemplated had long been regarded as difficult or impossible, such maximizing steps seemed warranted. The final pilot study is included in this dissertation as it was the prototype of the experiments that followed.

On the basis of the relevant literature discussed here, as supported by pilot research, certain hypotheses seemed tenable:

A. Temporal conditioning in a classical framework can be demonstrated for adult humans.

B. When a temporal response is acquired it will show improvement with continued amounts of periodic stimulation and extinction when anticipations are elicited in the absence of that periodic stimulation.

C. Performance observed in acquisition will be a function of ITI with performance at ITIs of more than 3 minutes and at 1 minute or less excelling performance of ITIs in between.

D. Performance observed in acquisition will be enhanced by increasing stimulus intensity at high ITIs and retarded by increasing stimulus intensity at low ITI s

E. Post—conditioning estimation of ITI length will be affected by some of the factors affecting temporal conditioning. Accuracy of estimation, for example, will increase with increasing ITI.

F. The more relaxed a subject before conditioning begins, the higher the subsequent level of conditioning obtained. Gsr drops obtained directly before acquisition will therefore be reliable predictors of subsequent performance.

G. As temporal conditioning occurs over trials, increased relaxation during the ITI will also be observed with trials. Gsr changes from the center of one ITI to the next will therefore show increased relaxation over trials in the presence of temporal conditioning.

H. Reported interoceptive process will vary with the subject and the ITI. Specifically, counting methods of synchrony will decrease in percentage of use as ITI length increases.

The following experiments attempted to gather sufficient basic data to support or reject these hypotheses and to lay the framework for a better understanding of respondent conditioning to an interval of time.

CHAPTER SEVEN

TEMPORAL CONDITIONING OF HUMANS I: PILOT RESEARCH

EXPERIMENT I

Experiment I, as the final pilot study, stood as basic prototype to the experiments following it. Its purposes were twofold. One was to demonstrate the feasibility of temporal conditioning at the stimulus conditions contemplated within the context of the experimental procedure and setting evolved for that purpose. Secondly, a first look at the differential effects of ITI and stimulus intensity was to be taken.

Method

Subjects.- - The Ss were 19 volunteer college students, or their wives, ranging in age from 19 to 25. There were 13 males and 5 females.

Apparatus. - - The experiment took place in a relatively light-tight single room. E sat at a desk directly behind S and collected data by the light of a red 60 watt bulb. The photic US was a bulb flash controlled by E with a Lafayette Stimulus Timer. The bulb was 7.5 watts white-frosted for the low intensity condition and was 100 watts white-frosted for the high intensity condition. The bulb was at eye level or below on a lamp 18 ins, in front of S. The bulb and lamp rested on a table which S faced. S's left hand rested on this table within the gsr finger electrodes. The gsr electrodes were connected to a Lafayette D.C. gsr unit placed over the Stimulus Timer at E's table. E also remained within reach of the room overhead lights. S sat in a comfortable wooden swivel chair with arm rests facing the lamp and US bulb which had a blank white wall behind it. E timed S's vocal responses with a Meylan stop watch, checking these readings at the shorter it is against tape recordings made during the experimental session. Dittoed data sheets (see Table 30) were used for uniform data recording; typed procedure and instructions for S were taped to E's desk.

Procedure.- - Before each S, E warmed up gsr and timer apparatus for 10 minutes. At the end of this time, S was allowed to enter the experimental room, minus any wrist watch, and settled in chair and gsr finger electrodes. At this time E recorded S's name, age, sex, and any other descriptive data that seemed relevant. E next handed S a carbon copy of the acquisition instructions. S followed this copy visually while E read the original out loud. The acquisition instructions were as follows:

> *This experiment is designed to measure your gsr or the electrical resistance of the skin. The finger electrodes are for measurement only and will not shock you. A brief explanation of the gsr's purpose will follow the experiment; any questions about our purpose will be answered at that time.*
>
> 1. *Because of the delicate balance of the electrical equipment please keep your left hand perfectly still throughout the experiment.*
> 2. *Find as comfortable a sitting position as you can, facing straight ahead.*
> 3. *The light in front of you will flash on and off very quickly every so often. The time between these flashes is a FIXED INTERVAL of time. There will be the same amount of time between each flash.*
> 4. *Your job is to say "NOW" whenever you think the bulb is about to flash. Try to say "NOW" as closely as possible to the actual flash. I will be scoring your accuracy. The closer you come to the flash, the more accurate the score.*
> 5. *Say "NOW" only once between flashes.*
> 6. *If you don't beat the flash; if the bulb flashes <u>before</u> you can say "NOW" please do not talk during the experiment.*
> 7. *Except for saying "NOW" please do not talk during the experiment.*
> 8. *When I turn off the lights the experiment will begin. When I turn them on it will be over.*

There will be a short wait of a few minutes before the first flash while the gsr warms up. Are there any questions?

E answered any questions by rereading the relevant portion of the instructions. Then E reclaimed the carbon copy of the acquisition instructions, shut the overhead lights, and turned on the red desk light. The stop watch was started. For some Ss, gsr readings were made at 0.5 minutes and at 2.5 minutes during the 3.0 minutes of habituation which now followed. At the end of these 3.0 silent minutes E set off the first photic flash. Twenty-one subsequent flashes separated by a common ITI followed (20 trials) with the time of Ss "NOW" anticipation recorded by E in every case. Various gsr measures were made by E throughout the trials. After the last flash, the following instructions were read to S:

You've done very well. Before I turn on the lights I'd like you to guess how much time there was between each pair of flashes.

(Bakan, 1955) has shown that lack of response set does not significantly affect temporal estimation.) After these estimation instructions, E recorded S's answer, and turned on the overhead lights. E then recorded S's introspections on methods of synchrony used, percent of time devoted to each method, and subjective unpleasantness of the flash. Finally, S was given a brief lecture on the history and uses of the gsr and released from the experimental situation. Ss were not told the exact ITI they had been run at until Experiment I was completed for all Ss.

Experimental Design. - - ITIs of 45, 135, and 240 sec. were used at either high or low US intensity. This formed six ITI—Int. conditions and 3 Ss were randomly assigned by card draw to each condition.

Results

Table 1* summarizes the most important abbreviations used in this and subsequent experiments. Table 2 summarizes the important S data for Experiment I. Looking first to temporal conditioning as a function of ITI and Int., mean occurrence of the temporal CR for these variables is depicted in Figure 1. As Table 1 indicates, a temporal CR or CR_{80} is any response anticipating the US within the last 20% of the ITI (Dmitriev and Kochigina, 1959). With this criterion, analysis of the binomial probabilities (Siegel, 1956) indicated that a frequency of occurrence of the CR_{80} of 55% or higher in a 5—trial block or 38% or higher in 20 trials would be significant at p < .05. Figure 1 shows the predicted near chance level dip at the (135 sec.) ITI falling between previously successful short American ITIs and long Soviet ITIs. An analysis of variance (Table 3) showed this ITI effect to be highly significant (F = 7.10, df = 2, 12, p < .01). Int. also looked as predicted with L Int. excelling H Int. at the short ITI and vice versa at the long ITI. However, neither the Int. nor its interaction with ITI were significant in the analysis of variance (Table 3). Figure 2 illustrates temporal conditioning over blocks. The overall increase in level of conditioning with blocks of 5 trials was highly significant as gauged by analysis of variance (F 1038, df = 3, 36, p<.005). Note in Figure 2 that this increase was only evident for the short and long ITIs after the second block of trials. Blocks at the 135 sec. ITI remained at or below chance level. Note also that conditioning at the long 240 sec. ITI levels off or drops after the third block of trials. This may have been the result of fatigue. The curves generally demonstrated that temporal conditioning in the experimental setting of Experiment I was demonstrably present or absent by the end of 10 to 15 trials. Analysis of variance showed none of the interactions between blocks of trials and ITI or Int. to be significant (Table 3).

---

*All tables are at the end of chapter 11

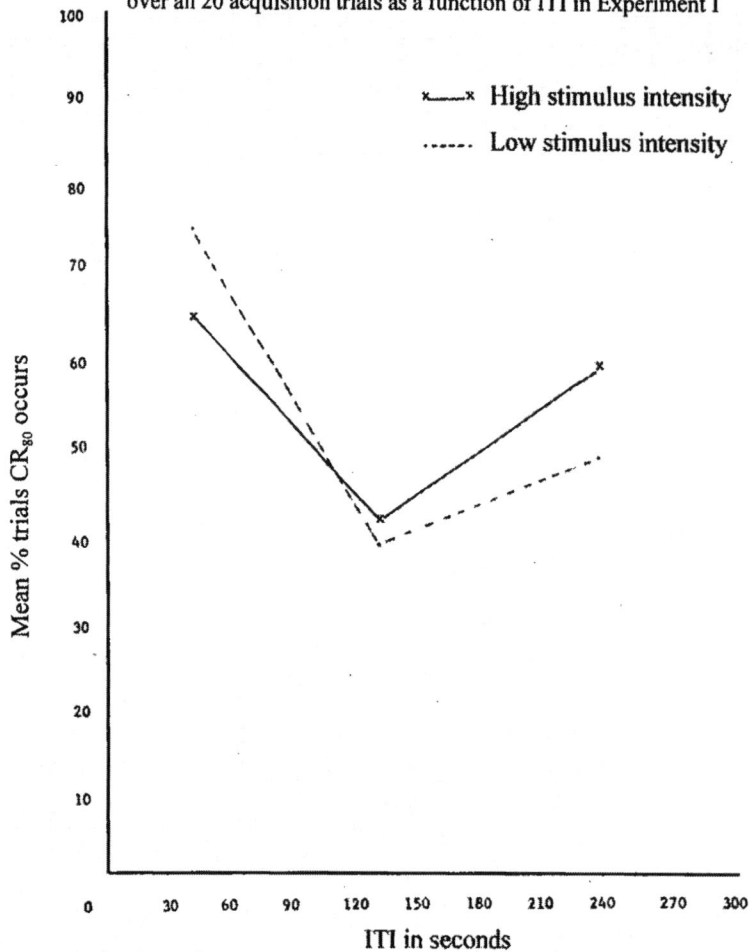

Figure 1. – - Mean % occurrence of CR_{80} at both stimulus intensities over all 20 acquisition trials as a function of ITI in Experiment I

x—x High stimulus intensity

····· Low stimulus intensity

Mean % trials CR_{80} occurs

ITI in seconds

As for estimation of ITI length, a product—moment correlation between A. Est. and CR_{80} scores for all blocks was +.26 or not significant at the 5% level for the number of Ss involved. Those Ss showing the best conditioning did not necessarily show the most accurate estimation. An analysis of variance of per cent A. Est. as a function of ITI and Int. (Table 4) showed significant effects for ITI (F 8.63, df = 2, 12, p < .005), Int. (F 55.38, df 1, 12, p. < .005), and their interaction (F = 12.12, df = 2, 12, p < .005). Estimation grew in mean accuracy as ITI length grew, had greater mean accuracy at H Int. than L Int., and showed a more dramatic increase with ITI for the L Int. Ss than for the H Int. Ss. These results from this miniature experiment suggested that the estimation process is sensitive to the same variables as the conditioning process.

Three Ss had their gsr changes gauged during the habituation period. The change from 0.5 minutes to 2.5 minutes, designated 11 gsr (for habituation), is plotted in Table 5 opposite the respective and subsequent CR_{80} score over all trial blocks in acquisition. The Product-moment correlation between H gsr and CR_{80} score for these 3 Ss was -.985 (P < .02). This finding was suggestive enough to give it more thorough consideration with the substantial number of Ss in Experiment IT. Various methods of gsr just guessed. Some Ss used a "Feel"or intuition method which, as opposed to blind guessing, gave them some definite physical sensation of anticipation prior to the US. One S, scoring 6 out of 20 possible CR_{80}s, visualized a clock with a second hand in motion at a constant rate of speed. He relaxed and let his thoughts wander at random until his "Feel" indicated a flash was close at which time he checked his imaginal clock to see how much time was left. Here was a real biological clock? (See Table 6.)

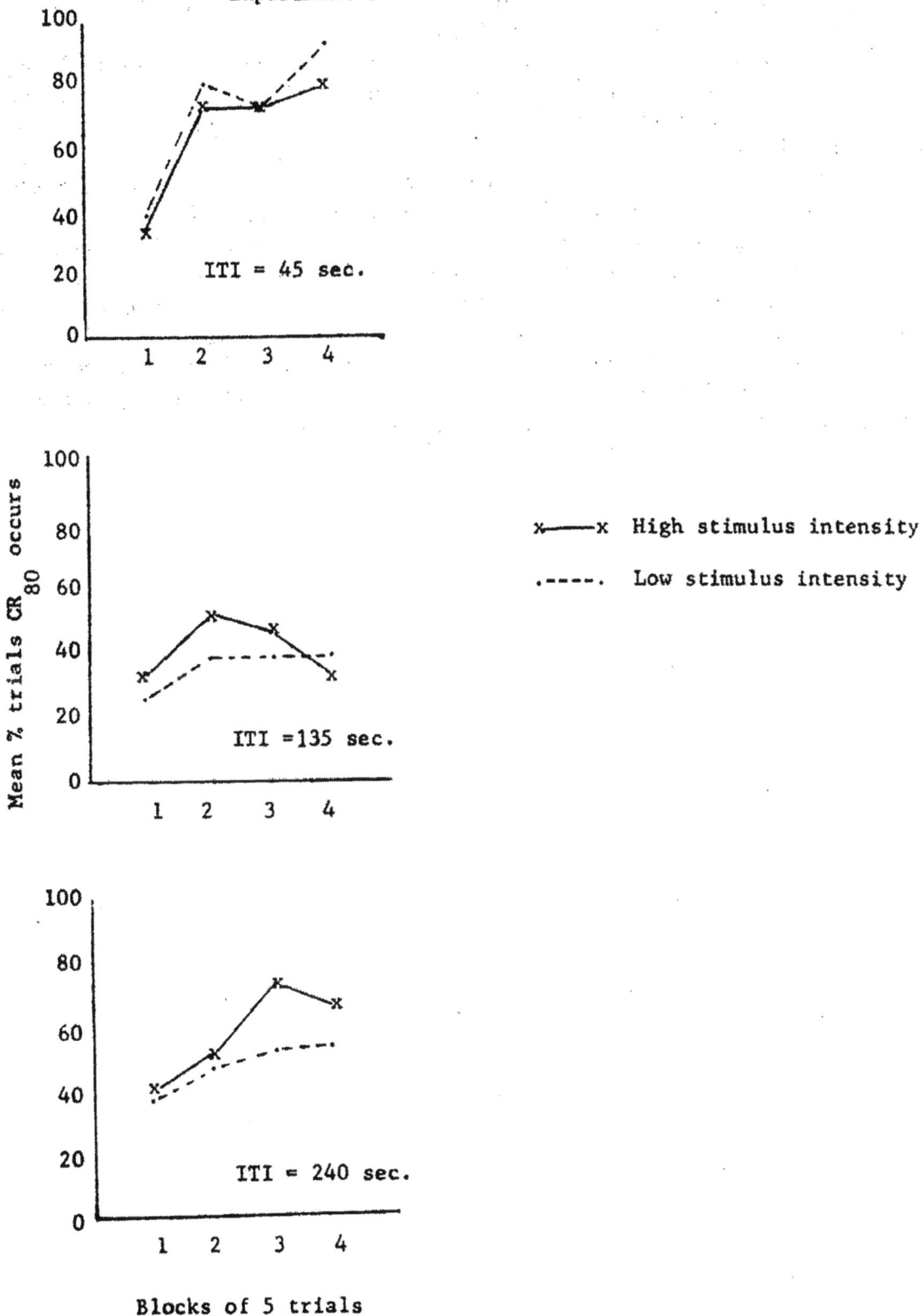

Figure 2.--Mean % occurrence of CR_{80} at both stimulus intensities for each ITI as a function of 5-trial acquisition block in Experiment I

Discussion

Experiment I demonstrated that temporal conditioning could occur as a result of the experimental procedure and surrounds evolved from prior pilot research. Furthermore, the occurrence of the conditioning was significantly related to the stimulus conditions.

ITI showed the predicted dip in the gap area between Soviet and American explored ITI ranges. Int. was as predicted in effect but was not significant for the number of Ss tested. Level of conditioning significantly Improved with trial blocks. Since there was the suggestion of fatigue at the long 240 sec. ITI after three 5—trial blocks. subsequent experiments will restrict themselves to three blocks of acquisition trials. Classical conditioning studies with humans had usually demonstrated significant effects within 20 trials (Kimble, Mann, and Dufort, 1955; Prokasy, Grant and Myers, 1958).

Introspections were suggestive and seemed worthy of expansion. It was decided that the next experiment would also collect methods of synchrony and per cent of time spent on each, as well as estimates of ITI length with additional estimates of the direction and magnitude of error of that estimate, and, again, introspective proof that the H Int. US was more subjectively unpleasant than the L Int. US.

Experiment I allowed for the evolution of the most experimentally feasible, reliable, and theoretically meaningful gsr measures for subsequent experiments. Besides the general refinement of measures and procedures, critical variables demanding further scrutiny had been delineated.

CHAPTER EIGHT

TEMPORAL CONDITIONING OF HUMANS II: BASIC METHOD

EXPERIMENT II

Experiment II was an extended replication of Experiment I. It was conducted under improved, refined, and expanded conditions, across a wider spectrum of critical ITIs, and, most important, with a much more substantial number of Ss.

Method

Subjects.- - The Ss were 120 volunteer college students from an introductory psychology course. Males outnumbered females 79 to 41. Age was restricted to from 18 to 22 years; nearly half the sample was 18 (58 Ss) with a mean age of 18.7 years for the full sample. All Ss received course credit for their time in the experiment.

Apparatus.- - This and subsequent experiments took place in a new light-tight room which was also sound-proofed to outside noise by virtue of being the insulated inner chamber of a double room. Figures 3 and 4 illustrate this. Otherwise the apparatus was exactly as described in Experiment I.

Procedure.- - The procedure was substantially identical to that of Experiment I with a few additions and changes which will be noted here. The positions of S and E in relation to each other and the apparatus remained the same (see Figures 5 and 6). The acquisition instructions read to S̲ by E̲ (still followed by S̲ on a carbon) were not re-worded. Again, after the overhead lights were turned off, there was a 3 minute habituation wait before the first US was presented. In this experiment all Ss had their gsrs recorded at the 0.5 minute and 2.5 minute marks of the habituation period. This H gsr change represented an increase or decrease in arousal as a function of the habituation wait. After the first flash, 16 subsequent US flashes separated by a common ITI (15 trials) followed with the time of S's "NOW" anticipation recorded by E̲ in every case. E̲ recorded S's gsr at the midpoint of every ITI up to and including the midpoint of the ITI following the last US flash. The mean gsr change from midpoint to midpoint for each block of 5 trials was termed the I gsr after inhibition (since Pavlovian inhibition theory predicted this mean change would be towards greater relaxation over trials). From these readings, E was also able to measure an overall experimental gsr or OE gsr by subtracting the pre—treatment 2.5 minute habituation reading from the very last or post—treatment ITI midpoint reading. This gave a before and after measure on arousal of the effect of the experiment as a whole. After the last midpoint gsr reading, E̲ asked S̲ for a verbal estimate of the ITI length. Following this estimate, additional retrospective information was collected. S̲ was asked to indicate the direction magnitude of the error in his initial estimation. The overhead lights were then put on and further introspective information gathered. S̲ was again asked what methods of synchrony were used, what per cent of the time they were used and when they were used. S̲ was again asked to classify the US as "pleasant:' "unpleasant," or "neutral." Following any final comments, S̲ was lectured on the gsr. All Ss received credit slips and were then released.

Experimental Design.- - ITIs of 30, 60, 90, 120, 150, 180, 210, 240, 270, 300 sec. were used at either high or low US intensity. This formed 20 ITI-Int. conditions and 6 Ss were randomly assigned by card draw to each condition.

Results

Table 7 summarizes the data for Experiment II. Again, abbreviations are defined in Table 1.

A first consideration was the pre-treatment composition of the sample in terms of the major independent variables. Chi square analyses (Table 20) did not show S distribution by sex, age, or pre-treatment H gsr to be significantly clustered on any one Int. or ITI. A similar check of H gsr by ITI and Int. was made with analysis of variance (Table 8) and, again, H gsr scores were not found significantly different by ITI, Ints. or their interaction. These results supported the random assignment of Ss to conditions as not biasing the stimulus variables with differential S characteristics.

Another preliminary consideration was the nature of the interrelationship of S characteristics. Both sexes had a mean age of 18.7 years. However, females had H gsrs significantly more relaxed than males as tested by t-test ($t = 3.28$, $df = 118$, $p < .01$). Age (18 years vs. 19-22 years) and H gsr (+ vs. -, 0) showed no significant relationship by chi square analysis nor did "excited" Ss (+ H gsr) differ significantly by age from "relaxed" Ss (0 or - H gsr) as gauged by t-test.

(In Experiment TI: all non-significant and significant chi squares can be observed in chi square Table 20; all t-test analyses can be observed in Table 19; all correlational analyses can be observed in Table 19; all correlational analyses can be observed in Table 16.)

Figure 3. -- Mean % occurrence of CR_{80} at both stimulus intensities
over all 15 acquisition trials as a function of ITI in
Experiment II

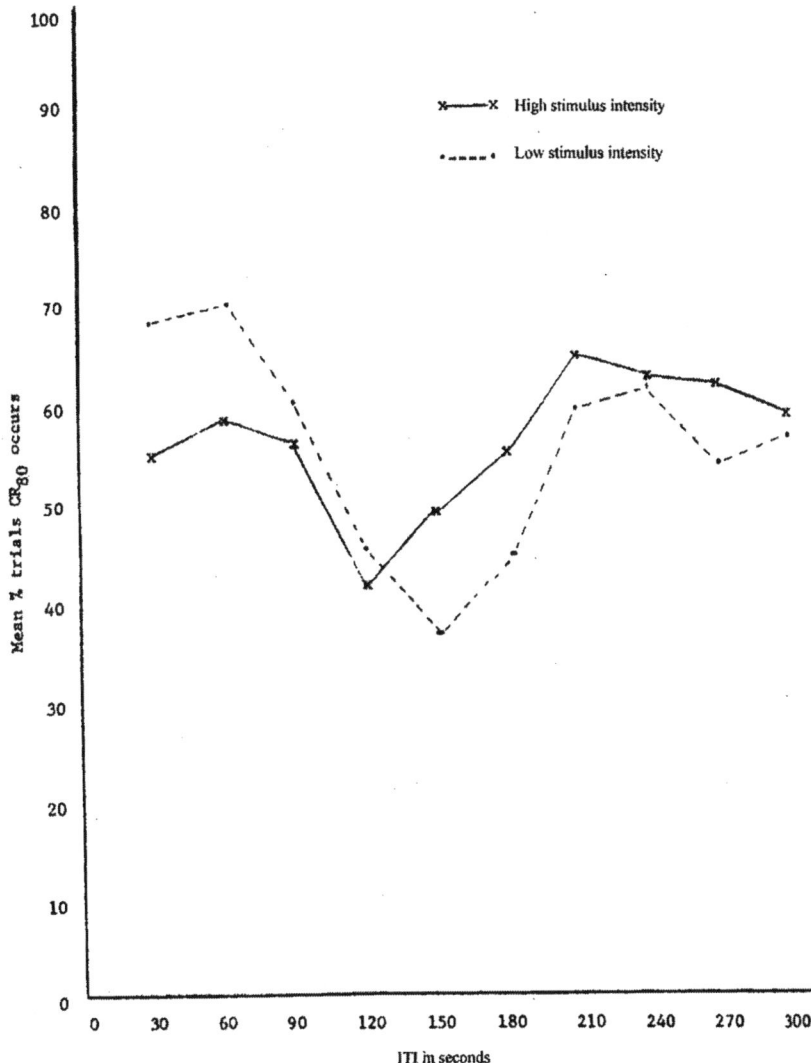

Subjective unpleasantness of the US (Sb Un) was found to bear no significant relationship to ITI, or the sex, age, or H gsr of S as analyzed by chi square. As expected, Ss at high stimulus intensity (H Int.) significantly more frequently labeled the US as "unpleasant" than Ss at the low stimulus intensity (L Int.) as tested by chi square (chi square = 8.89, df = 1, p <.01). At H Int. 53% of the Ss chose "unpleasant" as opposed to 27% of the Ss at L Int.

Figure 3 illustrates the mean per cent occurrence of CR_{80} over all acquisition trials as a function of ITI and Int. Binomial probabilities (Siegel, 1956) indicated that a frequency of occurrence of the CR_{80} over 15 trials of 41% or higher would be significant at p < .05. Once again, there was a dip of level of conditioning between ITIs of 1 and 4 minutes. The bottom of the dip was at or below chance level. Analysis of variance (Table 9) showed ITI to significantly affect the level of conditioning (F = 3.54, df = 9,100, p < .005). Int. appears to interact with ITI as in the last experiment with L Int. excelling H Int. at short ITIs and vice versa beyond the 120 sec. ITl. Analysis of variance (Table 9) did not show Int. or its interaction with ITI to be significant over all the ITIs. However, it must be noted that for the four shortest ITIs mean level of conditioning was higher for the L. Int. groups while for the six longer ITIs mean level of conditioning was higher for the H Int. conditions. The cross-over was between 120 and 150 seconds. Tukey (1949) developed a procedure for testing the significance of individual comparisons between condition means following an analysis of variance. Winer (1962), labeling it the "honestly significant difference" procedure, gave it laurels as a widely applicable but conservative measure. Edwards (1960a) referred to the procedure more simply as "Tukey's significant gap test." Basically it employs the error mean square of the analysis of variance as a common measure of error variance for t—test comparisons and converts this by formula to a minimum difference necessary to all comparisons for a specific level of significance. Table 10 lists selected comparisons and their significance at the 5% level (where applicable) according to Tukey's gap test. Returning now to the question of Int., it is seen from Table 10 that L Int. significantly excelled H Int. at both the 30 and 60 sec. ITIs thus supporting the hypothesis that short ITIs lead to this kind of result. On the other hand, only at 150 and 180 sec.

ITIs did H Int. excel L Int. to a significant extent. The evidence for superiority of H Int. was supportive then only at middle range ITI lengths. Tukey's gap test also allows for another look at the effect of ITI length at both intensities. Comparing each ITI to its next highest and next lowest neighbor in time, Table 10 illustrates that the subsequent ITI groupings were quite familiar. At H Int., level of conditioning separated 30, 60 and 90 sec. ITIs from middle range 120, 150, and 180 sec. ITIs, while the latter group was separated from the longer ITIs of 210 to 300 sec. This same division was found at L Int. with the additional isolation of the 90 sec. group from both shorter and longer ITIs. Here again are the American, Soviet, and untouchable ranges. Further analysis of these data- determined ITT groupings (ITT gps.) was made according to the following schema: 30 and 60 sec. ITIs were considered as the "short" (s) ITI group; ITIs of 120, 150, and 180 sec. were considered "medium" (m) length ITIs; ITIs of 210, 240, 270, 300 sec. were considered "long" (l) ITIs. The 90 sec. ITI, not clearly a member of the "short" group for both Ints., was not included in the groupings. Note that the "short," "medium," and "long" ITI groups each correspond to a different area of past American vs. Soviet exploration or lack of exploration.

Figure 4 illustrates the general increase in level of conditioning with blocks of acquisition trials observed at most ITIs and intensities. Again, a 5-trial block needed 55% frequency of occurrence of CR_{80} or better to show conditioning significant at p <.05. The overall increase was significant (F = 26.54, df = 2,200, p <.005) by analysis of variance (Table 9) although none of the interactions between trial blocks and ITI or Int. were significant.

100

Figure . – – Mean % occurrence of CR_{80} at both stimulus intensities
by 5-trial acquisition block for each ITI in Experiment II

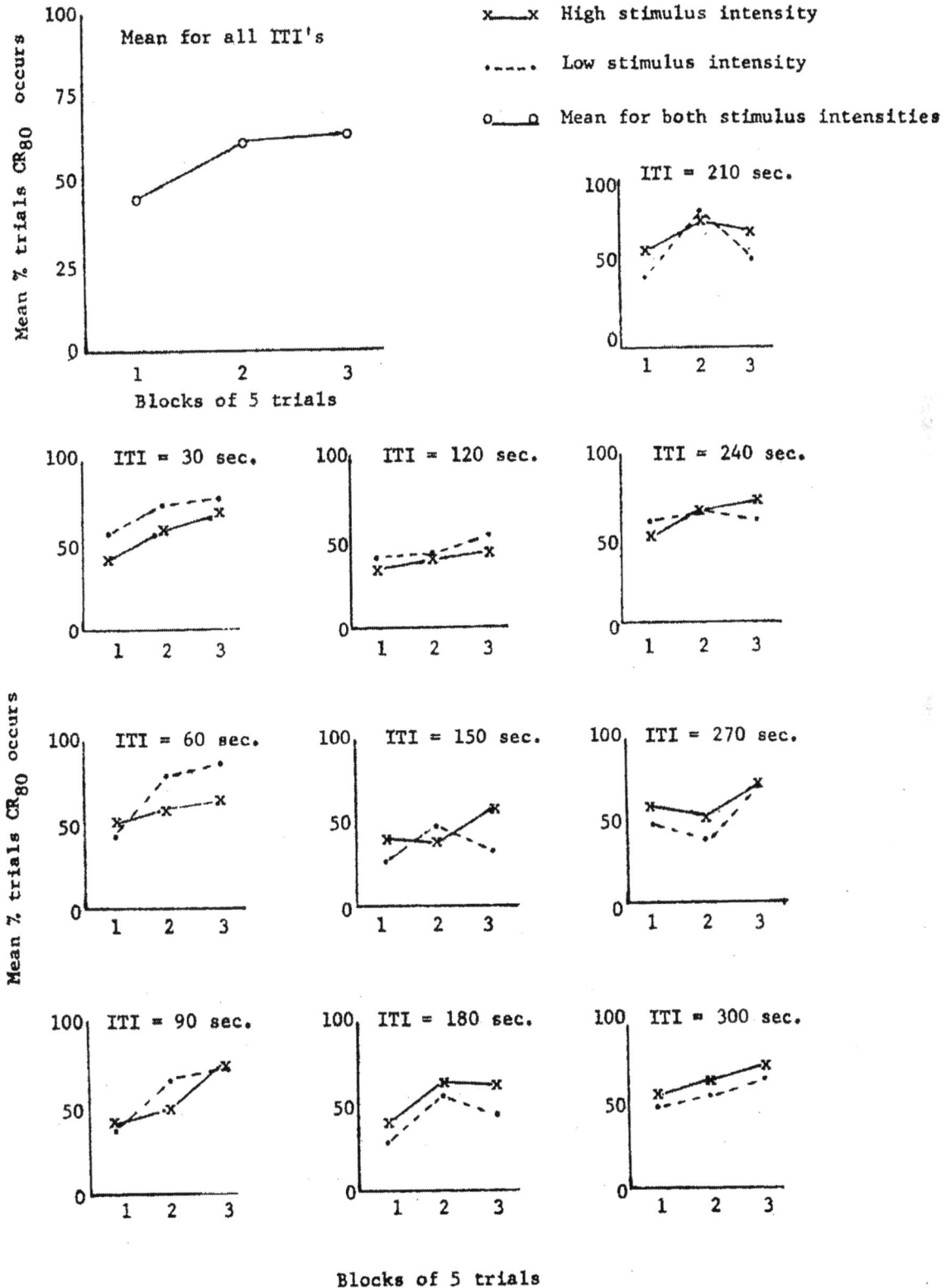

101

Figure 1. – - Mean % occurrence of CR_{80} at both stimulus intensities
over all 15 acquisition trials as a function of ITI lentgh
group in Experiment II

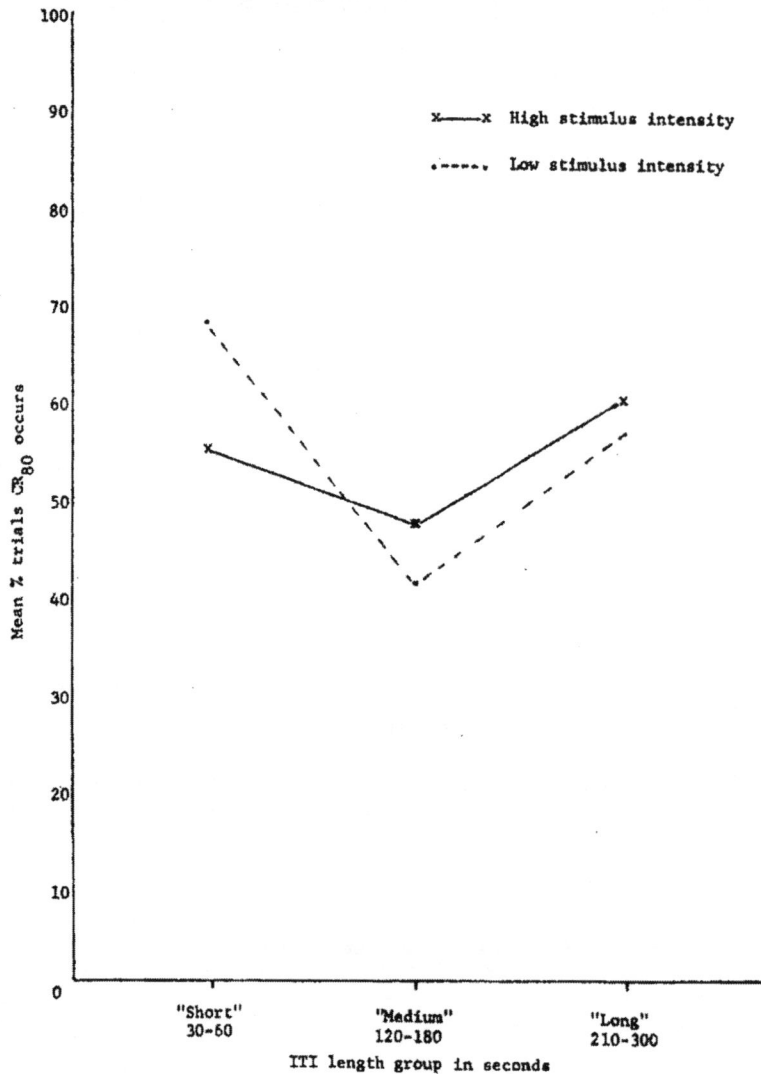

Figure 5 demonstrates the mean per cent occurrence of CR_{80} for all acquisition blocks as a function of ITI and Int. when ITI conditions were pooled into "short," "medium," and "long" groupings. Note the striking similarity between the "V" shapes in this figure and the "V" shapes in Figure 1 of Experiment I. In Figure 1, each point represents a single ITI falling in the derived ranges of "short," "medium," and "long" as used in Figure 5.

Differences between the ITI groupings depicted in Figure 5 were analyzed by t-test. As for intensity differences, only the "short" ITI group showed a significant difference (t = 2.23, df = 22, p < .05). As for ITI differences, at H Int. "long" ITIs significantly excelled "medium" ITIs (t = 3.06, df 40, p <.01) while "short" ITIs did not differ significantly from either "medium" or "long" ITIs (this, of course, reflected the debilitating effect on conditioning of H Int. at "short" ITIs); at L Int. "short," "medium," and "long" ITIs all differed significantly. These data are included in Table 19.

While statistical analyses with the CR_{80} measure appeared satisfactory, it was felt that another measure of conditioning might be briefly investigated and described. Magnitude of response seemed like a good companion to frequency of occurrence in such an effort. To guarantee maximum independence of the second kind of conditioning measure from the first, every S's median error of anticipation, whether a CR_{80} or not, was determined for each block of acquisition trials and over all blocks of trials. Medians rather than mean anticipations were used since occasionally S would make no anticipation in a given trial. The median values were more unstable than the CR_{80} measures, of course, as they reflected a different number of values from one S to the next. However, the median error of anticipation (E. Ant.) measure followed a pattern strikingly similar to the frequency of occurrence measure. Figure 6 illustrates that, as might be expected, the absolute error in seconds increased with increasing ITI length. Figure 7, plotting the median E. Ant. as a per cent of the ITI it was associated with, illustrates the same over—lapping "V" curves for the "short," "medium," and "long" ITI groups as was observed in Figure 5 with the frequency of occurrence measure.

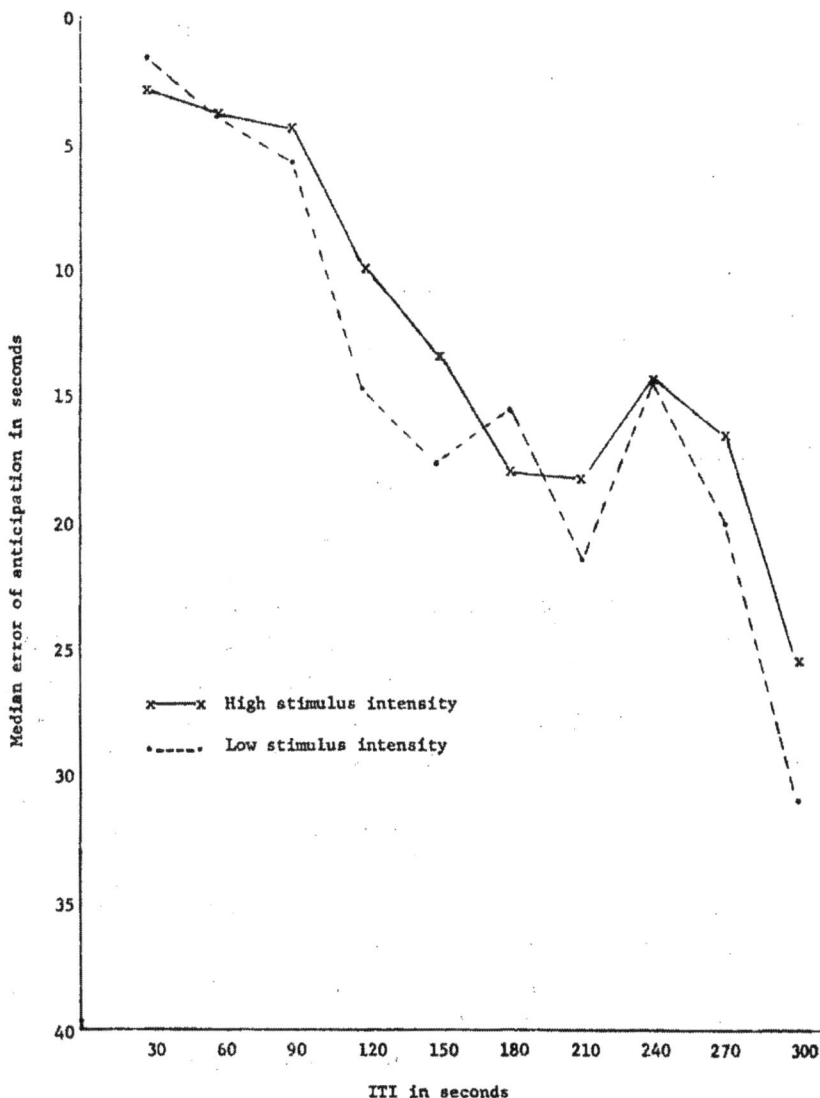

Figure 6. - - Median error of anticipation at both stimulus intensities over all 15 acquisition trials as a function of ITI in Experiment II

103

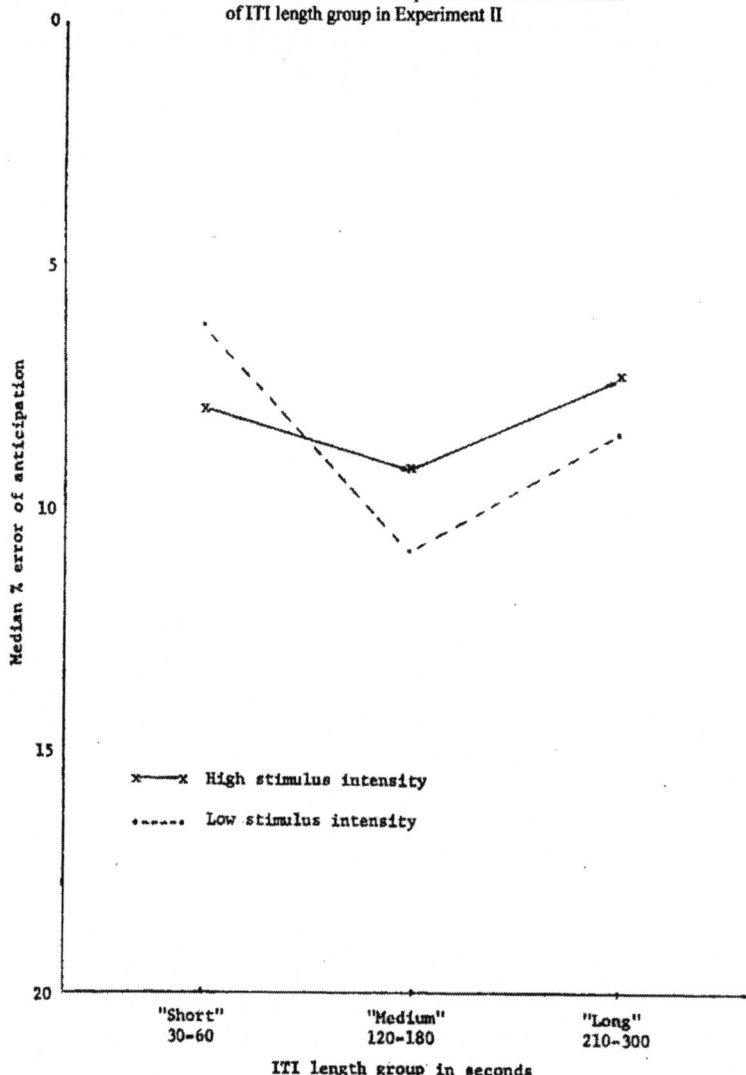

Figure 7. - - Median % error of anticipation at both stimulus intensities over all 15 acquisition trials as a function of ITI length group in Experiment II

Returning to the frequency of occurrence measure, it was decided to gauge the effects of the S̲ variables of age, sex, and H gsr on temporal conditioning. Since the independent variables had been shown effective in this regard, a derived or standard score was computed to allow common analysis of the full 120 S̲ sample. This was done by dividing every S̲'s CR_{80} score for all trial blocks by the mean CR_{80} score of the ITI—Int. condition group to which that S belonged. Bartlett's test (Edwards, 196Gb) had shown absence of significant heterogeneity of variance by ITI—Int. condition. The derived conditioning score (CR_d) represented S's frequency of occurrence of CR_{80} s in comparison to the other Ss undergoing the identical stimulus conditions.

Neither sex evidenced a significantly higher mean CR_d score as determined by t-test comparison. However, 18 year olds had a significantly lower mean CR_d score than 19—22 year olds (t = 2.39, df = 118, p <.02). "Excited" Ss (+ H gsr) had a significantly lower mean CR_d score than "relaxed" (0 or — H gsr) Ss (t = 3.28, df = 118, p < (.01). To further examine the pre-treatment H gsr measure of arousal as a predictor of conditioning, a product-moment correlation was computed for H gsr and CR_d

It was -.300 (df = 118, p <.01). Since the plot of these variables seemed somewhat curvilinear, the correlation ratios were also computed. These were -.408 and -.483. A final check with the more conservative Spearman rank order correlation produced a value of -.309 (df = 118, p <.01). Thus it seemed fairly safe to conclude that the magnitude of pre-treatment arousal was significantly related to subsequent level of temporal conditioning. This relationship is depicted in Figure 8 as are the relatively normal distributions of Ss over the values of each variable.

I gsr was not significantly influenced by either ITT, Int., or their interaction as analyzed by analysis of variance (Table 11). However, I gsr did become more relaxed with successive trial blocks as predicted (F = 17.23, df = 2,200, p <.005); none of the interactions of trial blocks with ITI or Int. were significant (Table 11). If ITI was not a significant factor for I gsr over all acquisition blocks, it did become meaningful when observed a block of trials at a time. Figure 9 illustrates the mean I gsr for "short," "medium," and "long" ITI groups for each successive block of trials. By block 3 the ITI groups had assumed the customary "V" shape common to the conditioning curves with "medium" ITIs showing an I gsr change towards greater arousal while "short" and "long" ITIs showed a mean I gsr movement towards greater relaxation. Analysis by t-test found no significant difference of I gsr between "short" and "long" ITI groups at any block. These groups were therefore pooled and compared to the "medium" ITI length group. The latter showed a significantly less relaxed mean I gsr only in block 3, the last 5-trial block (t = 2.47, df = 106, p <.02). Thus by the last block of trials, Ss at "medium" ITIs were showing substantially less relaxation from one ITI midpoint to the next than Ss at the more fruitful ITIs in the "short" or "long" range.

I gsr was not significantly related to S's sex or age as analyzed by chi square. Product-moment correlations between I gsr and H gsr were not significant for any block of trials. Thus H gsr and I gsr seemed to be measuring relatively independent processes.

The OE gsr decreased with increasing ITI as measured by product-moment correlation (r was -.230, df = 118, p <.02). This decline in arousal with ITI length increase is illustrated in Figure 10. Might this overall change in arousal have influenced the I gsr results? To control for this likelihood, an analysis of variance of I gsr as a function of trial blocks was conducted for only those Ss (n = 83) showing a + OE gsr. Trial blocks still showed a significant successive relaxation for I gsr (F = 20.80, df = 2,246, p <.005). Thus, even for those 83 Ss showing an overall increase in arousal as a result of the experiment, the gsr change from the midpoint of one ITT to the next showed a mean decrease in arousal or increase in relaxation (inhibition) with continuing acquisition trials (Table 8).

An analysis of variance of OE gsr (Table 9) showed it to vary significantly with ITI (F - 2.22, df = 9, 100, p <.05), as has already been reported, but not to vary significantly with Int. or the interaction of ITI with Int. as to S variables, OE gsr was significantly less relaxed for males (t = 4.66, df = 118, p <.01) than for females while age had no significant influence as gauged by t-test or chi square. A product-moment correlation of +.226 (df = 118, p <.05) between OE gsr and H gsr suggested some commonality in process. This would explain the sex difference common to both gsr measures.

Moving now to methods of synchrony, an analysis of variance of per cent time per S spent counting showed no significant relationship between this variable and ITI, Int., or their interaction (Table 14). The mean per cent time spent counting per S decreased from 88% at "short" ITIs to 86% for "medium" ITIs to 81% for "long" ITIs but none of these decreases proved to be statistically significant by t-test.

Table 17 breaks down the mean per cent time per S by every method of synchrony used. Counting methods were again predominant in a free choice situation but "Feel" and internal clock methods as

Figure 8. - - Median CRd over all 15 acquisition trials as a function
of pre-treatment Hgsr in Experiment II

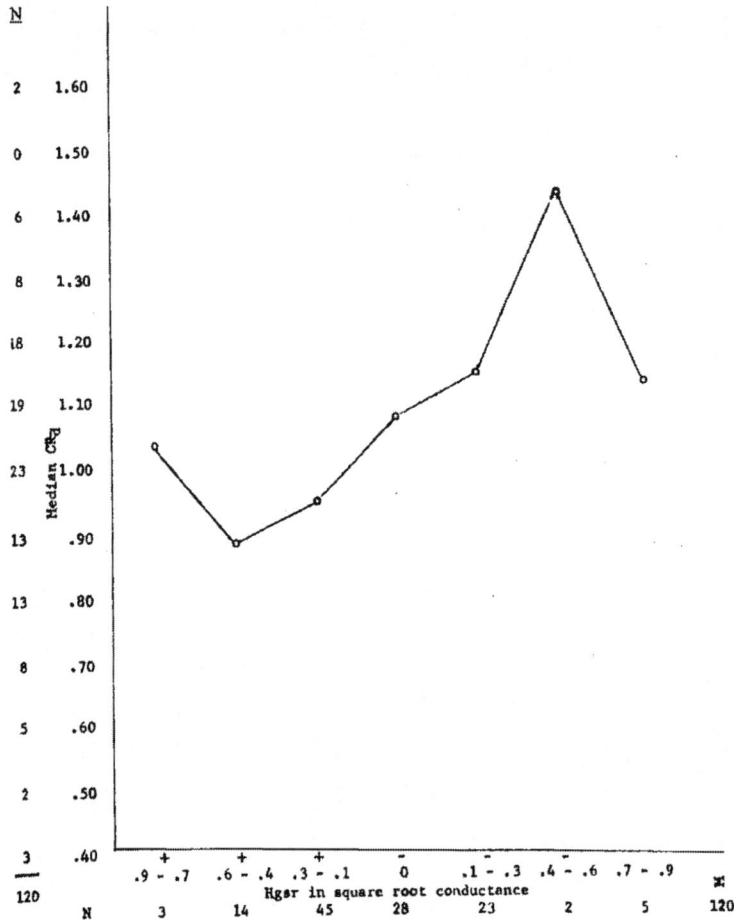

well as wild guessing were all in evidence. Table 18 relates the methods used at least 51% of the time per 5, "majority method," to the number of Ss using them and to the median CR_d score associated with that particular method. Note that only those Ss using a breath counting method scored significantly higher on CR_d than the guessers (Mann—Whitney U2.0,n_1 = 6, n_2 = 4, p <.05). Those 5 Ss using the "Feel" method a majority of the time did no better or worse than Ss using any counting method. All of these 5 intuitioners choosing to "Feel" the imminence in time of the US as a majority method were males (p <.06 by chi square); no other method showed any significant clustering by sex. As to age, all 6 Ss counting breaths a majority of the time were over 18 (p < .02 by chi square) while the 4 Ss using repeated mental events as a majority method of synchrony were all 18 (p < .05 by chi square). No other age clusterings by method approached significance. "Excited" (+ H gsr) Ss did not spend more time counting per S than "relaxed" (0 or - H gsr) Ss as tested by t-test although "excited" Ss more often chose a counting method of synchrony as majority method than did "relaxed" Ss (p < .01 by chi square). Thus pre-treatment arousal as measured by H gsr affected a S's choice of whether or not to count, the more relaxed Ss choosing less often to do so.

The methods classified in Table 17 and Table 18 should be clarified further. Counting by successive numbers meant counting in the absence of conscious listening to any internal rhythm or S- produced periodic events. Those counting these independent numbers in common still managed individual

Figure 9. - - Mean Igsr averaged over both stimulus intensities by
each 5-trial acquisition block as a function of ITI length
group in Experiment II

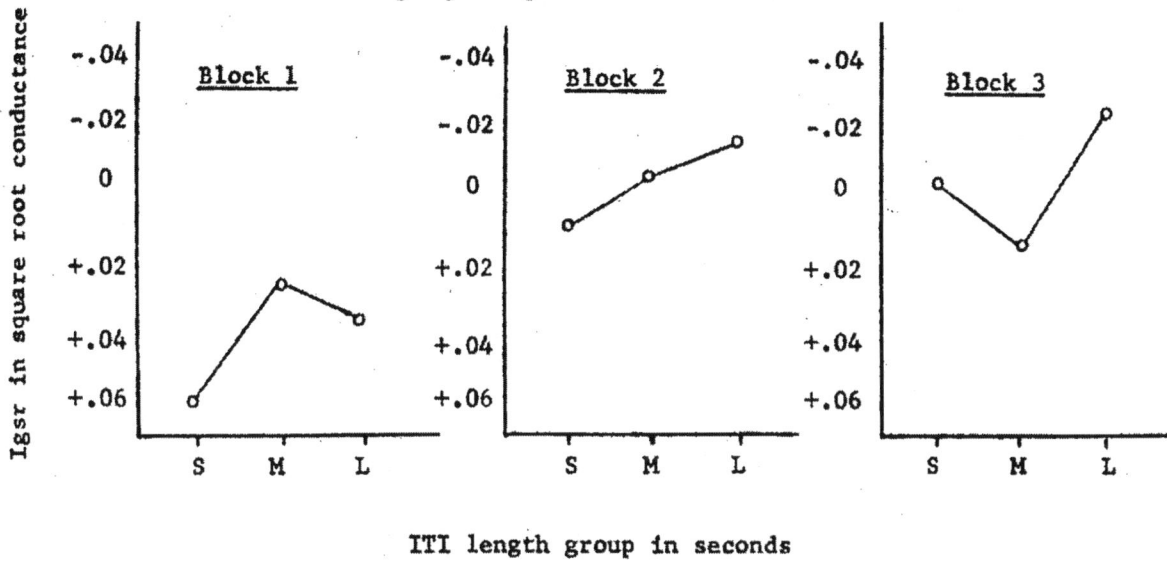

ITI length group in seconds

Figure 10. - - Mean OEgsr averaged over both stimulus intensities as a
function of ITI length group in Experiment II

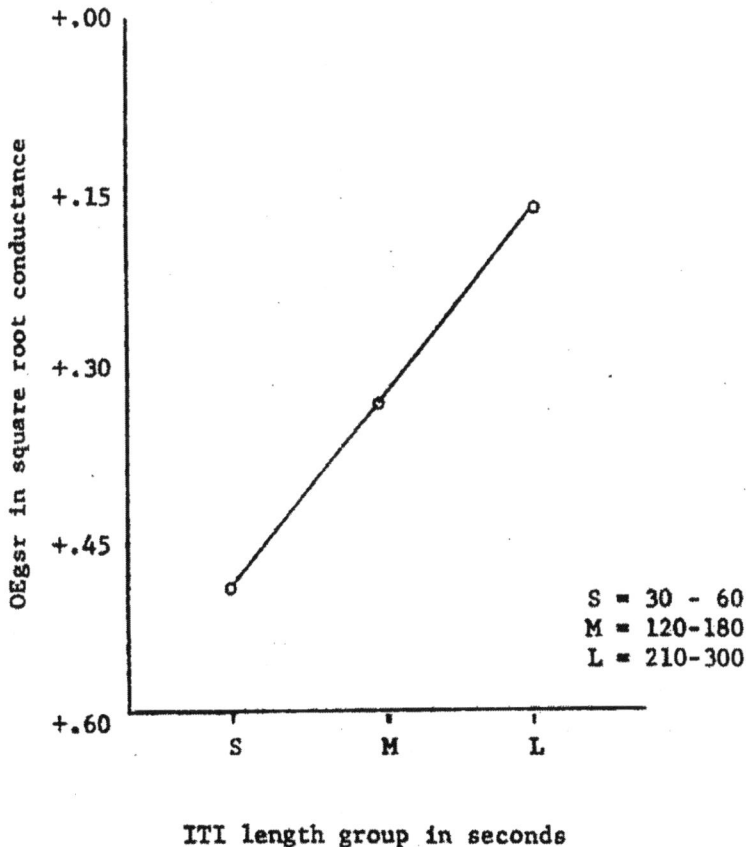

S = 30 - 60
M = 120-180
L = 210-300

ITI length group in seconds

differences of style. Such personal tempo styles ranged from the traditional "1 and 2 and 3..." to "1 hippopotamus, 2 hippopotamus, 3 hippo-...." Those who tapped for a method of synchrony tapped fingers, toes, toes within a cast, or even tapped fingers and toes simultaneously while rubbing eyebrows. Those who listened for pulse or breaths generally did so intently and without elaboration. S's choosing to synchronize with repeated mental events naturally showed a good deal of individuality in events chosen. These included "a graduation march with endless encores," the Gettysburg address, "running along a figure eight with each circuit as one count," imaginary swimming strokes, etc. Those Ss using the intuitive "Feel" method all experienced active sensations prior to the US, reporting: "I felt excitement just before the flash"; "I got nervous just before the flash"; "I sensed it when it was about to go off." Guessers were able to report no conscious methods or tip-off experiences whatever. Again one S created an imaginary clock to check with whenever the time grew short before a US. A few Ss at higher ITIs admitted dozing off shortly. One S, thinking he was in a non-temporal conditioning experiment, wasted his first few trials listening for a CS. A female S counted off "Hail Marys" through all trials but without above average temporal success.

Accuracy of estimation (A. Est.) of the ITI by S after the experiment was concluded did not, in this experiment, relate significantly to ITI, Int., or their interaction as analyzed by analysis of variance (Table 15). The ITI groupings reflected this as, although per cent accuracy increased slightly from "short" ITIs to "medium" and "long" ITIs. no t-tests showed significant differences. Thus for the 30-300 sec. ITI range, the findings of Experiment I regarding accuracy of estimation were not replicated. Nor did t-test indicate per cent accuracy of estimation differed significantly for sex or age of S. A product moment correlation of per cent A. Est. with H gsr was not significant. A. Est. was therefore sensitive to none of the independent variables affecting level of temporal conditioning over the range of values tested.

As Bakan (1962) indicated it would be, retrospective judgement of the direction of error of estimate was correct for a significant majority (62%) of the Ss (binomial probability = .016). Choosing the correct estimate of direction of error (CEDE) was not significantly related to ITI, Int., sex, age, or H gsr as analyzed by chi square. Since assessing the magnitude as well as the direction of error of the first estimate actually comprised a retrospective second estimate, both estimates were included in the analysis of variance gauging the effect of ITI and Int. on A. Est. There was no significant order effect for these estimates nor were any of the first order interactions with ITI or Int. significant (Table 15). Both estimates averaged a per cent A. Est. of 67%; i.e., the second more retrospective estimate was no more accurate than the first when magnitude as well as direction was taken into account.

Direction or error of estimation (DEE) of the initial estimate was approximately evenly divided between over estimators (52 Ss) and under estimators (49 Ss). DEE was not found to be significantly related to ITI, Int., sex, age, or H gsr as analyzed by chi square.

The 19 Ss initially estimating their ITI with 100% accuracy could not be significantly related to the stimulus conditions of ITI or Int. nor the S characteristics of sex, age, and H gsr as analyzed by chi square.

Another question that might be asked about the initial retrospective estimate of ITT length is what it most reflects. Does it relate more to S's memory of the time between the last two US flashes (the last S-S gap) or does it relate more to S's memory of the time between the second last US flash and S's subsequent response of anticipation (the last S-R gap)?

Since over estimators would by definition fall closer to the S-S interval, a fair test of the S-R hypothesis would consider only those 68 Ss who did not over estimate their ITI. The estimated ITI in seconds for these Ss was correlated with the last S-S gap in seconds and the last S-R gap in seconds. The product-moment correlation between the last S-S and S-R gaps was +.973 (df = 66, p <.01), a value which suggests that by the last trial S's anticipation quite closely approximated the ITI. The product-moment correlation between S's initial estimate and the last S-S gap was +.849 (df = 66, p <.01) while the product-moment correlation between S's initial estimate and the last S-R gap was +.790 (df 66, p <.01). Hotelling's (1940) test showed the S-S correlation to significantly excel the S-R correlation (t = 3.99, df = 65, p <01).

Final analyses of results in Experiment 11 concerned the interrelationships of the dependent variables. Comparing the two conditioning measures of frequency of occurrence (CR_{80}) and median error of anticipation (E. Ant.), Spearman rank order correlations of .338 (df = 118, p < .001) for block 3 and -.423 (df = 118, p <.001) for all blocks were obtained. CR_d correlated nonsignificantly with per cent A. Est.; with I gsr for each block; with OE gsr. Chi square analyses showed no significant relationship between CR_d score and CEDE, DEE, Sb Un. Those 19 Ss achieving 100% A. Est. ("ons") were compared to all other Ss and to the 19 Ss of lowest per cent A. Est. ("offs") in terms of CR_d: chi square analysis showed no significant differences.

Analysis by t-test found no significant relation of per cent A. Est. to CEDE, Sb Un, or use of the breathing method of synchrony. On the other hand, t-test analysis showed under estimators significantly more accurate at estimation than over estimators (73% as opposed to 49%) (t = 3.97, df = 99, p < .01). A check on this finding with Mann-Whitney $\underline{U}$ procedures yielded the same significant result (U — 833.5, n_1 = 49, n_2 52, Z = 3.01, p <.005). Product-moment correlations showed no significant relationship between per cent A. Est. and per cent counting per $\underline{S}$ or OE gsr. However, the product-moment correlation between per cent A. Est. and I gsr (block 3) was +.201 (df = 118, p <.05). In other words, the more aroused Ss became over the last block of trials, the less inhibition developing, the greater the per cent A. Est.; development of inhibition inhibited accurate estimation.

CEDE was not significantly related to DEE, I gsr (block 3), OE gsr, or Sb Un by chi square analysis.

"Ons" were not significantly related to I gsr (block 3), or Sb Un by chi square analysis comparing "ons" with "off s' and "ons" with all other Ss. However, being an "on" vs. being an "off" was significantly related to OE gsr (p = <.02 by chi square); a comparison between "ons" and all other Ss by OE gsr was also significant (p <.05 by chi square). Greater overall experimental arousal led to the 100% A. Est. of the "ons."

Product-moment correlations between OE gsr and I gsr by block were as follows: block 1 was +.783 (df = 118, p <.01); block 2 was +.362 (df = 118, p <.01); block 3 was +.312 (df = 118, p <.01). Thus the OE gsr was more a product of gsr change during the first block of trials than subsequent blocks of trials. That the correlation was significant is a natural reflection of the fact that the I gsr measures arithmetically summed would in total equal the OE gsr measure; i.e., they were different aspects of the same overall process.

Neither I gsr nor OE gsr were significantly related by chi square analysis to Sb Un.

Discussion

The findings of Experiment II supported and elaborated on the findings of Experiment I.

Again the more intense stimulus intensity elicited significantly more "unpleasant" ratings after the experiment, supporting its status as a more noxious US. The choosing of "unpleasant" as a descriptive term for the US was not significantly related to any other independent or dependent variable besides stimulus intensity.

Some of the S characteristics had interesting effects. Females were more relaxed than males both before the experiment (H gsr) and as a result of it (OE gsr). Females did not however evidence a significantly higher level of conditioning or a greater development of inhibition over trials (I gsr). Nor did females show performance significantly different from males on any of the aspects of temporal estimation gauged. Both sexes averaged the same age. Age differences had no significant effect on any of the gsr measures or temporal estimation measures. However, 18 year old Ss did not show as high a level of temporal conditioning as Ss 19 to 22 years did. The S characteristic of pre-treatment arousal or H gsr had significant consequences for temporal conditioning as theory predicted it would. By this measure, "relaxed" Ss significantly out-performed "excited" Ss, supporting Birmans's (1953) similar observations. Furthermore, the magnitude of the pre-treatment H gsr was found to be a significant predictor of subsequent level of temporal conditioning thus supporting the Pavlovian inhibition research findings (where inhibition has been operationally defined as relaxation). The correlation between H gsr and QE gsr was low, but positive and significant. Those Ss relaxing before the experiment generally relaxed as a result of it. However, H gsr was not significantly correlated with the buildup of inhibition at the midpoint of the ITI (I gsr). The inference was that these are independent system. H gsr did not significantly relate to any of the measured aspects of temporal estimation.

Thus it was demonstrated that, of the S characteristics, age and pre-treatment arousal (but not sex) affected the level of temporal conditioning achieved. The stimulus variables of ITI and Int. were also shown to be effective in this regard. Measures of frequency of occurrence of the CR and magnitude of error of anticipation, correlating significantly with each other, both confirmed the drop in level of conditioning at ITIs between 1 and 4 minutes as well as the performance depressing effect of increased stimulus intensity at short ITIs of a minute or less. Significant facilitation of level of conditioning by increased stimulus intensity was evident only at "medium" range ITIs. Apparently, beyond a maximum ITI length, stimulus intensity may no longer be a critical variable for temporal conditioning.

Level of conditioning significantly rose over blocks of acquisition trials and I gsr grew progressively and significantly more relaxed with it. This Pavlovian theory and practice predicted and it held true even when analyzed solely for those Ss whose overall reaction to the experiment (OE gsr) was one of greater arousal rather than greater relaxation. However, the I gsr did not take on the customary "V" shape as a function of ITI group until the third and last block of acquisition trials. At this block, the "medium" Washington-Moscow ITI gap ITIs showed significantly less relaxation by I gsr than "long" Soviet range ITIs or "short" American range ITIs. There was, therefore, an inhibition differential by the last block of trials. I gsr in this last block of trials was also found to correlate significantly and positively with accuracy of estimation. Apparently, then an increase in I gsr (a decrease in growth of relaxation or inhibition) is associated with an increase in estimation accuracy; the growth of inhibition thus is positively associated with temporal conditioning level and negatively associated with temporal estimation accuracy.

The OE gsr demonstrated less arousal as ITI length increased. This might have been a function of the ITI length in itself or the overall increased experiment length which naturally grew with the length of the ITI. Correlations with I gsr by block of acquisition trials suggested that OE was based more on change in the first block of trials than in subsequent blocks of trials. OE gsr had no demonstrable relationship to level of conditioning but those Ss scoring 100% accuracy of temporal estimation were less relaxed by OE gsr than their peers. This ties in with the finding that less relaxed I gsrs in the last acquisition block were associated with superior estimation performance.

Methods of synchrony were catalogued as to commonality and conditioning efficacy. The emergence of breathing as the only method to significantly excel guessing on level of conditioning was consistent with the literature available on the subject. It is interesting, for example, that Rozin (1959) made a point of observing breathing movements in his dogs (but did not relate it to level of conditioning as translated). This method might well be further scrutinized in its own right in future temporal conditioning investigations.

It was also of interest that per cent counting per S did not significantly decline from "'short" to "long" ITI group. ITIs of more than 5 minutes seemed necessary to bring out this decline if it in fact exists.

Accuracy of estimation was shown to be an ability independent of temporal conditioning performance. Furthermore, Experiment 1 estimation results were not replicated in that accuracy of estimation in Experiment II was not significantly related to the stimulus variables of ITI or intensity. Nor did A. Est. vary with sex, age, or H gsr as has already been mentioned.

Bakan's (1962) findings that retrospective judgement added information to temporal estimation was borne out in the sense that a majority of Ss correctly identified the direction of their error. However, the identification of the magnitude of error in conjunction with direction of error did not produce a second estimate any more accurate than the initial one. Neither knowing the correct direction of error nor the actual direction of error were found to be significantly related to any of the independent or dependent variables in this experiment. For example, none of the gsr arousal measures related to over estimation. As has already been discussed, however, accuracy of temporal estimation did increase with arousal as gauged by the OE gsr and I gsr measures. This supported the study of Burns and Gifford (1961) although it must be recognized that the interval estimated after temporal conditioning was unique in that it had been presented a number of times prior to estimation and had been synchronized with actively by S each of these times; there is evidence that accuracy of estimation can be affected by this procedure (Elkin, 1964). Therefore, the finding that arousal relates significantly to accuracy of estimation at the end of temporal conditioning must for now be limited to the context of temporal conditioning.

The magnitude of the temporal estimate was found to reflect the last S-S interval more closely than the last S-R interval even when analysis excluded Ss over-estimating the ITI (putting them by definition closer to the S-S interval).

Experiment II generally supported, replicated, and elaborated all the conditioning results of Experiment I. On the other hand, some temporal estimation results were not replicated nor did amount of counting per S significantly decrease over the III range explored.

CHAPTER NINE

TEMPORAL CONDITIONING OF HUMANS III:
TWICE OVER AND OUT

Experiment III

Experiments I and II dealt with the acquisition of a temporal CR over trials in a single one day session. Experiment III analyzed the acquisition process as a function of two successive daily sessions with subsequent extinction procedure.

Method

Subjects.-- The $\underline{Ss}$ were 12 volunteer college students drawn from the same introductory psychology course as in Experiment II. Males outnumbered females 8 to 4; a ratio nearly identical to that of the last experiment. Age, again restricted to from 18 to 22 years, averaged 19.0 with exactly half the sample 18 years old.

Apparatus. -- The apparatus was identical to that of Experiment 11.

Procedure. -- On day 1, $\underline{Ss}$ were run through a procedure identical to that of experiment II with the single following. After the last post-treatment data were collected, $\underline{S}$ received no explanation or credit slip but was told to return the next day at the same start time for part II of the experiment. On day 2, $\underline{S}$ was again run through the full acquisition procedure. Following collection of post-treatment data, $\underline{S}$ was read the following instructions by $\underline{E}$:

We have one more phase of the experiment to complete and then we'll be finished.

1. You will be given two more flashes. They will be the same time apart as all the flashes so far.
2. After the second flash, whenever you think another flash is due, say "NOW."
3. There will be no more flashes after the second flash but continue to say "NOW" anyway every time a flash would have been due. Keep this up until I turn on the lights.

These were the extinction instructions. As in acquisition, the times of $\underline{S}$'s anticipations were recorded and this recording continued until 15 such responses had been made. Following the last extinction response, the overhead lights were turned on, $\underline{S}$ lectured on the gsr, given a credit slip, and released.

Experimental Design. -- ITIs of 60 and 240 sec. were used at high US intensity only. This formed two ITI conditions with 6 $\underline{Ss}$ randomly assigned by card draw to each condition. The same $\underline{Ss}$ returned on day 2 to run under the same stimulus conditions as they had on day 1.

Results

The sample of Experiment III resembled the sample run under the same stimulus conditions in Experiment II in both $\underline{S}$ characteristics and day 1 performance. Fisher's exact test of probability (Siegel, 1956) did not show the distribution of sex, age, or H gsr to be significantly different for either sample or significantly different by ITI for the Experiment III $\underline{Ss}$.

Carrying the comparison between $\underline{Ss}$ at 60 and 240 sec. ITIs (H Int.) in both experiments further, analysis of variance found no significant difference in level of conditioning of the 240 and 60 sec. ITIs over both experiments; the analysis of variance also found the experiment x ITI interaction to be nonsignificant (Table 22). (The measure of conditioning analyzed throughout this results section was in all cases the CR_{80} or frequency of occurrence measure.)

Having established the comparability of the day 1 acquisition results at both ITIs in this experiment with the last experiment, analysis moved exclusively to Experiment III data. An analysis of variance of level of conditioning for day 1 alone (Table 23) found no significant difference by ITI, trial blocks, or their interaction. However, block 3 was at a significantly higher level of conditioning than block 1 ($t = 2.13$, df = 22, p <.05). Figure 11 illustrates this increase by block for day 1. ITIs have been pooled due to lack of significant difference between them.

An analysis of variance of level of conditioning over acquisition trials for day 2 alone (Table 24) found no significant difference by ITI, trial blocks, or their interaction. However, again block 3 was at a significantly higher level of conditioning than block 1 ($t = 2.36$, df = 22, p <.05). The ITIs pooled again, Figure 15 illustrates this increase by block for day 2. Note that all acquisition blocks (except the first on day 1) showed significant (55% or better) conditioning levels.

In analysis of the extinction results, an anticipatory response was considered a CR_{80} only if it occurred in that last 20% of the ITT which <u>would have</u> been defined if the US had not been deactivated. An analysis of variance of level of conditioning over extinction trials alone (Table 25) found no significant difference by ITI or the interaction of ITI with trial blocks. However, the F for trial blocks (F = 4.01, df = 2.20, p <.05) indicated the drop in level of conditioning over blocks of extinction trials was significant. This is also illustrated, with ITIs pooled, in Figure 11. Note also that <u>all</u> extinction blocks show less than significant (55% or better) levels of conditioning.

Complete t-test analyses of these data are presented in Table 21. The t-tests indicated that it was not until block 2 of acquisition on day 2 that level of conditioning significantly excelled block 1 of day

Figure 11. - - Acquisition and extinction of a temporal CR: Mean %
occurrence of CR80 at high stimulus intensity averaged
over both ITIs by 5-trial blocks in Experiment III

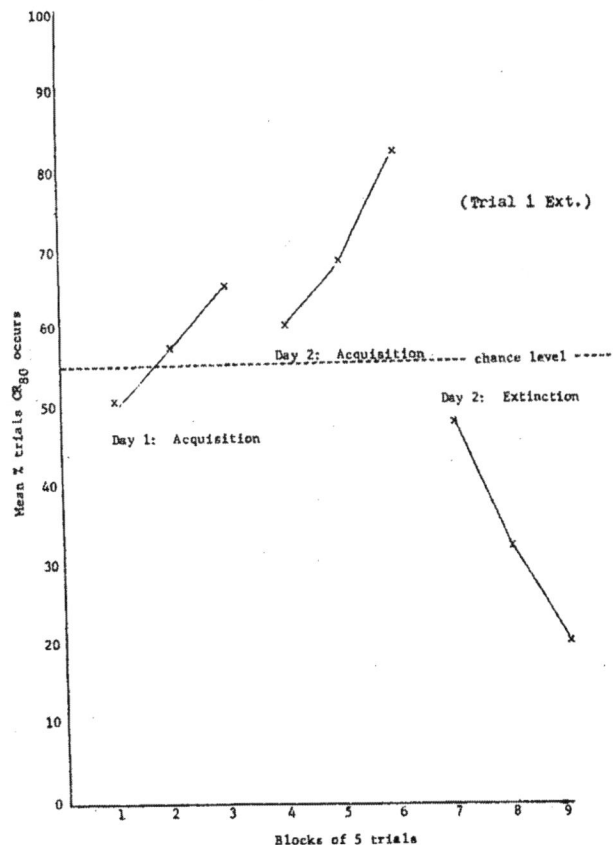

115

1, but that by block 3 of day 2 acquisition was significantly beyond all the blocks of day 1. The analyses further bore out what Figure 15 suggests: the extinction was quite rapid in comparison to acquisition. The second block of extinction trials was already significantly below the level of conditioning of all the day 2 acquisition blocks while the third block of extinction trials was significantly below <u>all</u> acquisition blocks for days 1 and 2. In fact, the mean 20% frequency of occurrence for the third block of extinction was what would most be expected by chance since a CR_{80} was any anticipation, occurring in the last fifth of the ITI. In other words, the results indicated 15 trials to have fully extinguished the temporal CR at both ITIs, with even 5 trials of extinction sufficient to drop CR_{80} occurrence below the normally accepted chance level.

Conditioning level in acquisition day 1 correlated +.617 (df = 10, p <.05) with conditioning level in acquisition day 2. Conditioning level in extinction correlated -.967 (df = 10, p <.01) with acquisition level on the same day and -.337 (df = 10, p <.25) with acquisition level of the day before (day 1). In all cases conditioning level was represented by the overall CR_{80} score for 15 trials. Thus the correlation between the same process on different processes on the same day. Time relations again seem to have had some relevance.

An analysis of variance was used to evaluate the effect of ITI, initial and secondary estimation, and day of testing, on per cent A. Est. (Table 26). ITI had no significant effect nor did order of estimate nor any of the interactions. However, there was a significant <u>decrease</u> in per cent A. Est. from 83.5% on day 1 to 76.2% on day 2 (F = 7.35, df = 1.30, p < .05). Estimation was made directly after acquisition on both days.

An analysis of variance of OE gsr by ITI and successive days of acquisition (Table 27) found the OE gsr to be significantly less relaxed on day 2 than on day 1 (F = 9.98, df = 1.10, p < .05). ITI and the interaction were not significant.

An analysis of variance of I gsr by ITI, trial blocks, and successive days of acquisition (Table 28) found no significant effects from ITI, successive days, or any of the interactions. However, as in Experiment II, I gsr grew significantly more relaxed with blocks of trials on both days of acquisition (F = 5.71, df = 2, 50, p <.01).

Discussion

In this experiment, level of temporal conditioning was shown to improve from one day of 15 acquisition trials to the next day of 15 acquisition trials. Temporal conditioning also showed significant extinction after 5 trials in the absence of periodicity from the US. The extinction process thus appeared to be more rapid than the acquisition process and was highly (negatively) correlated with conditioning level in acquisition the same day. However, extinction failed to correlate significantly with the acquisition of the day before. Despite the high significant correlation between acquisitions on subsequent days, extinction only related significantly to acquisition results of the same day. Here was evidence that human conditioning can be more similar for separate learning processes the same day than for the same learning process on separate days.

It is worth noting that although a "short" and a "long" ITI were tested in this experiment, there were virtually no significant differences between the two on any of the conditioning blocks or on any of the other dependent variables investigated. Temporal acquisition, savings in re-acquisition, and extinction were thus demonstrated at ills in both the American and Soviet investigated ranges.

The finding that accuracy of estimation decreased from one day to the next has no obvious explanation in terms of any of the theory or findings presented on past pages of this dissertation. It should be regarded as highly tentative pending replication in a future experiment. Difficulty of interpretation is compounded by the significant increase in OE gsr arousal (from day 1 to day 2) which, in Experiment II, was associated with those Ss reaching 100% accuracy of estimation. Perhaps a conservative but more accurate statement of findings would be that there was no evidence that accuracy of estimation improved after the second day of acquisition despite the observed significant improvement in level of conditioning.

That there was less relaxation (a larger OE gsr) as a result of the total acquisition segment of the experiment on day 2 may merely be a reflection of S's expectancy of the second (extinction) part of the experiment awaiting him. At any rate, it is interesting that even though the OE gsr averaged a daily increase in arousal which was significantly larger the second day, I gsr showed the same daily relaxation over blocks of trials as in the last experiment.

This build-up of inhibition or relaxation reflected by the I gsr in the last two experiments seemed to be an all-or-none process. Whenever temporal conditioning occurred there it was, even in Ss showing a net decrease in relaxation as a result of the experiment; but not necessarily in demonstrable relation to the magnitude of level of conditioning. Although it was premature to integrate this finding with previously cited elicitation theory (Denny and Adelman, *1955;* Ratner and Denny, 1964) on the basis of these parametric studies alone, such a relationship was suggested by the data. According to elicitation theory, omission of the US elicits responses antagonistic to the UR. This "secondary elicitation" means omission of a noxious US elicits relaxation. Thus the converging elicitation and Neo-Pavlovian inhibition theories both would have predicted relaxation during the ITI pending S's discrimination of that ITI as temporally distinct from the noxious US.

Alternate Methods of CR Definition in Extinction in Experiment III

I. CR is defined as any vocal response within the last 10% of the ITI before the periodic flash would have occurred or within the first 10% of the ITI after the periodic flash would have occurred.

	Mean % Occurrence of CR by Block of 5 Trials		
S	Block 1	Block 2	Block 3
1	60	40	60
2	40	0	60
3	100	100	80
4	40	40	20
5	100	100	100
6	0	0	0
7	100	80	100
8	80	100	20
9	100	100	60
10	0	40	20
11	100	80	100
12	80	60	0
Mean	67	62	52

II. CR is defined as any vocal response within the last 20% of the ITI before the periodic flash would have occurred or within the first 20% of the ITI after the periodic flash would have occurred. Note that this method doubles the acceptable time range for a CR as compared to the above definition as well as the definition used in Experiment III.

Mean % Occurrence of CR by Block of 5 Trials

S	Block 1	Block 2	Block 3
1	80	100	100
2	60	20	60
3	100	100	100
4	100	100	100
5	100	100	100
6	0	0	0
7	100	100	100
8	100	100	60
9	100	100	100
10	40	100	80
11	100	100	100
12	100	80	0
Mean	82	83	75

Secondary Elicitation and Relaxation During the Acquisition of a Temporally Conditioned Response

Elicitation theory (Denny and Adelman, 1955) is basically an S-R contiguity theory of learning. One of the major postulates is that of secondary elicitation which deals with the omission of an unconditional stimulus or consistent elicitor. Secondary elicitation is defined as the elicitation of a new characteristic class of response which is typically antagonistic to the original response, and which occurs with the omission of the original elicitor (US). As used in an avoidance learning context, secondary elicitation means that cues discriminated by S as occurring in contiguity with non-shock (a safe chamber) will acquire the property of eliciting relaxational response, just as the cues associated with shock come to elicit arousal and escape responses. Extinction is explained by assuming secondary elicitation brings about relaxational response in the shock area when shock is omitted. While secondary elicitation has thus generally been used to explain the extinction of avoidance behavior, the temporal conditioning situation suggests another application.

The acquisition and extinction of a temporally conditioned response take place in the presence of common external cues. The CS or cue to be discriminated must of necessity be some periodic interoceptive process. Such a discrimination does in fact occur with repeated presentations of the periodic US. As mentioned earlier, the photic US of the preceding experiments elicited immediate URs of arousal as gauged by gsr. The omission of the photic flash during the ITI, once S has discriminated that ITI as not associated with the noxious flash, should therefore lead to relaxational response according to secondary elicitation. The secondary elicitation postulate is being applied here to explain differential behavior during the ITI (as a function of perceiving the ITI as a relaxational cue) rather than an explanation of extinction. Reynierse (1964) used the same sort of explanation to account for the effect of a delayed avoidance trial on resistance to extinction (in rats).

Interestingly enough, the gsr data support this point of view. As Figure 13 shows, those ITIs associated with significant acquisition of the temporal response showed significant relaxation (as measured by gsr) from the midpoint of one ITI to the next by the third block of trials. Those ITIs not associated with significant acquisition of the temporal response showed greater mean arousal from the midpoint of one ITI to the next. Whether this differential relaxation was a result or a cause of the temporal discrimination cannot yet be determined from the data. That the latter is also a possibility is suggested by the significant correlation between pre-treatment relaxation and level of conditioning.

CHAPTER TEN

TEMPORAL CONDITIONING OF HUMANS IV: PAVLOV'S PAUSE

Experiment IV

Pavlov (1927) decreed that any length ITI could be temporally conditioned although none longer than 30 minutes had been attempted. Feokritova (1912) claimed the establishment of a CR within the last minute of this ponderous ITI after several trials only. It was the purpose of Experiment IV to attempt a replication of this conditioning of a 30 minute ITI, but in the context of the conditioning procedures used in the three previous experiments. A secondary purpose was to go beyond the 30 minute ITI and attempt conditioning at a 60 minute ITI. Pavlov's faith that ITIs of 30 minutes or longer could be conditioned was in this way assessed.

Method

Subjects. -- The Ss were six paid male college students. Four Ss were 18; two were 19.

Apparatus. -- The conditioning apparatus was identical to that of Experiments II and III. However, there were some changes in positioning. E, with the data control and recording apparatus, moved to the outer chamber of the double experimental room. S remained in the inner room facing the stimulus bulb, hand in gsr electrodes. Food, water, urinal, and the dim red light were left in the inner chamber with S. Since the shut door between E and S blocked out most sound as well as all light from outside, a microphone (connected to the PA system of a tape recorder next to E) was taped to the wall next to S. This recorder allowed E to time S's anticipations and even many of his activities.

Procedure. -- The procedure was basically the same as in Experiment II. S was read the standard instructions; additionally instructed to use the food, water, and urinal when necessary. S was not told how long "this phase" of the experiment would be although all Ss had set aside a full day of their time for psychological testing. When E had finished the instructions he left the inner chamber, shut the door, and began the timing of the habituation period. E was now abit to use full overhead lighting, in the outer chamber while S, as in past experiments, had light only from the dim red bulb. S received 15 full acquisition trials with a common ITI. E kept notes on behavior as picked up by the microphone throughout the experiment. At the end of the last gsr reading, E opened the door, entered S's inner chamber and collected the normal post-treatment introspective data. Afterwards, S was lectured on the gsr and given a voucher of payment for hours put in. Ss were not told the actual time of their ITI until all Ss had been run.

Experimental Design. -- ITIs of 30 and 60 minutes were used at high US intensity only. This formed two ITI conditions with 3 Ss haphazardly assigned to each condition.

Results

Table 29 summarizes the data for both ITIs in Experiment IV as compared to summary data from Experiment II. Sample characteristics were well balanced between the two ITIs in Experiment IV. All Ss were males and there were two 18 year olds and one 19 year old at each condition. There were "excited" and "relaxed" Ss, as gauged by H gsr, on each condition. Only one S (at the 30 minute ITI) had an H gsr varying by more than a standard deviation from the mean H gsr of the 120 Ss in Experiment II. All Ss but this highly "excited" S rated the US as "unpleasant" after the experiment.

Occurrence of the CR_{80} at these ITIs was far from as frequent as observed in Experiment II. Figure 12 illustrates this. Level of conditioning at the 30 minute ITI was, over all 15 acquisition trials, not (at

Figure 12. -- Mean % occurrence of CR_{80} at high stimulus intensity over all 15 acquisition trials as a function of ITI length in Experiments II and IV

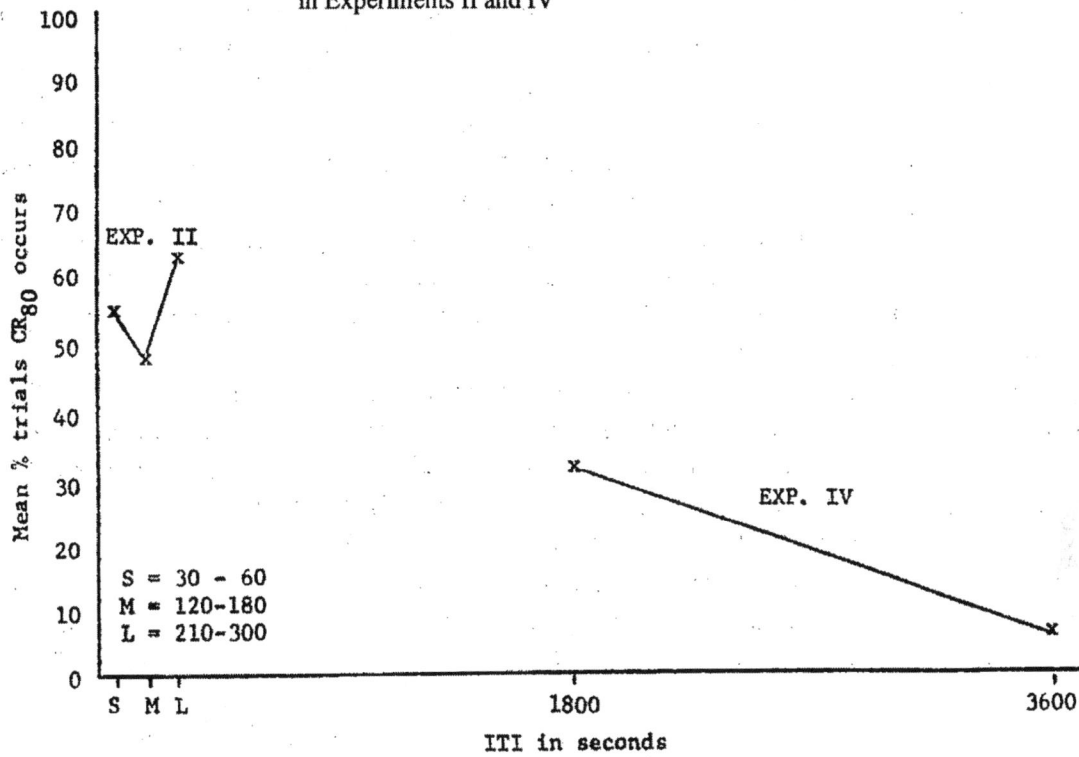

EXP. II

EXP. IV

S = 30 - 60
M = 120-180
L = 210-300

Mean % trials CR_{80} occurs

ITI in seconds

Figure 13. -- Median % error of anticipation at high stimulus intensity over all 15 acquisition trials as a function of ITI length in Experiments II and IV

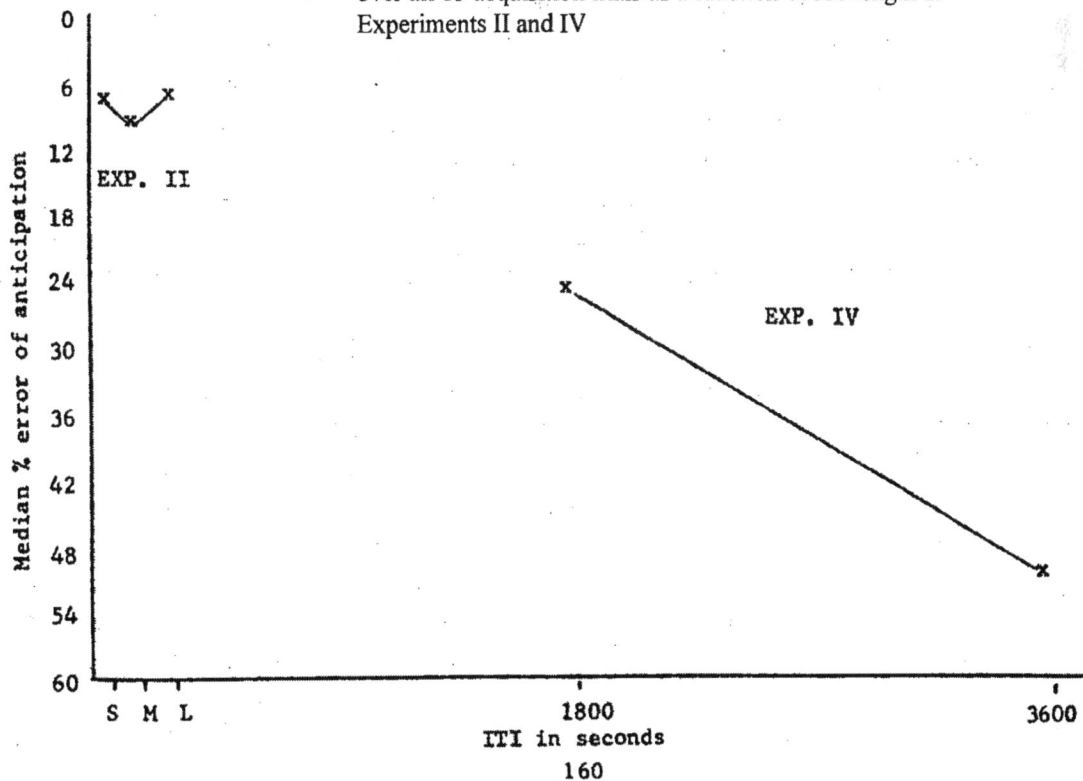

EXP. II

EXP. IV

Median % error of anticipation

ITI in seconds

160

31%) significantly better than would be expected by chance. Performance at the 60 minute ITI was even lower (6%). That this may not exclusively be a fatigue effect is indicated by the fact that mean number of CR_{80}s increased somewhat with trials at both ITIs although no block exceeded 40% occurrence. Looking at the median error of anticipation by block of trials as it is cited in Table 29, fatigue effects were more noticeable. Block 2 had a <u>larger</u> median error of anticipation than block 1 at both ITIs although there was a slight improvement in block 3 at both ITIs. Figure 13 illustrates this error of anticipation measure over all acquisition blocks. Again, the results were congruent with the frequency of occurrence measure graphed in Figure 12. While the 120 <u>S</u>s of Experiment II averaged an error of anticipation of 8% of the ITI over all blocks, <u>S</u>s in Experiment IV averaged 21% error at the 30 minute ITI and 50% error at the 60 minute ITI. Thus there was no substantial evidence of conditioning at either of the long ITIs of Experiment IV. Figures 14 and 15 illustrate level of conditioning over blocks at these ITIs for both conditioning measures.

The change in I gsr with blocks of trials reflected the lack of conditioning. As listed in Table 19 and as illustrated in Figure 14, I gsr was moving in the direction of increased relaxation for the <u>S</u>s in Experiment II by the second block of trials; this trend continued for the third. In Experiment IV, I gsr showed no mean change in either direction at the 30 minute ITI for the first two blocks of trials, but showed a slight movement towards relaxation at the ITI midpoint in the third block of trials. At the 60 minute ITI, I gsr was moving towards greater relaxation on block 2 but dropped to a mean change of zero on block 3. In other words, inhibition or relaxation as gauged by the I gsr measure was not consistently apparent at the 60 minute ITI and occurred slightly only at the last block of trials at the 30 minute ITI.

The OE gsr (see Table 29 and Figure 17) continued the trend of growth with ITI length observed in Experiment II. The experiment as a whole substantially reduced level of arousal from 30 to 60 minute ITIs. <u>S</u> comments indicated that this was more a function of fatigue than habituation.

The mean per cent time per <u>S</u> spent counting is tabulated in Table 29 and illustrated in comparison to the ITI groups of Experiment II in Figure 18. Where this per cent averaged in the 80s for the 120 <u>S</u>s of Experiment II (overall mean was 84%), the mean per cent counting per <u>S</u> dropped to 52% at the 30 minute ITI and to 32% at the 60 minute ITI. Thus, at an ITI range of 0.5 minutes to 60 minutes, per cent counting did show a decrease. On the other hand, even the lengthy ITI of 60 minutes, taking close to 16 hours for 15 acquisition trials, still averaged counting per <u>S</u> approximately a third of that time. One <u>S</u> at this 60 minute ITI found himself counting to 1850 with every trial. Human counting methods then, while diminished with highly increased ITI length, remained a substantial method of synchrony at all ITIs.

Methods of synchrony at the Experiment IV ITIs included visualized clocks and guessing as well as the counting methods of successive numbers, tapping, and repeated mental events. An additional method attempted briefly by two <u>S</u>s at the 30 minute ITI was synchrony with automatically flushing toilets which could be heard faintly through the vent in the inner chamber. This method was soon abandoned by both <u>S</u>s as the flushing ITI of approximately 20 minutes would be disrupted by a periodic consumer use.

Although the number of <u>S</u>s in Experiment IV was far too small to justify the full classificatory listing of per cent use of methods of synchrony done in Experiment II, certain comments might be made. For one, no <u>S</u> synchronized with his physiological "Feel" prior to the flash although one <u>S</u> reported having such anxiety reactions within seconds of each US presentation. This method of synchrony could not therefore be evaluated at the extra long ITIs. Time spent guessing substantially increased in Experi-

Figure 14. – – Mean % occurrence of CR_{80} at high stimulus intensity
by 5-trial acquisition block over all ITIs in Experiments II
and for both ITIs in Experiment IV

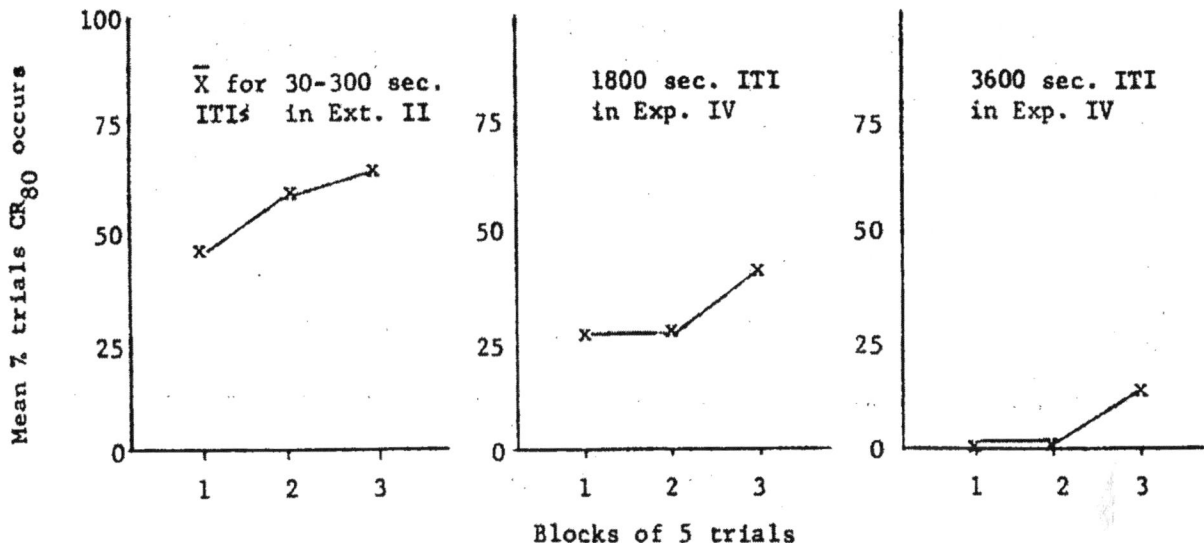

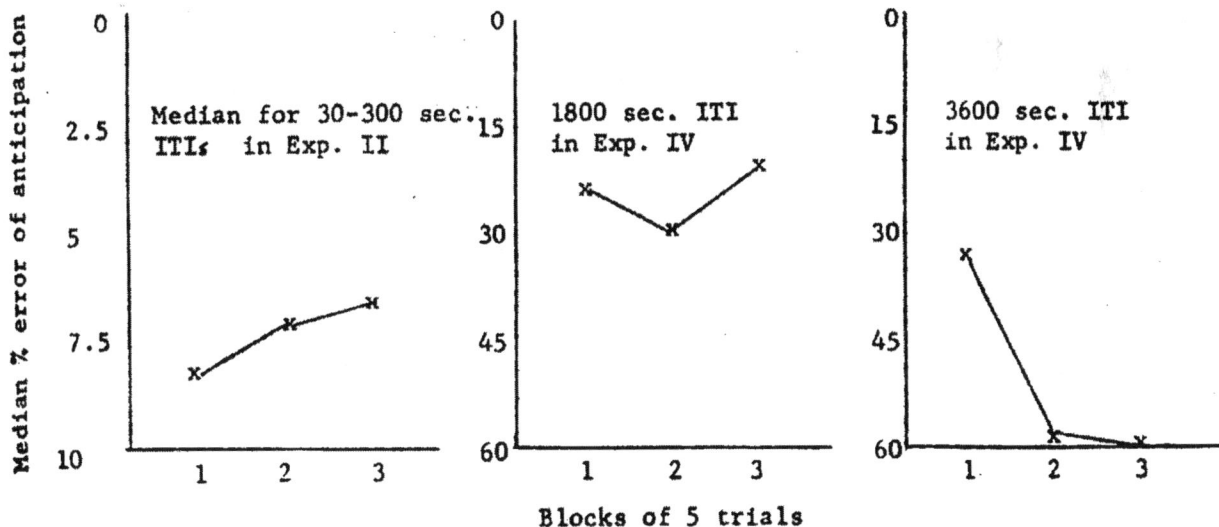

Figure 15. – – Median % error of anticipation at high stimulus intensity
by 5-trial acquisition block over all ITIs in Experiments II
and for both ITIs in Experiment IV

* Note that ordinate scale is expanded for Experiment IV
figures to accommodate larger % error of anticipation.

Figure 16. – – Mean Igsr as a function of 5-trial acquisition block
over all ITIs in Experiments II and for both ITIs in Experiment IV

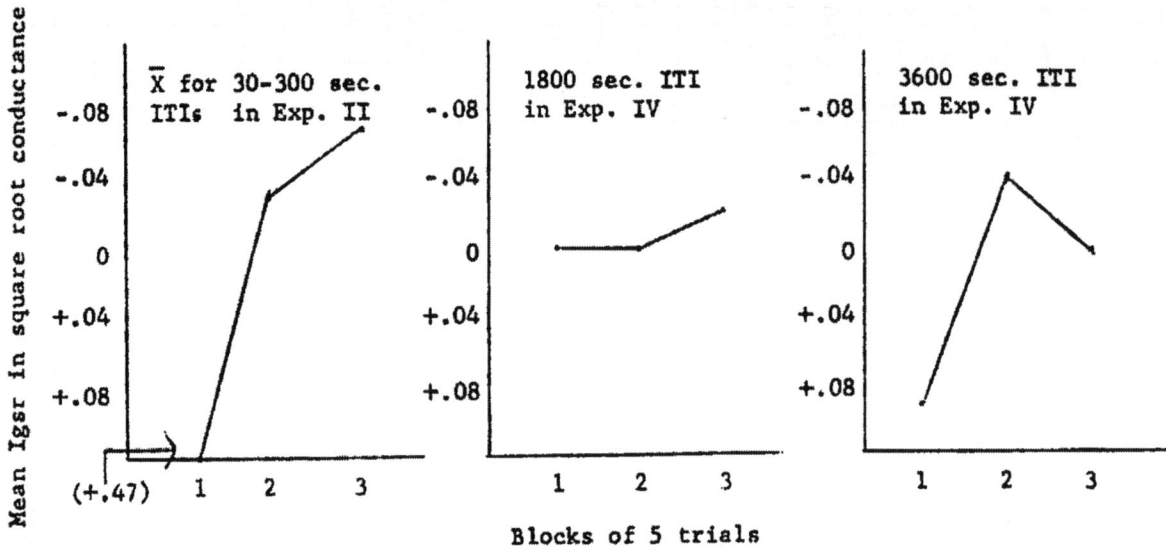

Figure 17. – – Mean OEgsr at high stimulus intensity as a function of ITI
length in Experiments II and IV

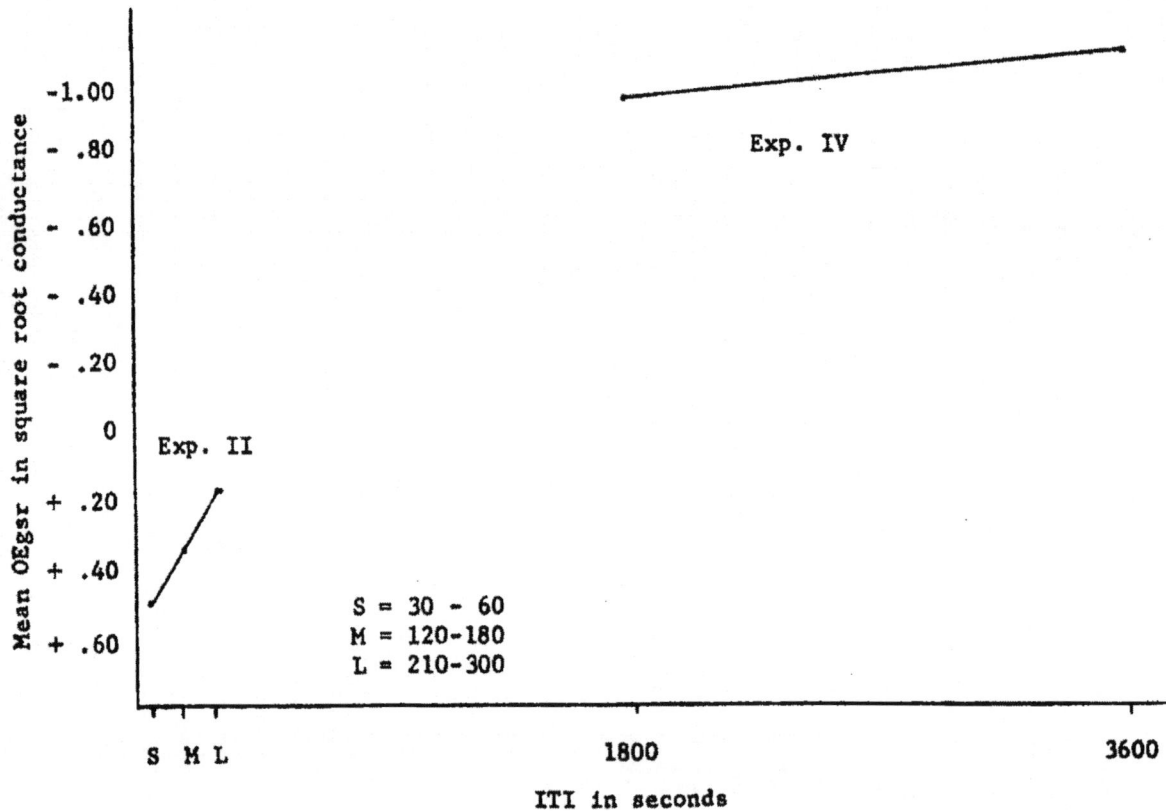

ment IV. Where approximately 5% of S's time was spent guessing at the 30 to 300 second ITI range of Experiment II, 48% and 35% of S's time was spent guessing at the ITIs of 30 minutes and 60 minutes respectively. The S (S2) using the visual clock method used it 100% of the time and was the most accurate on the error of anticipation measure of the three Ss at his 60 minute ITI. The bulk of counting time was spent on successive numbers or tapping methods just as in Experiment II. Repeated mental events included song choruses and mental jigsaw puzzles. Only one S counted pulse and that briefly; no one synchronized with breathing.

Figure 18. – - Mean % time per subject spent counting (for method
of synchrony) as a function of ITI length in Experiments II and IV

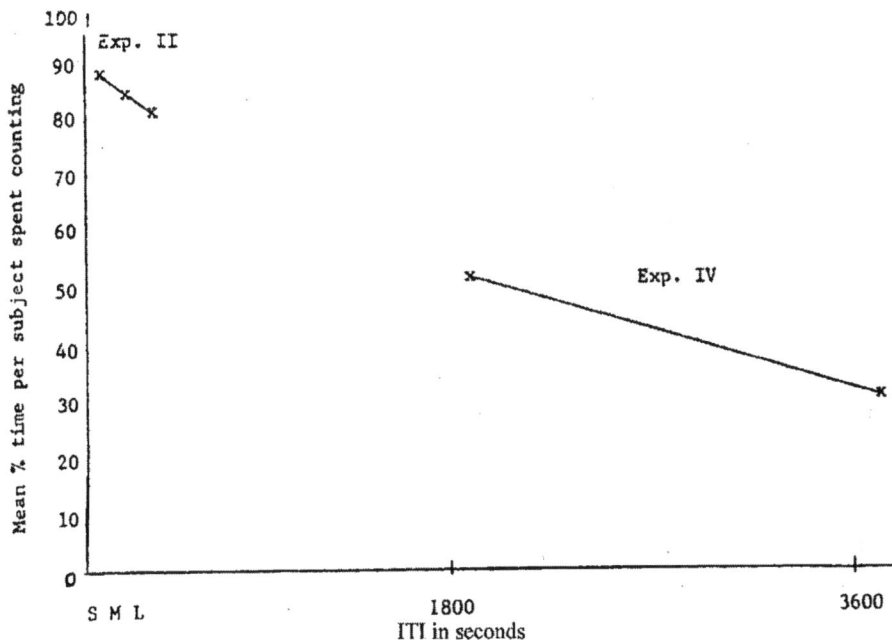

Figure 19. – - Mean % accuracy of estimate of ITI length as a function
of ITI length in Experiments II and IV

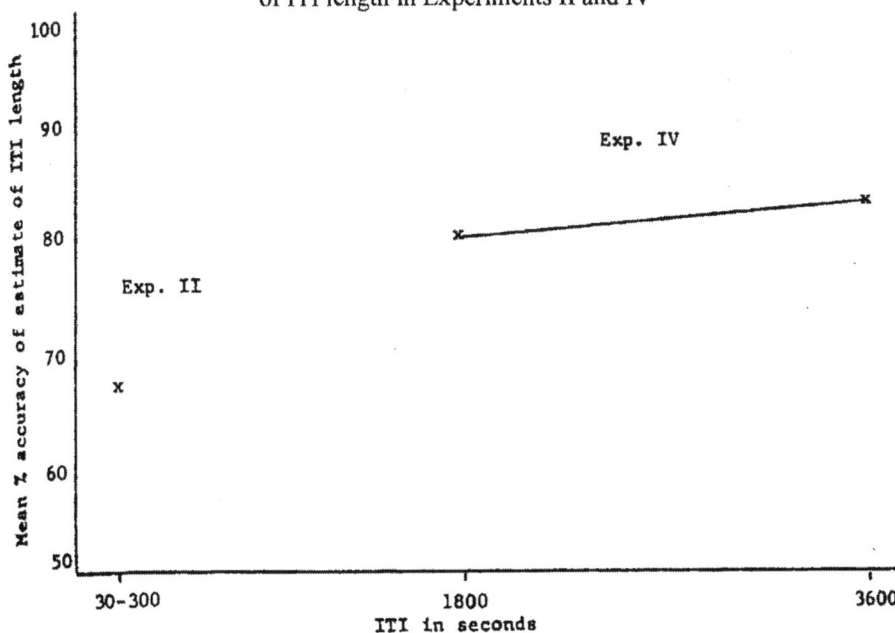

127

Figure 19 illustrates the mean per cent accuracy of estimation at the long ITIs of Experiment IV as compared to the mean 67% accuracy for the ITIs of Experiment II. Accuracy did increase to a mean of 80% for the 30 minute ITI and 83% for the 60 minute ITI. Half the Ss in Experiment IV showed 100% accuracy with their initial estimate. The other Ss all underestimated their ITI length. Only 2 of the 6 Ss had a second retrospective estimate more accurate than the initial one. Two of the 3 Ss making an initial error of estimate knew the correct direction of their error. These data are all included in Table 19.

Detailed behavioral logs were kept on each S. None quit the experiment before its completion although occasionally morale slackened enough to elicit caustic comments. Theses usually came in the middle block of trials and were never reflected in the attitude of S once the door to the inner chamber was opened at the experiment's end. Ss whenever face to face with E were cooperative and in good spirits. However, frequent lows in this attitude were recorded for the isolated hours spent by S in the inner chamber. A carbon of the instructions left with S during one acquisition session was found afterwards to have been crumpled, torn, and dipped in the urinal. Another S managed to remove the screws from his table with his free hand during the experiment. In general, however, hostility was covert and cooperation was always beyond the minimum necessary for a successful acquisition procedure.

Discussion

Pavlov's (1927) statement that temporal conditioning was possible at any ITI was not supported by the data of Experiment IV. Level of conditioning at ITIs of 30 and 60 minutes, as depicted by two measures of learning, remained well below that established at ITIs of 0.5 to 5.0 minutes in Experiment II. On the other hand, Feokritova's (1912) observation that conditioning at a 30 minute ITI occurred after only two or three trials is understandable in the sense that all Ss at the 30 minute ITI in Experiment IV achieved at least one or two CR_{80}s in the first block of 5 trials. However, frequency of occurrence never got much better than this over further blocks. Furthermore, an occurrence of one CR_{80} on any 5 trials is highly likely by chance alone. It is interesting that no replication of Feokritova's 30 minute ITI was included in the Soviet literature. While Experiment IV may have supported her observation, it has not supported her conclusions or those of Pavlov.

Again I gsr reflected the presence or absence of conditioning. It was relatively absent in Experiment IV. Low conditioning levels were paralleled by a lack of clearcut progressive movement towards relaxation at ITI midpoints as gauged by the I gsr. The OE gsr, on the other hand, continued to show less arousal with greater ITI length. Per cent time counting per S decreased and accuracy of estimation increased with increasing ITI. Apparently the ITI differential for these events must be as much as 25 minutes before their effects grow marked.

Unfortunately, neither breath counting nor "Feel" methods were attempted at the 30 to 60 minute ITI and their efficacy with conditioning remains to be tested in this context.

CHAPTER ELEVEN

TEMPORAL CONDITIONING HYPOTHESES SURVIVING THE RESEARCH

To sum up: past decades of Soviet research on the classical conditioning of a temporal response to a periodic stimulus led to the formation of several testable theories and attitudes. Pavlovians consider temporal conditioning to be a respectable member of the conditioning family, subject to the laws of inhibition and differential stimulus intensity; without upper limit as to size of intertrial interval (ITI). Over the years, accumulated Soviet evidence indicated ITIs below three to five minutes were difficult or impossible to condition. Sporadic American research came to an opposite conclusion: temporal conditioning became more difficult as ITIs increased to one minute or larger. Major purposes of the following experiments were to resolve the apparent American-Soviet ITI contradiction and to study temporal conditioning phenomena in depth through the use of the larger subject ($\underline{S}$) samples, statistical evaluation, and experimental control common to less neglected areas of North American experimental psychology.

Male and female volunteer college student Ss vocally anticipated a periodic photic stimulus (US) once each trial in all experiments. Anticipations occurring in the last fifth of the ITI were defined as conditioned responses (CRs).

Experiment I gauged conditioning efficacy over 20 trials at ITIs of 45, 135, or 240 seconds and at high (100 watt) or low (7 watt) US intensity. With 3 $\underline{S}$s at each ITI—intensity condition, conditioning level at 135 seconds trailed the shorter and longer ITIs. High US intensity depressed conditioning level at the shortest ITI, raising it at the highest ITI. Introspective reports of methods of synchrony, estimation of ITI length, and stimulus unpleasantness were analyzed in this and the following experiments.

Experiment II replicated Experiment I's conditioning results in 15 trials at ITIs of 30, 60, 90, 120, 150, 180, 210, 240, 270, 300 seconds with high or low US intensity. With 6 Ss at each ITI-intensity condition (120 $\underline{S}$s total), conditioning level at ITIs of 60 seconds or less and of 210 seconds or more excelled that of ITIs in between. High US intensity again depressed performance at short ITIs (30, 60, sec.) but enhanced performance significantly only at middle range ITIs (150, 180 sec.). Independent conditioning measures of CR frequency and error magnitude showed similar results, demonstrating general increase in conditioning level with blocks of trials. Galvanic skin response (gsr) measures yielded a highly significant positive relationship between pre-experimental relaxation and subsequent performance. Gsr readings taken at the midpoint of every ITI showed a significantly increasing level of relaxation at the midpoint over blocks of acquisition trials in the presence of temporal conditioning which was absent or inconsistent when such conditioning was absent. This held true even for $\underline{S}$s having overall gsr decrease in relaxation in response to the entire experiment. Gsr findings supported neo-Pavlovian inhibition theory prediction and a complementary discrimination-production hypothesis.

Experiment III demonstrated conditioning for 12 Ss at high US intensity ITIs of 60 or 240 seconds to significantly improve with a second day of 15 acquisition trials and to significantly extinguish with 15 subsequent trials lacking the periodic US.

Experiment IV failed to demonstrate significant Pavlov—predicted temporal conditioning over 15 high US intensity acquisition trials with ITIs of 30 and 60 minutes. The 3 $\underline{S}$s at each ITI did show higher estimation accuracy and less mean per cent time counting than $\underline{S}$s at the lower ITIs of the earlier experiments.

These experiments generally reconciled American and Soviet thrusts towards the demonstration and understanding of the parameters of temporal conditioning, a gateway to the psychology of time.

These data allowed consideration of the hypotheses the research was designed to evaluate (Chapter six).

Hypothesis A was strongly supported by Experiments I, II, and III. Temporal conditioning was demonstrated for adult humans such that it could not statistically be classified as a chance event.

Hypothesis B was supported by Experiment III. Level of conditioning was found to show significant improvement with successive days of acquisition while showing significant extinction in the absence of the periodic stimulus. General Improvement in level of conditioning with 5-trial blocks of acquisition was observed in Experiments I and II as well as in Experiment III.

Hypothesis C was supported by Experiments I and II. Performance in temporal conditioning at ITIs of more than 3 minutes and at ITIs of 1 minute or less excelled the performance level of the ITIs in between. Experiment IV, in addition, suggested no support for significant temporal conditioning of humans at ITIs as long as 30 and 60 minutes. ITI was thus shown to be a critical variable for temporal conditioning.

Hypothesis D was partially supported in Experiments I and II. High stimulus intensity was shown to depress performance level in temporal conditioning at low ITIs of 60 sec. or less. However, the enhancing effect of high stimulus intensity on level of temporal conditioning was significant in Experiment II only at the middle length ITIs of 150 and 180 sec. Beyond ITIs of 3 minutes in duration, an intensity difference of the magnitude tested in these experiments did not lead to differential performance.

Hypothesis E was partially supported by Experiments II and IV in that accuracy of estimation did appear to increase substantially from ITIs of 0.5 and 5.0 minutes to ITIs of 30 and 60 minutes. Within the 0.5 to 5.0 minute range, however, the observed increase was not significant. Furthermore, the significant relationship between accuracy of estimate and the variables of ITI and stimulus intensity observed in Experiment I was not replicated with a larger number of Ss in Experiment II.

Hypothesis F was strongly supported by Experiment II. The relationship between relaxation before the experiment and the subsequent level of conditioning was positive and highly significant. Thus the work of Birman (1953), Dmitriev and Kochigina (1959), and Fraisse (1963) in this regard was confirmed. These and the present study, however, all based this conclusion on the time oriented conditioning procedures of trace or temporal conditioning. Generalization to other methods of learning on the basis of these data would not be justified. Pavlov (1927) related the importance of pre-treatment relaxation to the subsequent development of cortical inhibition. It has been suggested in this dissertation that another plausibility would be that conscious or unconscious perception and symmetric production of the interoceptive rhythms upon which time conditioning is based would be sensitive to S's degree of relaxation.

Hypothesis G was supported by Experiment I through IV. Increased relaxation during the ITI (of uncorrelated magnitude) was generally observed wherever temporal conditioning occurred and was absent or inconsistent when temporal conditioning failed to occur. This was even true for those Ss evidencing an overall decrease in relaxation as a result of the entire experiment. Insofar as neo-Pavlovians have operationally equated inhibition with overt relaxation rather than a cortical event, these data support the Pavlovian as well as the American "secondary elicitation" point of view.

Hypothesis H was supported by Experiments I, II, and IV. As in the case of accuracy of estimation, the time spent counting per S did not appreciably drop with ITI increase until ITI increased to 30 to 60 minutes. The methods of synchrony chosen by Ss were many and varied in popularity, time used per S, and efficacy in conditioning. In Experiment II, only those Ss counting breaths as a method of synchrony significantly excelled the level of conditioning of Ss guessing a majority of the time. Future experiments might well devote themselves to the conditioning efficacy of breath counting, "Feel," guess, and other methods through the pre-treatment instruction (to use a-single method) of equivalent groups of Ss. One underlying inference of this approach is that what turns out to be the best conscious method of temporal synchrony might well be, at a given ITI range, the dominant interoceptive rhythm for unconscious temporal conditioning. Among other interesting findings in these experiments were the parallelism of the two independent measures of conditioning; the increase in accuracy of estimation with the decrease of inhibition during the ITI; the enhanced conditioning observed with a small increment of adult age; the significantly greater anxiety of the college male over the college female. These and other second order findings fill out the picture of temporal conditioning in humans but demand serendipity's companions: further replication, research, and explanation.

Temporal conditioning offers a method of analyzing many more learning problems than synchrony to time in its own right. Perhaps the simplest of conditioning procedures, only conditioning to time directly hinges the CR and the UR to the same external flash or event. The growing awareness that time is periodicity and periodicity is basic to perception, learning, and all behavior will continue to bring about a convergence of approaches from a wide variety of disciplines on this single concern: the psychology of time. Temporal conditioning methods provide one of the strongest approaches of an old fertile direction.

Table 1.--Some abbreviations and definitions used
in Experiments I, II, III, and IV

Abbreviations	Definitions
Acq.	Acquisition
A. Est.	Accuracy of estimation of ITI
Blk. 1, Blk. n	First 5-trial block, nth 5-trial block
CEDE	Correct estimation of direction of error in estimation of ITI
CR_{80}	Response anticipating US within last 20% of ITI
CR_d	A CR score derived by dividing $\underline{S}$'s CR_{80} score by the mean $\overline{CR}_{80}$ score of $\underline{S}$'s ITI-Int. condition
D-1, D-2	Day 1, Day 2
DEE	Direction of error of estimate of ITI
E. Ant	Error of anticipation of US
Ext.	Extinction
F	Female
Gsr	Galvanic skin response
H gsr	Pre-treatment measure of gsr change during habituation
I gsr	Mean gsr change from midpoint of one ITI to midpoint of next by acquisition block
Int.	Intensity of photic US (H for high, L for low)
ITI	Intertrial interval
ITI groups (gps):	
"Short"	ITIs of 30-60 seconds
"Medium"	ITIs of 120-180 seconds
"Long"	ITIs of 210-300 seconds

Table 1.--<u>Continued</u>

Abbreviations	Definitions
M	Male
N	No
OE gsr	Gsr change over entire experiment (after minus before)
"Offs"	The 19 Ss with lowest A. Est. in Experiment II (Median was 0% A. Est.)
"Ons"	The 19 Ss with 100% A. Est. in Experiment II
Sb Un	Subjective unpleasantness of US as rated by S after the experiment
src	Square root conductance (gsr units converted from ohms)
+ src	A gsr change in the direction of greater arousal
- src	A gsr change in the direction of greater relaxation
0 src	No gsr change in either direction
y	Yes

Table 2.—Data summary for ITI-Int. conditions in Experiment I: sex, age, Sb Un, occurrence of CR_{80}, estimation of ITI, counting per S

Data Category	H INT.									L INT.								
	45 sec ITI			135 sec ITI			240 sec ITI			45 sec ITI			135 sec ITI			240 sec ITI		
	S1	S2	S3	S1	S2	S3	S1	S2	S3	S1	S2	S3	S1	S2	S3	S1	S2	S3
Age by S	19	19	18	19	18	19	18	18	19	20	20	20	21	22	20	25	18	25
Sex by S	M	M	M	M	M	M	M	F	M	M	F	F	M	M	F	F	M	M
Sb Un by S	Y	N	Y	Y	Y	Y	Y	Y	N	Y	Y	N	N	N	N	Y	N	N
% CR80:																		
X̄ Blk 1		33			33			40			40			27			40	
X̄ Blk 2		73			53			53			80			40			47	
X̄ Blk 3		80			47			73			73			40			53	
X̄ Blk 4		80			33			67			93			40			53	
X̄ All Blks		65			42			58			75			39			48	
ITI Est.:																		
Sec. by S	51	58	40	135	120	150	200	196	150	13	75	90	210	75	90	165	180	170
X̄ % A. Est		82			93			76			21			51			72	
Counting:																		
% by S	100	90	100	50	90	85	100	85	85	100	100	80	0	100	60	10	40	100
Median %		100			85			50			100			60			40	

Table 3.--Analysis of variance of occurrence of CR_{80} by ITI,
Int., and trial blocks in Experiment I

Source	SS	df	MS	F
A: ITI	28.7	2	14.35	7.10*
B: Int.	0.2	1	0.25	0.12
A x B	3.1	2	1.53	0.76
error (a)	24.2	12	2.02	
C: Trial Blks.	16.5	3	5.50	10.38**
A x C	6.6	6	1.10	2.08
B x C	1.1	3	0.38	0.72
A x B x C	1.5	6	0.24	0.45
error (b)	19.1	36	0.53	
Total	101.0	71		

$*\ p < .01$
$**\ p < .005$

Table 4.--Analysis of variance of per cent A. Est. by ITI
and Int. in Experiment I

Source	SS	df	MS	F
A: ITI	1819.5	2	909.8	8.63*
B: Int.	5839.2	1	5839.2	55.38*
A x B	2555.0	2	1277.5	12.12*
error	1265.2	12	105.4	
Total	11478.9	17		

$*\ p < .005$

Table 5.--Occurrence of CR_{80} as a function of H gsr at
45 sec. ITI and H Int. in Experiment I

S	H gsr (src)	Total Number CR_{80}s in Acq.
1	+.23	15
2	+.75	12
3	+.89	12

Table 6.--Number of Ss at each method of synchrony used in
Experiment I

Method of Synchrony	Number of Ss using method at any time *
1. Counting by any means	15
a. Successive numbers	4
b. Tapping	4
c. Counting breaths	2
d. Repeated mental events	2
e. Pulse count	2
2. "Feel"	5
3. Guess	4

* Any one S may appear in more
than one category; n = 18 Ss

Table 7.--Data summary for ITI-Int. conditions in Experiment II: sex, age, H gsr, Sb Un, occurrence of CR_{80}, E. Ant., A. Est., CEDE, DEE, I gsr, OE gsr, counting per $\underline{S}$.

ITI-Int.	Sex (#Ss)		Age (# Ss)		H gsr (#Ss)		Sb Un (#Ss)		$\bar{X}$% Occurrence of CR_{80}			
	M	F	18	19-22	+	0.-	Y	N	Blk 1	Blk 2	Blk 3	All Blks
30 sec-H	3	3	2	4	4	2	2	4	40.0	56.6	66.7	54.5
30 sec-L	5	1	2	4	4	2	1	5	53.4	73.4	76.7	67.8
60 sec-H	3	3	2	4	3	3	4	2	50.0	60.0	63.4	57.8
60 sec-L	4	2	4	2	2	4	0	6	46.6	76.6	86.6	70.0
90 sec-H	3	3	6	0	3	3	3	3	40.0	50.0	76.7	55.0
90 sec-L	5	1	3	3	5	1	2	4	36.6	66.6	76.7	60.0
120 sec-H	5	1	0	6	5	1	3	3	36.6	40.0	46.6	41.1
120 sec-L	4	2	3	3	5	1	3	3	40.0	43.4	53.4	45.5
150 sec-H	5	1	2	4	4	2	2	4	43.4	43.4	60.0	48.9
150 sec-L	5	1	2	4	4	2	0	6	26.6	50.0	33.4	36.7
180 sec-H	4	2	1	5	2	4	2	4	40.0	63.4	60.0	54.5
180 sec-L	3	3	4	2	3	3	1	5	30.0	56.6	46.6	44.5
210 sec-H	5	1	5	1	2	4	5	1	53.4	73.4	66.6	64.5
210 sec-L	3	3	5	1	2	4	3	3	43.4	80.0	53.4	58.9
240 sec-H	2	4	4	2	2	4	3	3	50.0	66.6	70.0	62.2
240 sec-L	5	1	1	5	2	4	1	5	60.0	63.4	60.0	61.1
270 sec-H	4	2	4	2	2	4	4	2	60.0	53.4	70.0	61.1
270 sec-L	3	3	3	3	4	2	1	5	50.0	40.0	70.0	57.8
300 sec-H	4	2	3	3	3	3	4	2	43.4	60.0	70.0	57.8
300 sec-L	4	2	2	4	1	5	4	2	50.0	53.4	66.6	57.7
Σ	79	41	58	62	62	58	48	72	----	----	----	----
$\bar{X}$	---	---	18.7 yrs.		+.07 src		---		44.6	58.4	63.6	55.5
S.D.	---	---	2.3		.30		---		7.9	7.3	7.9	15.5

138

Table 7.--Continued.

ITI-Int.	Median E. Ant. in sec.				Median E. Ant. in %				% A. Est.		CEDE DEE (#Ss)		
	Blk 1	Blk 2	Blk 3	All Blks	Blk 1	Blk 2	Blk 3	All Blks	Est 1	Est 2	#Ss	Under	Over
30 sec-H	5	2	2	3	17	7	7	9	48	49	4	3	2
30 sec-L	3	2	2	3	10	4	4	6	70	59	3	1	3
60 sec-H	2	5	6	4	3	8	10	7	68	65	2	2	4
60 sec-L	6	4	3	4	10	7	4	7	63	69	3	2	3
90 sec-H	4	4	4	4	4	4	5	5	63	69	1	1	4
90 sec-L	9	5	7	6	10	6	8	6	27	26	3	3	3
120 sec-H	7	8	13	10	6	7	11	8	77	78	3	3	2
120 sec-L	16	8	8	14	13	13	7	12	82	87	6	1	2
150 sec-H	22	16	12	13	15	11	8	9	82	77	5	2	3
150 sec-L	29	13	20	18	19	9	13	12	82	86	3	3	3
180 sec-H	34	20	12	18	19	11	7	10	86	78	4	3	1
180 sec-L	37	12	20	15	21	7	11	8	58	55	2	2	3
210 sec-H	20	12	12	15	10	5	6	9	61	55	2	4	1
210 sec-L	32	10	16	18	15	7	8	10	82	80	4	4	2
240 sec-H	14	16	16	14	6	7	6	6	67	76	6	3	2
240 sec-L	21	16	13	14	6	6	6	6	72	71	2	3	3
270 sec-H	22	17	15	17	8	6	6	6	63	65	2	1	5
270 sec-L	21	16	38	20	8	6	14	7	65	64	2	1	2
300 sec-H	24	23	22	26	8	8	7	8	69	62	4	3	1
300 sec-L	26	45	24	31	9	15	8	10	61	63	6	3	2
Σ/X̄	—	—	—	—	—	—	—	—	—	—	82	49	52
X̄	—	—	—	—	—	—	—	—	67	56	—	—	—
S.D.	—	—	—	—	—	—	—	—	33	33	—	—	—
Median	20.5	12.5	12.0	14.0	10	7	7	8	67	67	—	—	—

Table 7.--Continued.

ITI-Int.	X̄ I gsr in src			X̄ OE gsr in src	.X̄ % Time spent counting per S	N
	Blk 1	Blk 2	Blk 3			
30 sec-H	+.08	+.01	0	+.02	65	6
30 sec-L	+.03	+.01	0	+.04	96	6
60 sec-H	+.04	+.03	+.01	+.07	92	6
60 sec-L	+.10	-.02	-.03	+.07	100	6
90 sec-H	+.07	+.03	+.02	+.10	78	6
90 sec-L	+.16	+.03	-.04	+.11	93	6
120 sec-H	+.06	+.02	0	+.06	92	6
120 sec-L	+.05	-.02	0	+.04	82	6
150 sec-H	+.12	+.04	+.04	+.11	80	6
150 sec-L	0	-.08	+.02	+.02	100	6
180 sec-H	-.01	+.02	+.02	.01	83	6
180 sec-L	-.04	-.03	0	+.03	78	6
210 sec-H	+.03	+.02	-.04	+.02	78	6
210 sec-L	+.02	-.01	+.03	+.04	75	6
240 sec-H	0	-.01	-.02	+.02	82	6
240 sec-L	+.10	-.03	-.07	+.01	81	6
270 sec-H	+.03	-.03	0	+.01	93	6
270 sec-L	+.01	+.01	+.03	+.02	72	6
300 sec-H	+.09	0	-.01	+.04	82	6
300 sec-L	+.02	-.06	-.09	+.01	87	6
Σ	---	---	---	---	--	120
X̄	+.05	.00	-.01	+.04	84	
S.D.	.11	.06	.07	.08	29	

140

Table 8.--Analysis of variance of H gsr by ITI and Int. in Experiment II

Source	SS	df	MS	F
A: ITI	39.21	9	4.36	0.48
B: Int.	0.00	1	0.00	0.00
A x B	96.75	9	10.75	1.18
error	908.83	100	9.08	
Total	1044.79	199		

Table 9.--Analysis of variance of occurrence of CR_{80} by ITI, Int., and trial blocks in Experiment II

Source	SS	df	MS	F
A: ITI	48.0	9	5.33	3.54*
B: Int.	1.0	1	1.00	0.66
A x B	15.5	9	1.72	1.14
error (a)	150.5	100	1.51	
C: Trial Blks	58.0	2	29.00	26.54*
A x C	31.0	18	1.72	1.58
B x C	0.0	2	0.00	0.00
A x B x C	13.5	18	0.75	0.67
error (b)	218.5	200	1.09	
Total	536.0	359		

$* \ p < .005$

Table 10.--Tukey (1949) significant gap test for selected differences in level of conditioning of ITI-Int. conditions in Experiment II

Comparison	Mean % difference* of % occurrence of CR_{80} for all blks.
1. ITI (sec.): H Int.	
30 vs. 60	+ 3.2
60 vs. 90	- 2.3
90 vs. 120	-14.4**
120 vs. 150	+ 7.8
150 vs. 180	+ 5.6
180 vs. 210	+10.0**
210 vs. 240	- 2.3
240 vs. 270	- 1.1
270 vs. 300	- 3.3
2. ITI (sec.): L Int.	
30 vs. 60	+ 2.2
60 vs. 90	-10.0**
90 vs. 120	-14.5**
120 vs. 150	- 8.8
150 vs. 180	+ 7.8
180 vs. 210	+14.4**
210 vs. 240	+ 2.2
240 vs. 270	- 7.8
270 vs. 300	+ 3.4
3. ITI (sec.): H vs. L Int.	
30	+13.3**
60	-12.2**
90	+ 4.5
120	+ 4.4
150	-12.2**
180	-10.0**
210	- 5.6
240	- 1.1
270	- 7.8
300	- 1.1

* A + sign indicates increase in per cent occurrence of CR_{80} from first to second condition in the comparison; a - sign indicates a decrease.

** p < .05 or a critical difference exceeding 9.35 %.

Table 11.--Analysis of variance of I gsr (all 120 Ss) by ITI, Int., and trial blocks in Experiment II

Source	SS	df	MS	F
A: ITI	936	9	104	1.48
A: Int.	271	1	271	3.86
A x B	1094	9	122	1.74
error (a)	7020	100	70	
C: Trial Blks	2102	2	1051	17.23*
A x C	1549	18	86	1.41
B x C	191	2	96	1.57
A x B x C	1167	18	65	1.07
error (b)	12191	200	61	
Total	26521	359		

* p < .005

Table 12.--Analysis of variance of I gsr (for 83 Ss having a + OE gsr) by trial blocks in Experiment II

Source	SS	df	MS	F
Trial blocks	2587	2	1293.5	20.80*
error	15302	246	62.2	
Total	17889	248		

* p < .005

Table 13.--Analysis of variance of OE gsr by ITI and Int. in Experiment II

Source	SS	df	MS	F
A: ITI	1369	9	152	2.22*
B: Int.	23	1	23	0.34
A x B	388	9	43	0.63
error	6839	100		
Total	8619	119		

* p < .05

Table 14.--Analysis of variance of per cent time per $\underline{S}$ spent counting by ITI and Int. in Experiment II

Source	SS	df	MS	F
A: ITI	3334	9	370	0.44
B: Int.	399	1	399	0.47
A x B	10128	9	1125	1.34
error	84210	100		
Total	98071	119		

Table 15.--Analysis of variance of per cent A. Est. by ITI, Int., and estimate order in Experiment II

Source	SS	df	MS	F
A: ITI	23395	9	2599.4	1.26
B: Int.	149	1	149.0	0.07
A x B	18616	9	2068.4	1.00
error (a)	206698	100	2067.0	
C: Estimates	4	1	4.0	0.05
A x C	1	9	0.1	0.00
B x C	22	1	22.0	0.30
A x B x C	1403	9	155.9	2.11*
error (b)	14300	200	71.5	
Total	264488	239		

* p < .05

Table 16.--Correlation analyses in Experiment II

Comparison	df	Correlation
CR_d (all blks) vs. % A. Est.	118	PPM r = +.028
CR_d (all blks) vs. H gsr	118	PPM r = -.300***
CR_d (all blks) vs. H gsr	118	Eta r = -.408*** (X.Y)
		Eta r = -.483*** (Y.X)
CR_d (all blks) vs. H gsr	118	SRO r = -.309***
CR_d (blk 1) vs. I gsr (blk 1)	118	PPM r = -.037
CR_d (blk 2) vs. I gsr (blk 2)	118	PPM r = -.067
CR_d (blk 3) vs. I gsr (blk 3)	118	PPM r = -.120
CR_d (all blks) vs. OE gsr	118	PPM r = -.095
I gsr (blk 1) vs. H gsr	118	PPM r = +.164
I gsr (blk 2) vs. H gsr	118	PPM r = +.066
I gsr (blk 3) vs. H gsr	118	PPM r = -.043
I gsr (blk 1) vs. OE gsr	118	PPM r = +.783***
I gsr (blk 2) vs. OE gsr	118	PPM r = +.362***
I gsr (blk 3) vs. OE gsr	118	PPM r = +.312***
I gsr (blk 3) vs. % A. Est	118	PPM r = +.201*
OE gsr vs. ITI length	118	PPM r = -.230**
OE gsr vs. H gsr	118	PPM r = +.226*
OE gsr vs % A. Est.	118	PPM r = +.040
% A. Est vs. H gsr	118	PPM r = +.084
% A. Est. vs % counting per S	118	PPM r = -.024
Final S-S interval vs. final S-R interval	66	PPM r = +.973***
Final S-R interval vs. ITI Est.	66	PPM r = +.790***
Final S-S interval vs. ITI Est.	66	PPM r = +.849***
CR_{80} (all blks) vs. Med. % E. Ant.:		
Block 3:	115	SRO r = -.338***
All blks:	118	SRO r = -.423***

PPM - Pearson product moment   * p < .05
SRO - Spearman rank order   ** p < .02
Eta - Correlation ratio   *** p < .01

Table 17.--Mean per cent time spent per $\underline{S}$ on each method of synchrony used in Experiment II

Method of Synchrony	Mean per cent time per $\underline{S}$
Counting methods	
a) successive numbers	60.5
b) tapping	15.0
c) counting breaths	5.4
d) repeated mental events	4.4
e) pulse count	3.4
"Feel"	6.1
Guess	4.8
Internal clock	0.2
Sleep	0.1
Listen for cues	0.1
N = 120	100.0

Table 18.--Median CR_d and number of $\underline{S}$s by majority method of synchrony in Experiment II

Majority method of synchrony	N	Median CR_d	U*
Counting methods			
a) successive numbers	69	1.00	76.5
b) tapping	17	1.10	14.5
c) counting breaths	6	1.10	2.0**
d) repeated mental events	4	1.10	3.0
e) pulse count	4	1.10	6.0
"Feel"	5	1.00	6.5
No majority method	11	1.00	9.0
Guess	4	0.85	---
	120		

    * $\underline{U}$ is the Mann-Whitney $\underline{U}$ (Siegel, 1956) and is based on the comparison of the CR_ds of $\underline{S}$s in each method group with the CR_ds of the $\underline{S}$s in the Guess group.

    ** p < .05

Table 19.--t-test analyses in Experiment II

Comparison	df	t
Age by sex (M vs. F)	118	0.00
H gsr by sex	118	3.28***
Age by H gsr (+ vs. -,0)	118	1.72
CR_d by sex	118	0.69
CR_d by age	118	2.39**
CR_d by H gsr	118	3.28***
CR_{80} of ITI groups by Int.:		
"Short" (H vs. L)	22	2.25*
"Medium" (H vs. L)	34	0.93
"Long" (H vs. L)	46	1.07
CR_{80} of H Int. by ITI gp.:		
"Short" vs. "Long"	34	0.98
"Short" vs. "Medium"	28	1.28
"Long vs. "Medium"	40	3.06***
CR_{80} of L Int. by ITI gp.:		
"Short" vs. "Long"	34	2.80***
"Short" vs. "Medium"	28	6.15***
"Long" vs. "Medium"	40	3.42***
I gsr by ITI gp.:		
"Long" vs. "Short" (Blk 1) . . .	70	0.71
"Long" vs. "Short" (Blk 2) . . .	70	0.93
"Long" vs. "Short" (Blk 3) . . .	70	0.07
"Long & Short" vs. "Medium" (Blk 1)	106	0.82
"Long & Short" vs. "Medium" (Blk 2)	106	0.04
"Long & Short" vs. "Medium" (Blk 3)	106	2.47**
OE gsr by sex	118	4.66***
OE gsr by age	118	0.61
% time per S̲ counting by H gsr . . .	118	1.06
% time per S̲ counting by ITI gp.:		
"Short" vs. "Long"	70	1.04
"Short" vs. "Medium"	58	0.35
"Medium" vs. "Long"	82	0.66
% A. Est. by order of est. (1st vs. 2nd)	238	0.06
% A. Est. by ITI gp.:		
"Short" vs. "Long"	70	0.61
"Short" vs. "Medium"	58	1.66
"Long" vs. "Medium"	82	1.58
% A. Est. by sex	118	1.56
% A. Est. by age	118	0.48
% A. Est. by CEDE (Y vs. N) . . .	99	0.70
% A. Est. by DEE (under vs. over) . .	99	3.97***
% A. Est. by Sb Un (Y vs. N) . . .	118	0.27
% A. Est. by breath counting method		
(users vs. non-users)	118	0.93

* p < .05
** p < .02
*** p < .01

Table 20.--Chi square analyses in Experiment II

Comparison	df	Chi sq.
Sex (M vs. F) & ITI (all 10) . . .	9	3.22
Sex & Int. (H vs. L)	1	0.33
Age (18 vs. 19-22) & ITI	9	12.74
Age & Int.	1	0.07
H gsr (+ vs. -,0) & ITI	9	13.90
H gsr & Int.	1	0.13
Sex & Age	1	0.78
Sex & H gsr	1	12.70***
Age & H gsr	1	2.50
Sb Un (Y vs. N) & ITI	9	13.05
Sb Un & Int.	1	8.89***
Sb Un & Sex	1	0.15
Sb Un & Age	1	0.23
Sb Un & H gsr	1	0.07
Blk 3 I gsr (+ vs. -,0) & Sex . . .	1	1.96
Blk 3 I gsr & Age	1	2.29
OE gsr (+ vs. -,0) & Sex	1	13.97***
OE gsr & Age	1	0.00
Counting methods (Y vs. N) & Sex . .	1	0.26
Counting methods & Age	1	0.00
Counting methods & H gsr	1	8.18***
Counting successive numbers & Sex . .	1	0.82
Counting successive numbers & Age . .	1	1.68
Counting successive numbers & H gsr .	1	0.00
Tapping & Sex	1	1.24
Tapping & Age	1	0.00
Tapping & H gsr	1	0.00
Counting breaths & Sex	1	0.00
Counting breaths & Age	1	6.38**
Counting breaths & H gsr	1	0.00
Repeated mental events method & Sex .	1	0.00
Repeated mental events method & Age .	1	4.87
Repeated mental events method & H gsr	1	0.04
Counting pulse & Sex	1	1.38
Counting pulse & Age	1	0.00
Counting pulse & H gsr	1	0.00
"Feel" method & Sex	1	3.49
"Feel" method & Age	1	0.00
"Feel" method & H gsr	1	3.07
No majority method & Sex	1	0.43
No majority method & Age	1	0.00

** p < .02
*** p < .01

Table 20.--Continued.

Comparison	df	Chi sq.
No majority method & H gsr	1	1.32
Guess method & Sex	1	0.00
Guess method & Age	1	0.00
Guess method & H gsr	1	0.19
CEDE (Y vs. N) & ITI	9	12.27
CEDE & Int.	1	0.15
CEDE & Sex	1	0.03
CEDE & Age	1	2.80
CEDE & H gsr	1	0.03
DEE & ITI	9	7.10
DEE & Int.	1	0.01
DEE & Sex	1	0.04
DEE & Age	1	2.90
DEE & H gsr	1	0.68
"Ons" (Y vs. N) & ITI	9	3.15
"Ons" & Int.	1	2.25
"Ons" & Sex	1	1.10
"Ons" & Age	1	0.02
"Ons" & H gsr	1	0.02
"Ons" vs. "Offs" & ITI	9	4.74
"Ons" vs. "Offs" & Int.	1	1.24
"Ons" vs. "Offs" & Sex	1	1.12
"Ons" vs. "Offs" & Age	1	0.01
"Ons" vs. "Offs" & H gsr	1	0.00
CR_d over 1.00 (Y vs. N) & CEDE	1	0.29
CR_d over 1.00 & DEE	1	0.01
CR_d over 1.00 & "Ons" (Y vs. N)	1	0.71
CR_d over 1.00 & "Ons" vs. "Offs"	1	0.11
CR_d over 1.00 & Sb Un	1	0.01
CEDE & DEE	1	0.64
CEDE & Blk 3 I gsr	1	0.00
CEDE & OE gsr	1	2.98
CEDE & Sb Un	1	0.92
DEE & Blk 3 I gsr	1	1.12
DEE & OE gsr	1	0.05
DEE & Sb Un	1	0.00
"Ons" (Y vs. N) & Blk 3 I gsr	1	2.45
"Ons" & OE gsr	1	5.57**
"Ons" & Sb Un	1	0.32
"Ons" vs. "Offs" & Blk 3 I gsr	1	0.91
"Ons" vs. "Offs" & OE gsr	1	3.96*
"Ons" vs. "Offs" & Sb Un	1	0.00
Blk 3 I gsr & Sb Un	1	0.01
OE gsr & Sb Un	1	0.47

* p < .05
** p < .02

Table 21.--$\underline{t}$-test analyses of occurrence of CR_{80} with ITIs pooled by trial block and stage of learning in Experiment III

Comparison ($\overline{X}$ % occur. in paren.)	df	t
Acq. D2 vs. Acq. D1:		
Blk 1 (60) vs. Blk 1 (50)	22	1.07
Blk 1 (60) vs. Blk 2 (57)	22	0.34
Blk 1 (60) vs. Blk 3 (65)	22	0.56
Blk 2 (68) vs. Blk 1 (50)	22	2.30*
Blk 2 (68) vs. Blk 2 (57)	22	1.35
Blk 2 (68) vs. Blk 3 (65)	22	0.46
Blk 3 (82) vs. Blk 1 (50)	22	4.08**
Blk 3 (82) vs. Blk 2 (57)	22	2.95**
Blk 3 (82) vs. Blk 3 (65)	22	2.31*
All Blks (70) vs. All Blks (57)		
Ext. D2 vs. Acq. D 2:		
Blk 1 (48) vs. Blk 3 (82)	22	2.91**
Blk 1 (48) vs. Blk 2 (68)	22	1.72
Blk 1 (48) vs. Blk 1 (60)	22	0.92
Blk 2 (32) vs. Blk 3 (82)	22	4.46**
Blk 2 (32) vs. Blk 2 (68)	22	3.25**
Blk 2 (32) vs. Blk 1 (60)	22	2.31*
Blk 3 (20) vs. Blk 3 (82)	22	5.92**
Blk 3 (20) vs. Blk 2 (68)	22	4.57**
Blk 3 (20) vs. Blk 1 (60)	22	3.45**
All blks (33) vs. All Blks (70)	22	6.10**
Ext. D2 vs. Acq. D1:		
Blk 1 (48) vs. Blk 1 (50)	22	0.14
Blk 1 (48) vs. Blk 2 (57)	22	0.67
Blk 1 (48) vs. Blk 3 (65)	22	1.48
Blk 2 (32) vs. Blk 1 (50)	22	1.62
Blk 2 (32) vs. Blk 2 (57)	22	2.12*
Blk 2 (32) vs. Blk 3 (65)	22	3.05**
Blk 3 (20) vs. Blk 1 (50)	22	2.83**
Blk 3 (20) vs. Blk 2 (57)	22	3.27**
Blk 3 (20) vs. Blk 3 (65)	22	4.41**
All Blks (33) vs. All Blks (57)	22	4.25**

* $p < .05$
** $p < .01$

Table 22.--Analysis of variance of occurrence of CR_{80} in Acq. at H Int. by ITI (60 and 240 sec.) and by Experiment II vs. Experiment III (D1)

Source	SS	df	MS	F
A: ITI	1.4	1	1.40	0.89
B. Experiment	0.5	1	0.50	0.32
A x B	0.0	1	0.04	0.02
error	31.6	20	1.58	
Total	33.5	23		

Table 23.--Analysis of variance of occurrence of CR_{80} in acq. (D1) by ITI and trial blocks in Experiment III

Source	SS	df	MS	F
A: ITI	0.4	1	0.39	0.34
error (a)	11.6	10	1.16	
B: Trial blks	3.1	2	1.54	1.60
A x B	1.7	2	0.85	0.89
error (b)	19.2	20	0.96	
Total	36.0	35		

Table 24.--Analysis of variance of occurrence of CR_{80} in Acq. (D2) by ITI and trial blocks in Experiment III

Source	SS	df	MS	F
A: ITI	0.0	1	0.00	0.00
error (a)	4.3	10	0.43	
B: Trial blks	7.2	2	3.58	2.28
A x B	2.2	2	1.09	0.70
error (b)	31.3	20	1.57	
Total	45.0	35		

Table 25.—Analysis of variance of occurrence of CR_{80} in Ext. (D2) by ITI and trial blocks in Experiment III

Source	SS	df	MS	F
A: ITI	1.8	1	1.78	0.31
error (a)	57.6	10	5.76	
B: Trial Blks	12.2	2	6.09	4.01*
A x B	2.1	2	1.02	0.67
error (b)	30.4	20	1.52	
Total	104.1	35		

* $p < .05$

Table 26.—Analysis of variance of per cent A. Est. by ITI, successive estimate, and successive day in Experiment III

Source	SS	df	MS	F
A: ITI	88	1	88.0	0.10
error (a)	8599	10	859.9	
B: Successive Days	653	1	653.0	7.35*
C: Successive Estimates	99	1	99.0	1.11
A x B	143	1	143.0	1.61
A x C	1	1	1.0	0.01
B x C	2	1	2.0	0.02
A x B x C	77	1	77.0	0.87
error (b)	2664	30	88.8	
Total	12326	47		

* $p < .05$

Table 27.--Analysis of variance of OE gsr by ITI and successive days of Acq. in Experiment III

Source	SS	df	MS	F
A: ITI	23563	1	23563	2.79
error (a)	84322	10	8432	
B: Successive Days	18593	1	18593	9.98*
A x B	73	1	73	0.04
error (b)	18631	10	1863	
Total	145182	23		

* p < .05

Table 28.--Analysis of variance of I gsr by ITI, trial blocks,
and successive days of Acq. in Experiment III

Source	SS	df	MS	F
A: ITI	29	1	29.00	0.50
error (a)	581	10	58.10	
B: Successive Days	162	1	162.00	3.12
C: Trial Blk	593	2	296.50	5.71*
A x B	12	1	12.00	0.23
A x C	91	2	45.50	0.88
B x C	162	2	81.00	1.56
A x B x C	70	2	35.00	0.67
error (b)	2596	50	51.92	0.67
Total	4296	71		

* p < .01

Table 29.--Data summary for ITI conditions in Experiment IV as opposed to Experiment II: age, sex, H gsr, Sb Un, occurrence of CR80, E. Ant., A. Est., CEDE, DEE, I gsr, OE gsr, counting per S

Data Category	Experiment IV 3600 sec ITI (N=3) S1	S2	S3	1800 sec ITI (N=3) S1	S2	S3	Experiment II 30-300 sec ITI (N = 120)
Age: by S	18	19	18	18	18	19	18.7
$\overline{X}$ by ITI		18.3			18.3		
Sex: by S	M	M.	M	M	M	M	
Total N of Ms by ITI		3			3		79
H gsr: src by S	-.08	-.05	+.02	-.04	+1.04	+.02	
Median by ITI		-.05			+.02		$\overline{X}=+.07$; SD=.30
Sb Un: by S	Y	Y	Y	Y	N	Y	Y=33/60 Ss at H Int
Occurrence of CR80 Number by S,							
Blk 1	0	0	0	1	2	1	
Blk 2	0	0	0	2	1	1	
Blk 3	0	1	1	2	3	1	
All Blks	0/0	1/1	1/1	2/5	3/6	1/3	
$\overline{X}$ % by ITI,							
Blk 1		0			20		45
Blk 2		0			27		58
Blk 3		13			40		67
All Blks		6			31		56

Table 29.—Data summary for ITI conditions in Experiment IV as opposed to Experiment II: age, sex, H gsr, Sb Un, occurrence of CR80, E. Ant., A. Est., CEDE, DEE, I gsr, OE gsr, counting per S

Data Category	Experiment IV 3600 sec ITI (N=3) S1	S2	S3	Experiment IV 1800 sec ITI (N=3) S1	S2	S3	Experiment II 30–300 sec ITI (N = 120)
Age: by S	18	19	18	18	18	19	18.7
$\overline{X}$ by S by ITI			18.3			18.3	
Sex: by S	M	M	M	M	M	M	
Total N of Ms by ITI			3			3	79
H gsr: src by S	−.08	−.05	+.02	−.04	+1.04	+.02	$\overline{X}$=+.07; SD=.30
Median by S by ITI			−.05			+.02	
Sb Un: by S	Y	Y	Y	Y	N	Y	Y=33/60 Ss at H Int
Occurrence of CR80 Number by S,							
Blk 1	0	0	0	1	2	1	20
Blk 2	0	0	0	2	1	1	27
Blk 3	0	0	0	2	2	1	40
All Blks	0	0	0	5	5	3	31
					13/6		
$\overline{X}$ % by ITI,							
Blk 1	0						45
Blk 2	0						58
Blk 3	0						67
All Blks	0						56

Table 29.--Continued.

Data Category	Experiment IV 3600 sec ITI (N=3)			1800 sec ITI (N=3)			Experiment II 30-300 sec ITI (N = 120)
	S1	S2	S3	S1	S2	S3	
CEDE: by S	Y	–	–	Y	N	–	Y = 82/120
DEE: Under by S	Y	–	–	Y	Y	–	Y = 49/120
I gsr: src by S							
Blk 1	+.03	-.07	+.32	-.25	+.17	+.07	+.47
Blk 2	+.16	-.11	-.12	+.02	-.06	+.04	-.03
Blk 3	-.08	+.42	-.31	-.02	+.01	-.04	-.07
$\bar{X}$ src by ITI							
Blk 1			+.09			.00	
Blk 2			-.04			.00	
Blk 3			.00			-.02	
OE gsr: src							
by S	-.57	-1.56	-1.15	-1.36	-1.94	+.46	+.04
$\bar{X}$ src by ITI			-1.09			-.95	
Counting per S:							
% by S	27	0	69	65	50	41	84
$\bar{X}$ % by ITI			32			52	

Table 30.--Sample data sheet from all experiments

DATA SHEET   TEMPORAL CONDITIONING

Date _____ 1965   Age___   Sex___   ITI____   Bulb_____

Time_____   Name of S _____

Examiner _____

  I. GSR 0.50 min._____   2-50 min._____

 II. Acquisition (XX = UR)

Flash #	Seconds before flash "NOW" said	Time GSR Taken	GSR
1			
2			
3			
4			
5			
6			
7			
8			
9			
10			
11			
12			
13			
14			
15			
16			
17			

III. Estimation   Time in seconds_____
                     S: Over or under-estimated_____
                     How much? _____

 IV. Questions

	Method Count	When used

   1. Method of synchrony: _____

   2. Bulb flash pleasant, unpleasant, or neutral
       on average? _____

   3. Other comments:

BIBLIOGRAPHY

Aaronson, B.S. Behavior and the place names of time. American Journal of Hypnosis: Clinical, Experimental, & Theoretical, 1966, 9, 1—17.

Aaronson, B.S. Hypnotic alterations of space and time. International Journal of Parapsychology, 1968a, 10, 5—36.

Aaronson, B.S. Hypnosis, time rate perception, and personality. Journal of Schizophrenia, 1968b, 2, 11—41.

Adrian, E.D. Electrical activity of the nervous system. Arch. Neurol., 1934, 32, 1125—1134.

Anger, D. Discriminations in the reinforcement of Sidman avoidance behavior. J. Exp. Anal. Behav., 1963, 6, 477—506.

Anliker, J. Variations in alpha voltage of the electroencephalogram and time perception. Science, 1963, 140, 1317—1309.

Aschoff, J. Circadian rhythms in man. Science, 1965, 148, 1427—1432.

Baiandurov, B.I. Conditioned reflexes in birds. Tomsk, 1937. In Dmitriev and Kochigina, 1959.

Bakan, P. Effect of set and work speed on time estimation. Percept. Mot. Skills, 1955, 5, 147—148.

Bakan, P. Retrospective awareness of error in time estimation. Percept. Mot. Skills, 1962, 15, 342.

Barber, T.X. & Calverly, D.S. Toward a theory of "hypnotic" behaviour. Archives of General Psychiatry, 1964c, 10, 209.

Barch, A., Ratner, S.C., & Morgan, R.F. Extinction and latent reacquisition. Psychonomic Science, 1965, 3, 495—496.

Barnett, L. The Universe and Dr. Einstein. William Sloane Associates, New York, 1950, page 40.

Bell, C. and Provins, K. Relations between physiological responses to environmental heat and time judgments. J. E . Psychol., 1963, 66, 572—579.

Benussi, V. Zur experimentellen analyse des zeitvergleichS. Arch. Ges. Psychol., 1907, 9, 384—385.

Beritov, I.S. Individually acquired activity of the central nervous system. Tbilisi, 1932: In Dmitriev and Kochigina, 1959.

Birman, B.N. Essai clinico-psysiologique de détermination des différents types d'activité nerveuse supérieure. Cah. Med. Sov., 1953, 2, 123—134. In Fraisse, 1963.

Birren, J.E., Kenyon, G.M., Ruth, J., Schroots, J.J.F, Svenson, T. Aging & Biography: Explorations In Adult Development. New York: Springer, 1996.

Bolotina, 0.P. Motor conditioned reflexes to time in dogs. Proc. Pavlov Physiol. Inst., 1952a, 1, 29—34. In Dmitriev and Kochigina, 1959.

Bolotina, 0.P. Motor conditioned reflexes to time in monkeys. Proc. Pavlov Physiol. Inst., 1952b, 1, 196—204. In Dmitriev and Kochigina, 1959.

Bolotina, 0.P. Effect of bromide and caffeine on conditioned reflexes to time in dogs and monkeys. Proc. Pavlov Physiol. Inst., 1953, 2, 52—63. In Dmitriev and Kochigina, 1959.

Brown, J.S. A note on a temporal gradient of reinforcement. J. Exp. Psychol., 1939, 25, 221—227.

Bugelski, B.R. Psychology of Learning. New York: Holt, 1956.

Bugelski, B.R. and Coyer, R.A. Temporal conditioning versus anxiety reduction in avoidance learning. Amer. Psychol., 1950, 5, 264.

Burns, N., and Gifford, E. Time estimation and anxiety. J. Psychol. Studies, 1981, 12, 19—27.

Butler, B. The use of hypnosis in the care of the cancer patient. Cancer, 1954, 1, 1—14.

Casey, G.A. Hypnotic time distortion and learning. Unpublished doctoral dissertation, Michigan State University, East Lansing, Michigan, 1966.

Cheek, D.B. & LeCron, L.M. Clinical Hypnotherapy. New York: Grune & Stratton, 1968.

Cheek, D,B, HYPNOSIS: The Application of Ideomotor Techniques. Needham Heights, Mass: Allyn & Bacon, 1994.

Cohen, J. Psychological time in health and disease. Springfield, IL.: Charles C. Thomas, 1967.

Cohen, Cooper, and Ono, A. The hare and the tortoise: a study of the tau effect in walking and running. Acta Psychologica, 1963, 21, *387—393.*

Collier, G., Knarr, F.A., and Marx, M.H. Some relations between the intensive properties of the consummatory response and reinforcement. J. Exp. Psychol., 1961, 62, 484—495.

Collier, G., and Myers, L. The loci of reinforcement. J. Exp. Psychol., 1961, 61, 57—76.

Conrad, D.G. and Sidman, M. Sucrose concentration as reinforcement for lever pressing by monkeys. Psychol. Rep., 1956, 2, 381—384.

Cooper, L.F. Time distortion in hypnosis. Journal of Psychology, 1952, 34, 247—284.

Cooper, L.F. Time distortion in hypnosis. The Bulletin, Georgetown University Medical Center, 1948, 1 (April/May), 214—221.

Cooper, L.F. & Erickson, M.H. Time distortion in hypnosis. Baltimore: Williams & Wilkins, 1954.

Cooper, L.F. & Erickson, M.H. Time distortion in hypnosis II. The Bulletin, Georgetown University Medical Center, 1950, 4 (Oct/Nov), 50—68.

Cooper, L.F. & Rodgin, D.W. Time distortion in hypnosis and non-motor learning. Science, 1952, 115, 500—502.

Cooper, L.F. & Tuthill, C.E. Time distortion in hypnosis and motor learning. Journal of Psychology, 1953, 36, 67—76.

Crasilneck. H.B., Stirman, J.A., Wilson, B.J., McCranie, E.J., & Fogelman, M.J. Use of hypnosis in the management of patients with burns. J. Amer. Med. Ass., 1955, 158, 103—106.

Crawford, M.L. and Thor, D.H. Circadian activity and noise comparisons of two confined groups with and without reference to clock time. Percept. Mot. Skills, 1964, 19, 211—216.

Cutler, H.M. The effects of stress on the perception of time by normal and neurotic subjects. Unpublished doctoral dissertation, Purdue University, 1952.

Davidson, R.J., & Goleman, D.J. The role of attention in meditation and hypnosis: A psychobiological perspective on transformations of consciousness. Int. J. Clin. Exp. Hypnosis, 1977; 25, 291—308.

Dengrove, E. The uses of hypnosis in behavior therapy. International J. Clin. Exper. Hypnosis, 1973, 21(1), 13—17.

Denner, B., Wapner, S., McFarland, J., and Werner, H. Rhythmic activity and the perception of time. Amer. J. Psychol., 1963, 76, 287—292.

Denner, B., Wapner, S., and Werner, H. Rhythmic activity and the discrimination of stimuli in time. Percept. Mot.. Skills, 1964, 19, 723—7.29.

Denny, M.R., and Adelman, H.K. Elicitation theory: Analysis of two typical learning situations. Psychol. Rev., 1955, 62, 290—296.

Deriabin, V.S. Further material on the physiology of time as a conditioned stimulus of the salivary glands. Unpublished doctoral dissertation, St. Petersburg, 1916. In Dmitriev and Kochigina, 1959.

Dimond, S.J. The structural basis of timing. Psychol. Bulletin, 1964, 64, 348—350.

Dmitriev, A.S. & Kochigina, A. The importance of time as a stimulus of conditioned reflex activity. Psychological Bulletin, 1959, 56, 106—132.

Dmitriev, A.S. and Grebenkina. On switch-over of conditioned reflexes of the same type. Deiat., 1959, 9, 892—899. In Psychol. Abst., 1961, #4627.

Doehring, D., Helmer, J., and Fuller, E.A. Physiological responses associated with time estimation in a human operant situation. Psychol. Rec., 1964, 14, 355—362.

Dufort, R., and Kimble, G. Changes in response strength with changes in the amount of reinforcement. J. Exp. Psychol., 1956, 51, 185—191.

162

Duran, E. & Duran, B. Native American Postcolonial Psychology. Albany: State University of New York Press, 1995.

Edmunston, W.E. & Erbeck, J.R. Hypnotic time distortion: a note. American Journal of Clinical Hypnosis, 1967, 10, 79—80.

Edwards, A. Statistical Methods for the Behavioral Sciences. New York: Rinehart, 1960a.

Edwards, A. Experimental Design in Psychological Research. New York: Holt, Rinehart and Winston, 1960b.

Ehrenwald, H. Storung der zeitauffassung dér rá?umlichen orientierung, des zeichens und des rechnens bei einem hirnverletzten. A. Neurol. Psychiat., 1931, 132, 518—569.

Elkin, D.G. Anticipatory reflexes and the perception of time. Voprosy Psikhologii, 1964, 123—130. In Psychol. Abst., 1965, 39, #3399.

Elkind, L. Effects of hypnosis on the process of aging. Unpublished doctoral dissertation, California School of Professional Psychology, San Francisco, 1972. Reprinted in Chapter 3 of R.F. Morgan's, Growing Younger: How to Measure and Change Your Body Age, Fair Oaks, California: Morgan Foundation Publishers, 2000.

Erickson, M.H. & Erickson, E.M. Further considerations of time distortion: subjective time condensation as distinct from time expansion. American Journal of Clinical Hypnosis, 1958, 1, 83—88.

Erickson, M.H. Hypnotic investigation of psychosomatic phenomena. Psychosomatic Medicine, 1943, 5, 51—58.

Erickson, M.H. Collected writings, In J. Haley (editor), Advanced techniques of hypnosis and therapy: the collected writings of Milton H. Erickson. New York: Grune & Stratton, 1967.

Erickson, M.H. Hypnosis in painful terminal illness. Amer. J. Clin. Hypnosis, 1958, 1, 117—121.

Erickson, M.H. Development of apparent unconsciousness during hypnotic reliving of traumatic experience, Arch. Neurol. & Psychiat. 38: 1282—1288, Dec. 1937.

Feokritova, Y.P. Time as a conditioned stimulus to the salivary gland. Unpublished doctoral dissertation, St. Petersburg, 1912. In Dmitriev and Kochigina, 1959; Fraisse, 1963; Pavlov, 1927; Frolov, 1937.

Ferster, C.B., and Skinner, B.F. Schedules of Reinforcement. New York: Appleton-Century-Crofts, 1957.

Fischer, R. A cartography of the ecstatic and meditative states: The experimental and experiential feature of a perception-hallucination continuum are considered. Science, 1971, 174, 897—904.

Fischer, R. Biological time. In J.T. Fraser (editor), The voices of time. New York: Braziller, 1966.

Fraisse, P. The psychology of time. New York: Harper & Row, 1963.

Fraisse, P. and Jampolsky, M. Premiéres recherches sur l'induction rythmique des réactions psychogalvaniques et l'estimation de la durée. Année Psychol., 1952, 52, 363—381.
Francois, M. Contribution à l'étude du sens du temps. La température interne comme facteur de variation de l'appréciation subjective des durées. Année Psychol., 1927, 28, 188—204.

Francois, H. Influence de la température interne sur notre appréciation du temps. C.R. Soc. Biol., 1928, 108, 201—203.

Fraser, J.T., Haber, F.C., & Muller, G.H. The study of time: proceedings of the first conference of the International Society for the Study of Time in Black Forest, West Germany. New York: Springer-Verlag, 1972.

Frolov, Y.P. Pavlov and His School. New York: Oxford U. Press, 1937.

Fogel, S., & Hoffer, A. Perceptual changes induced by hypnotic suggestion for the posthypnotic state: I. General account of the effect on personality. J.Clin. Exp. Psychopath. Q4art. Rev. Psychiat. Neurol., 1962, 23, 24—35.

Geiwitz, J.P. Hypnotically induced boredom and time estimation. Psychonom. Sci., 1964, 1, 277—278.

Gill, M.M., & Brenman, J. Hypnosis and related states: Psychoanalytic studies in regression. New York: International Universities Press, 1959.

Gilliland, A., and Humphreys, D. Age, sex, method and interval as variables in time estimation. J. Genet. Psychol., 1943, 63, 123—130.

Graef, J.R. The influence of cognitive states on time estimation and subjective time rate. Doctoral dissertation, unpublished, at the University of Michigan, Ann Arbor, 1969.

Grant, D.A., McFarling, D., and Gormezano, 1. Temporal conditioning and the effect of interpolated UCS presentations in eyelid conditioning. J. Gen. Psychol., 1960, 63, 249—257.

Grunbaum, A. The status of temporal becoming. In R. Fisher (Ed.), Interdisciplinary Perspectives of Time, Annals of the New York Academy of Sciences. New York: New York Academy of Sciences, 1967, 138, 374—395.

Gulliksen, H. The influence of occupation upon the perception of time. J. Exp. Psychol., 1927, 10, 52—59.

Guttman, N. Operant conditioning, extinction, and periodic reinforcement in relation to concentration of sucrose used as reinforcing agent. J. Exp. Psychol., 1953, 46, 213—244.

Hardesty, and Bevan, W. Response latency as a function of the temporal pattern of stimulation. Psychol. Rec., 1965, 15, 385—392.

Hare, D. Anxiety, temporal estimation, and rate of counting. Percept. Mot. Skills, 1963, 16, 441—444.

Harrison, F. The hypothalamus and sleep. Res. Publ. Ass. Nerv. Ment. Dis., 1940, 20, 635—656.
Hilgard, E.R., & Hilgard, J.R. Hypnosis in the relief of pain. Los Altos, Calif.: Kaufmann, 1975.

Hilgard, E.R. Hypnotic susceptibility. New York: Harcourt, Brace & World, 1965.

Hilgard, J. Personality and hypnosis. Chicago, Ill.: University of Chicago Press, 1970.

Hoagland, H. The physical control of judgements of duration: evidence for a chemical clock. J. Gen. Psychol., 1933, 9, 267—287.

Hoagland, H. The physiological control of judgements of duration. Amer. J. Physiol., 1934, 109, 54.

Hoagland, H. Temperature characteristics of the Berger rhythm in man. Science, 1936a, 83, 84—84.

Hoagland, H. Electrical brain waves and temperature. Science, 1936b, 84, 139—140.

Hoagland, H. Pacemakers of human brain waves. Amer. J. Physiol., 1936c, 116, 604—615.

Hoagland, H. Some pacemaker aspects of rhythmic activity in the nervous system. Cold Spring Symposia on Quantitative Biology, 1936d, .3, 267—284.

Hoagland, H. The chemistry of time. Sci. Mon., 1943, 56, 56—61.

Hotelling, H. The selection of variates for use in prediction, with some comments on the general problem of nuisance parameters. Ann. Math. Statist., 1940, 11, 271—283.

Hyde, R., and Wood, A.C. Occupational therapy for lobotomy patients. Occup. Ther. Rehabilit., 1949, 28, 109—124.

Johnson, T.J. The influence of experimentally produced affect on time perception. Unpublished doctoral dissertation. Washington University, 1962.

Kayser, C. Le rythme nycthemeral des mouvements d 'énergie. Rev. Scient., 1952, 90, 173—188.

Kimble, G.A. Conditioning and Learning. New York: Appleton-Century-Crofts, 1961.

Kimble, G.A. Man, L., and Dufort, R. Classical and Instrumental eyelid conditioning. J. Exp. Psychol., 1955, 49, 407—417.

Kleitman, N. Sleep and Wakefulness as Alternating Phases in the Cycle of Existence. Chicago: U. Chicago Press, 1939.

Kleitman, N., Titelbaum, S., and Hoffmann, H. The establishment of the diurnal temperature cycle. Amer. J. Physiol., 1937, 119, 48—54.

Krauss, H., Katzell, R., & Krauss, B.J, Effect of hypnotic time distortion upon free-recall learning. J. Abnorm. Psychol., 1974, 83, 140—144.

Krzhishkovskii, K.N. On the physiology of conditioned inhibition. Proc. Russian Med. Soc. St. Petersburg, 1908. In Dmitriev and Kochigina, 1959.

LeCron, L.M. Self hypnotism: the technique and its use in daily living. New York: Signet, 1970.

LeCron, L.M. Experimental hypnosis. New York: Citadel Press, 1968.

Lehmann, H.E. Time and psychopathology. In R. Fischer (editor), Interdisciplinary perspectives of time, Annals of the New York Academy of Sciences, New York: New York Academy of Sciences, 1967, 138, 798—821.

Loomis, E.A. Space and time perception and distortion in hypnotic states. Personality, 1951, 1, 283.

Luce, G.G. Rhythms in psychiatry and medicine. Public Health Service Publication No. 2088, Washington, D.C., 1970.

Meares, A. A system of medical hypnosis. Philadelphia: Saunder, 1960.

Mo, S.S. Temporal reproduction of duration as a function of numerosity. Bulletin of the Psychonomic Society, 1975, 5, 165—167.

Morgan, R.F. Conquest of Aging: Modern Measurement & Intervention. Applied Gerontology Communications, Pueblo, Colorado: 1977.

Morgan, R.F. Memory and the senile psychoses: a follow-up note. Psychological Reports, 1967, 20, 733—734.

Morgan, R.F. Temporal conditioning in humans as a function of intertrial interval and stimulus intensity. Dissertation Abstracts, 1966, 27, No. 66— 6153. From the doctoral dissertation at Michigan State University, East Lansing, 1965.

Morgan, R.F. Note on the psychopathology of senility: senescent defense against the threat of death. Psychological Reports, 1965, 16, 305—306. 208

Morgan, R.F., and Bakan, P. Sensory deprivation hallucinations and other sleep behavior as a function of position, method of report, and anxiety. Percept. Mot. Skills, 1965, 20, 19—25.

Morgan, R.F., and Wilson, J., Growing Younger: How to Measure and Changer Your Body Age. Fair Oaks, California: Morgan Foundation Publishers, 2000.

Morgan, R.F. Electroshock: The Case Against Over Four Decades. Fair Oaks, CA: Morgan Foundation Publishers, 1999.

Morgan, R.F. No Place Like Home in P. Breggin's Psychosocial Approaches To Deeply Disturbed Persons. Hazelton, PA: Haworth Press, 141—183, 1996.

Morgan, R.F. Decades Of Research and Practice With The Adult Growth Examination, A Brief Standardized Test Of Adult Aging in A. Balin, Human Biological Age Determination. Boca Raton: FL: CRC Press, Ch. 12, 181—211, 1994.

Morgan, R.F., Ratner, S.C., and Denny, M.R. Response of earthworms to light as measured by the GSR. Psychonom. Sci.,1965, 3, 27—28.

Munsterburg, J. Beitrage zur experimentellen psychologie. Heft 2. Greiburg-Br.: Siebeck, 1889. In Woodrow, 1951.

Orme, J.E. Time, experience, and behaviour. New York: American Elsevier, 1969.

Orme, J.E. Personality, time estimation, and time experience. Acta Psychologica, 1964, 22, 430.

Orme, .J. E. Time estimation and personality. Journal of Mental Science, 1962, 108, 213.

Ornstein, R.E. The psychology of consciousness. New York; Viking, 1972.

Partridge, M. Prefrontal leucotomy. Oxford, England: Blackwell, 1950.

Passey, G.E. The influence of intensity of unconditioned stimulus upon acquisition of a conditioned response. J. Exp. Psychol., 1948, 38, 420—428.

Pavlov, I.P. Conditioned Reflexes: An Investigation of the Physiological Activity of the Cerebral Cortex. (Translated into English by G.V. Anrep), London: Oxford U. Press, 1927.

Pavlov, I.P. Lectures on Conditioned Reflexes: 25 Years of Objective Study of the Higher Nervous Activity of Animals. New York: International, 1928.

Pavlov, I.P. Experimental Psychology and Other Essays. New York: Philosophical Library, 1957.

Popov, N.A. Le facteur temps dans la théorie des réflexes conditionnes. C. R. Soc. Biol., 1948, 142, 156—158.

Popov, N.A. Action prolongée sur le cortex cérébral après stimulation rythmique. J. Physiol. Path. Gen., 1950a, 42, 51—72.

Popov, N.A. Etudes de Psychophysiologie. Paris: Editions du Cedre, 1950b.

Prokasy, W.F. Classical Conditioning: A Symposium. New York: Appleton-Century-Crafts, 1965.

Prokasy, W.F., and Chambliss, D.J. Temporal conditioning: negative results. Psychol. Rep., 1960, 7, 539—542.

Prokasy, W.F., Grant, D., and Myers, N. Eyelid conditioning as a function of UCS intensity and inter-trial interval. J. Exp. Psychol., 1958, 55, 2'2—246.

Ratner, S.C., and Denny, M.R. Comparative Psychology. Homewood, Illinois: Dorsey, 1964.

Remy, M. Contribution à l'étude de la maladie de Korsakow: étude anatomoclinique. Mschr. Psychiat. Neurol., 1942, 106, 128—180.

Reynierse, J.H. The effects of stimulus sampling on the retention of an avoidance response. Unpublished doctoral dissertation, Michigan State University, 1964.

Richards. W. Time estimates measured by reproduction. Percept. Mot. Skills, 1964, 18, 929—943.
Richardson, M.W. & Stalnaker, J.M. Time estimation in the hypnotic trance. Journal of General Psychology, 1930, 4, 362—366.

Rimoldi, H.J. Personal tempo. J. Abnorm. Soc. Psychol., 1951, 46, 283—303.

Rosenzweig, S., and Koht, A.C. The experience of duration affected by need tension. J. Exp. Psychol., 1933, 16, 745—775.

Rozin, M.I. The physiological mechanism of the conditioned reflex to time. Academy of Sciences I3ye-lorussian SSR Proc., 1959, 3, 318—321. From Tech. Transl. #60—21776, Clearinghouse, U.S. Library of Congress.

Sacerdote, P. Applications of hypnotically elicited mystical states to the treatment of physical and emotional pain. Internati. J. Clin. Exper. hypnosis, 1977, 25, 309—324.

Sacerdote, P. Theory and practice of pain control in malignancy and other protracted or recurring painful illnesses. Int. J. Clin. Exp. Hypnosis, 1970, 18, 160—180.

Sacerdote, P. Hypnosis in the emotional care of the cancer patient. In A.H. Kutscher (Ed.), Emotional care of the cancer patient, in press.

Shaefer, G., and Gilliland, A. The relation-of time estimation to certain physiological changes. J. Exp. Psychol., 1938, 23, 545—552.

Schlosberg, H., and Stanley, W.C. A simple test of the normality of twenty-four distributions of electrical skin conductance. Science, 1953, 117, 35—37.

Siegel, S. Nonparametric Statistics for the Behavioral Sciences. New York: McGraw-Hill, 1956.

Siegman, A.W. Anxiety, impulse control, intelligence, and the estimation of time. J. Clin. Psychol.

1962, 18, 103—105.

Spence, K., Haggard, D., and Ross, L. Intrasubject conditioning as a function of the intensity of the unconditioned stimulus. Science, 1958, 128, 774—775.

Spiegel, E., and Wysis, H. Physiological and psychological results of thalamotomy. Proc. Roy. Soc. Med., 1949, 42, 84—93.

Spiegel, E., Wysis, H., Orchinik, C.W., & Freed, H. The thalamus and temporal orientation. Science, 1955, 121, 771—772.

Spivack, G. and Levine, M. Consistency of individual differences in time judgements. Percept. Mot. Skills, 1964, 19, 83—92.

Still, H. Of time, tides, and inner clocks. Moonachie, New Jersey: Pyramid Publications, 1972.

Stolz, S. Vasometer response in human subjects: conditioning and pseudo-conditioning. Psychonom. Sci., 1965, 2, 181—182.

Stukova, M. Further contribution on the physiology of time as a conditioned excitant of the salivary glands. Unpublished doctoral dissertation. St. Petersburg, 1914. In Dmitriev and Kochigina, 1959.

Takala, M., and Partanen, N. Psychomotor expression and personality study: III. The problem of "personal tempo." Scandinavian J. Psychol., 1964, 5, 161—170.

Tukey, J.W. Comparing individual means in the analysis of variance. Biometrics, 1959, 5, 99—114.

Von Uexkull, .3. A stroll through the worlds of animals and men. In C.H. Schiller (editor), Instinctive behavior. New York: International Universities Press, 1957, 5—80.

Wallace, M., and Rabin, A.I. Temporal experience. Psychol. Bulletin, 1960, 57, 213—236.

Weitzenhoffer, A.M. Explorations in hypnotic time distortions. I. Acquisitions of temporal reference frames under conditions of time distortion. Journal of Nervous and Mental Diseases, 1964, 138, 354.

Welch, L. The space and time of induced hypnotic dreams. Journal of Psychology, 1935, 1, 171—178.

Werboff, J. The relationship between electroencephalographic activity and the estimation of short temporal intervals. Unpublished doctoral dissertation, U. of Washington, 1957.

Weybrew, B. Accuracy of time estimation and muscular tension. Percept. Mot. Skills, 1963, 17, 118.

Winer, B.J. Statistical Principles in Experimental Design. New York: McGraw-Hill, 1962.

Woodrow, H. Time perception. In S.S. Stevens (Ed.), Handbook of Experimental Psychology. New York: Wiley and Sons, 1951, 1224—1236.

Woodworth, R.S., and Schlosberg, H.S. Experimental Psychology. New York: Holt, Rinehart, and Winston, 1954.

Zelenyi, G.P. Reactions of the dog to auditory stimuli. Unpublished doctoral dissertation. St. Petersburg, 1907. In Dmitriev and Kochigina, 1959.

Zelkind, I., and Spilka, B. Some time perspective-time perception relationships. Psychol. Rec., 1965, 15, 417—421.

Zimbardo, P.G., Marshall, G., & Maslach, C. Liberating behavior from time-bound control: expanding the present through hypnosis. Journal of Applied Social Psychology, 1971, 1, 305—323.

Zimbardo, P.G. The human choice: Individuation, reason, and order versus deindividualation, impulse, and chaos. In W.J. Arnold & D. Levine (Eds.), Nebraska symposium on motivation. Lincoln, Nebraska University of Nebraska Press, 1969.

Dr. Robert F. Morgan
Psychologist

Robert Morgan is a Licensed Psychologist and Consultant. He is also a Fellow of the American Psychological Association (Div. 12 & 29 & *52)*.

In 1965, Dr. Morgan completed his psychology doctorate at Michigan State University as Fellow of the National Institute of Mental Health. During this time he had also served as City Human Relations Commissioner. Following postdoctoral work at Hawaii State Hospital, including the founding of its first inpatient therapeutic community Adolescent program, he served full time on the faculties of Saint Bonaventure University, Nova Scotia's Acadia University, the San Francisco (now Berkeley) and Fresno campuses of the California School of Professional Psychology, the University of Southern Colorado (USC), and the Howard University (Washington, D.C.), San Francisco State University, the University of Nevada in Reno, CSPP's San Diego Campus, San Diego State University, Wilfred Laurier University (WLU), and Montana State University.

In addition to chairing departments of Psychology at USC, MSU, and WLU, he was for many years the Dean of Faculty and then Campus Dean at CSPP-SF. He has also served on the Executive Council of CSPP's Board (Faculty Elected Director) as Treasurer, and as Vice President of CSPP's California Community Services, Inc. Subsequently, he was founding President of the USC-affiliated Southern Colorado Community Services, Inc. From 1982-1986, he was Professor of Psychology and Dean for Academic Affairs at the California School of Professional Psychology's Fresno Campus. From 1986-1990, he was professor of Psychology and Academic Vice President at the Pacific Graduate School of Psychology, Palo Alto, and then Professor of Psychology and Department Chair at Montana State University, Billings (1991-1993). From 1994-1996 he was Professor of Psychology and Director of the Psychology Doctoral Program at the California Institute of Integral Studies, San Francisco, and is currently Professor of Psychology and Program Director at the American School of Professional Psychology, Corte Madera.

Since 1965, Dr. Morgan has provided clinical and supervisory services to community mental health facilities in Hawaii, New York, Nova Scotia, California, North Carolina, Colorado, and Nevada He has been listed in the National Register of Mental Health Providers in Psychology since its inception in 1975, reflecting earlier licensing and certification at the state level. Professional consultation over the last three decades has included government agencies from Peace Corps to the U.S. Office of Education, community organizational change groups such as Dr. M.L. King's SCLC, evaluation and appraisal services, and communication media including Science Digest and the London Sunday Times. Consultation on clinical training, accreditation and program development as well as to individuals and practitioners is his current practice.

While on leave from USC in 1977, he accepted a two-year post with the State of Nevada as Chief, Human Services Education. In this role he organized and coordinated statewide mental health manpower, training, research, prevention, legislation, and university education liaison. The latter included representing Nevada on the Advisory Council for the Western Center for Continuing Education in Mental Health of the Western Interstate Commission in Higher Education (WICHE), a coordinating and advisory body for university education in the 13 western states. He continues to sit on the International Council of Psychologists, the Michigan Academy of Science, national and regional psychological and academic associations. He is Founding President of the Division of Gerontological Psychology, International Association of Applied Psychology; past Chair and CSPA Board of Directors Representative for the California Psychological Association's Division of Education and Training from 1986-1989 and sits on the CPA Mandatory Continuing Education Psychology Committee (MCEP). He was on the Scientific Program Committee of the American Psychological Association for the 1998 World Congress of Psychology in San Francisco and is a liaison for the 2002 World Congress in Singapore. In 1998 he joined APA's Committee on Aging as liaison for its International Psychology Division *(52)*.

More than 70 articles, chapters, books, and papers have been published in the psychological areas of international psychology, applied gerontology, life-span development, community, social, general-experimental, evaluation; cognition, perception, special education, psychopathology, statistics, professional ethics and issues, clinical testing, temporal, prevention of iatrogenic practice, and graduate education/training in psychology.

NAME INDEX

Name Index

AARON, H.	2
AARONSON, B.S.	2, 4, 14, 26, 79, 160
ADELMAN, H.H.	117, 118, 161
ADRIAN, E.D.	86, 87, 160
ANCIKER, J.	160
ANGER, D.	82, 160
ANREP, G.V.	160
ARNOLD, W.J.	160
ASCHOFF, J.	160
BAIANDUROV, B.I.	160
BAKAN, P.	xv, 93, 96, 107, 141, 160, 166
BARBER, T.X.	3, 160
BARCH, A	6, 160
BARNETT, L.	36, 63, 160
BELL, C.	94, 160
BENUSSI, V.	93, 160
BERITOV, I.S.	95, 160
BEVAN, W.	82, 161
BIRMAN, B.N.	98, 110, 160
BOLOTINA, O.P.	83, 84, 85, 161
BRENMAN, J.	69, 79, 164
BROWN, J.S.	82, 161
BUGELSKI, B.R.	83, 84, 161
BURNS, N.	161
BUTLER, B.	73, 79, 161
CALVERLY, D.S.	3, 161
CANNON, G.	xv
CASEY, G.A.	4, 161
CHAMBLISS, D.J.	161
CHEEK, D.B.	ix, xiii, 4, 161
COHEN, J.	14, 25, 38, 161
COLLIER, G.	85, 161
CONRAD, D.G.	85, 161
COOPER, L.F.	xv, 2, 3, 4, 6, 31, 34, 63, 66, 67, 161, 161
COYER, R.A.	83, 86, 162
CRAIK, K.H.	32
CRASILNECK, H.B.	73, 79, 162
CRAWFORD, M.L.	162
CUTLER, H.M.	162
D'AMBROSIO, S.	xv
DAVIDSON, R.J.	73, 79, 162
DENGROVE, E.	2, 162
DENNER, B.	162
DENNY, M. RAY	xv, 85, 117, 118, 162, 167
DERIABIN, V.S.	85, 162
DIMOND, S.J.	86, 162
DMITRIEV, A.S.	5, 82, 83, 84, 85, 86, 87, 96, 160, 161, 162, 168
DOEHRING, D.	88, 162
DUFORD, R.	85, 96, 162, 166

EDMUNSTON, W.E.	4, 32, 163
EDWARDS, A	100, 127, 163
EHRENWALD, H.	86, 163
EINSTEIN, A	2, 59
ELKIN, D.G.	xvi, 85, 98, 163
EKLIND, L.	4, 163
ERBECK, J.R.	4, 32, 163
ERICKSON, E.	xv, 36, 66, 163
ERICKSON, M.H.	xv, 2, 3, 4, 5, 6, 7, 31, 34, 36, 63, 66, 163, 164
ESHER, M.C.	v
FEOKRITOVA, Y.P.	83, 86, 122, 128, 163
FERSTER, C.B.	83, 163
FISCHER, R.	6, 31, 71, 163, 164
FOGEL, S.	71, 79, 164
FOGELMAN, M.J.	73, 164
FRAISSE, P.	6, 83, 86, 87, 164
FRANCOIS, M.	164
FRASER, S.	xv, 6, 32, 164
FREED, H..	86, 169
FROLOV, G.P.	89, 100, 164
FULLER, E.A.	98, 162
GEIWITZ, J.P.	164
GIFFORD, E.	160
GILL, M.M.	79, 164
GILLILAND, A.	86, 164, 168
GLUCKMAN, P.	32
GOLEMAN, D.J.	73, 79, 162
GORMEZAND, I.	164
GRAEF, J.R.	4, 164
GRANT, D.A.	85, 110, 164, 168
GREBENKINA, A.	84, 162
GRUNBAUM, A.	22, 26, 164
GULLIKSEN, H.	164
GUTTMAN, N.	85, 164
HABER, F.C.	164
HAGGARD, D.	83, 168
HALEY, J.	163
HARDESTY, W.	82, 165
HARE, D.	165
HARRISON, F.	86, 165
HELMER, J.	98, 162
HILGARD, E.R.	14, 23, 26, 73, 165
HILGARD, J.R.	165
HOAGLAND, H.	86, 165
HOFFER, A.	71, 79, 164
HOFFMAN, H.	86, 166
HOTELLING, H.	166
HUDSON, D.W.	xv
HUMPHREYS, D.	165
HYDE, R.	86, 165
INGLIS, N.R.	36, 63
JAMPOLSKY, M.	83, 164

JOHNSON, T.J.	165
KATZELL, R.	166
KAYSER, C.	86, 165
KIMBLE, G.A.	83, 85, 89, 96, 110, 162, 165
KLEITMAN, N.	86, 166
KING, J.A.	xv
KNARR, F.A.	85, 160
KOCHIGINA, A.	15, 82, 83, 84, 85, 86, 97, 160, 161, 162, 163, 166, 169
KOHT, A.C.	166
KRAUSS, B.J.	166
KRAUSS, H.	166
KRZHISHKOVSKII, K.N.	83, 166
KUGLELMASS, J.	26
KUTSCHER, A.H.	168
LeCRON, L.	4, 160, 166
LEHMAN, H.E.	26, 166
LEVINE, P.	169
LEVINE, M.	170
LINDSLEY, O.R.	31
LOOMIS, E.A.	3, 166
LUCE, G.G.	25, 26, 166
MANN, L.	96, 165
MANN, H.B.	106
MARSHALL, G.	xv, 2, 12, 41, 167
MARX, M.H.	85, 161
MASLACH, C.	xv, 2, 12, 167
MCCRANIE, E.J.	73, 161
MCFARLAND, J.	161
MCFARLING, D.	165
MEARES, A.A.	70, 79, 166
MEYERS, L.	85, 86, 96, 160
MISCHEL, W.	31
MO, S.S.	166
MORGAN, A.K.	iii
MORGAN, C.	iii
MORGAN, R.F.	xii, xiii, 2, 3, 6, 89, 160, 166, 167, 169
MULLER, G.H.	164
MUNSTERBERG, J.	166
MYERS, N.	168
ONO, A.	161
ORCHINIK, C.W.	168
ORME, J.E.	167
ORNE, E.C.	32
ORNSTEIN, R.E.	6, 41, 167
PARTANEN, N.	167
PASSEY, G.E.	167
PARTRIDGE, M.	86, 167
PAVLOV, I.P.	82, 83, 84, 85, 86, 87, 96, 122, 128, 162, 167
POPOV, N.A.	87, 167
PROKASY, W.F.	85, 96, 168
PROVINS, K.	86, 160
RABIN, A.I.	168
RATNER, S.C.	6, 85, 117, 160, 167, 168

REYNIERSE, J.H.	119, 168
RHINE, J.B.	36, 63
RICHARDS, W.	168
RICHARDSON, M.W.	5, 168
RIHOLDI, H.J.	168
RODGIN, D.W.	3, 161
ROSENZWEIG, S.	168
ROSS, L.	83, 168
ROZIN, M.I.	5, 111, 168
SACERDOTE, P.	xv, 4, 69, 71, 73, 79, 80, 168
SARGIN, T.R.	32
SCHLOSBERG, H.	98, 168
SHAEFER, G.	168
SHOR, R.E.	32
SIDMAN, M.	85, 161
SIEGEL, S.	100, 168
SIEGMAN, A.W.	168
SKINNER, B.F.	83, 164
SPEARMAN, C.	105
SPENCE, K.	84, 169
SPIEGEL, E.	86, 169
SPILKA, B.	169
SPIVACK, G.	86, 169
STALNAKER, J.M.	2, 169
STANLEY, W.C.	169
STEVENS, S.S.	6
STIRMAN, J.A.	73, 79, 161
STILL, H.	6, 169
STOLZ, S.	89, 100, 169
STUKOVA, M.	85, 169
TAKALA, M.	169
THOR, D.H.	161
TITELBAUM, S.	85, 165
TUKEY, J.W.	120, 169
TUTHILL, C.E.	3, 161
VON BAER, K.E.	3
VONNEGUT, K.	2
VON UEXKULL, J.	xv, 2, 6, 8, 169
WALLACE, M.	169
WAPNER, S.	162
WEIZENHOFFER, A.M.	4, 169
WELCH, L.	2, 36, 63, 169
WERBOFF, J.	86, 169
WERNER, HJ.	162
WEYBREW, B.	169
WHITE, G.	31
WHITNEY, D.R.	106
WILSON, B.J.	73, 161
WILSON, J.	169
WINER, B.J.	100, 169
WOOD, A.C.	86, 165
WOODROW, R.S.	6, 169
WOODWORTH, R.S.	89, 169

WYSIS, H.   86, 170
ZELENYI, G.P.   82, 84, 170
ZELKIND, P.G.   170
ZIMBARDO, P.G.   xiv, xv, 2, 4, 12, 14, 25, 31, 169, 170